graphis posters 80

The International Annual of Poster Art

Das internationale Jahrbuch der Plakatkunst

Le répertoire international de l'art de l'affiche

Edited by: / Herausgegeben von: / Réalisé par:

Walter Herdeg

Graphis Press Corp., Zurich (Switzerland)

Distributed in the United States by

Hastings House

Publishers

10 East 40th Street, New York, N.Y. 10016

PUBLICATION No. 158   [ISBN 0-8038-2707-5]

5-6-80

Contents

Inhalt

Sommaire

Advertising Posters

Werbeplakate

Affiches publicitaires

Cultural Posters

Kulturelle Plakate

Affiches culturelles

Social Posters

Soziale Plakate

Affiches sociales

Consumer Posters

Dekorative Plakate

Affiches décoratives

Abbreviations   Abkürzungen   Abréviations

Argentina	ARG	Argentinien	ARG	Afrique du Sud	SAF
Australia	AUS	Australien	AUS	Allemagne (Est)	GDR
Austria	AUT	Belgien	BEL	Allemagne (Ouest)	GER
Belgium	BEL	Brasilien	BRA	Argentine	ARG
Brazil	BRA	Bulgarien	BUL	Australie	AUS
Bulgaria	BUL	Chile	CHI	Autriche	AUT
Canada	CAN	Dänemark	DEN	Belgique	BEL
Chile	CHI	Deutschland (Ost)	GDR	Brésil	BRA
Czechoslovakia	CSR	Deutschland (West)	GER	Bulgarie	BUL
Denmark	DEN	Finnland	FIN	Canada	CAN
Finland	FIN	Frankreich	FRA	Chili	CHI
France	FRA	Grossbritannien	GBR	Corée	KOR
Germany (East)	GDR	Hongkong	HKG	Danemark	DEN
Germany (West)	GER	Irland	IRL	Espagne	SPA
Great Britain	GBR	Israel	ISR	Etats-Unis	USA
Hong Kong	HKG	Italien	ITA	Finlande	FIN
Hungary	HUN	Japan	JPN	France	FRA
Ireland	IRL	Jugoslawien	YUG	Grande-Bretagne	GBR
Israel	ISR	Kanada	CAN	Hongkong	HKG
Italy	ITA	Korea	KOR	Hongrie	HUN
Japan	JPN	Luxemburg	LUX	Irlande	IRL
Korea	KOR	Niederlande	NLD	Israël	ISR
Luxemburg	LUX	Norwegen	NOR	Italie	ITA
Netherlands	NLD	Österreich	AUT	Japon	JPN
Norway	NOR	Polen	POL	Luxembourg	LUX
Poland	POL	Schweden	SWE	Norvège	NOR
Spain	SPA	Schweiz	SWI	Pays-Bas	NLD
South Africa	SAF	Spanien	SPA	Pologne	POL
Sweden	SWE	Südafrika	SAF	Suède	SWE
Switzerland	SWI	Tschechoslowakei	CSR	Suisse	SWI
Turkey	TUR	Türkei	TUR	Tchécoslovaquie	CSR
Uruguay	URU	Ungarn	HUN	Turquie	TUR
USA	USA	Uruguay	URU	Uruguay	URU
Venezuela	VEN	USA	USA	Venezuela	VEN
Yugoslavia	YUG	Venezuela	VEN	Yougoslavie	YUG

Cover / Umschlag / Couverture: Ron Benvenisti

We would like to take this opportunity to warmly thank all contributors once again for their collaboration. Due solely to their support it has been made possible for us to provide a truly international survey and cross-section of the development and trends in poster design from the numerous posters submitted for consideration.

An dieser Stelle möchten wir wiederum allen Einsendern unseren herzlichen Dank für ihre Mitarbeit aussprechen. Allein durch ihre Unterstützung ist es uns möglich, anhand von mehreren hundert Beispielen einen wirklich internationalen Überblick über die Entwicklung und Trends auf dem Gebiet der Plakatgestaltung zu geben.

Nous tenons à remercier tous nos collaborateurs de nous faire parvenir régulièrement leurs travaux et de nous mettre ainsi à même de préparer, grâce aux nombreux exemples soumis, un compendium international présentant les tendances nouvelles dans le domaine de l'affiche.

On our dust jacket RON BENVENISTI has captured the fingerprint of chance, colourfully and formally fascinating yet veiled with a hint of melancholy, left upon these tatters of messages long grown meaningless. Apart from the camera, the most important tool in the production of a series of studies on this subject was the eye of the former painter, trained for some years at Cooper Union as well as in photographic practice. The New Yorker Ron Benvenisti belongs to a generation which has developed an alert eye for phenomena of this kind, a vision that would hardly have been thinkable without the influence of fine art.

RON BENVENISTI hat auf unserem Schutzumschlag das Spiel des Zufalls eingefangen, farbig und formal faszinierend, überdeckt von einem Hauch der Melancholie, die in diesen sinnlos gewordenen Signalfetzen liegt. Der während Jahren des Studiums an einer New Yorker Kunstschule und in der photographischen Praxis geschulte Blick des ehemaligen Malers war neben der Kamera das wichtigste Werkzeug, das eine Serie von Studien zu diesem Thema entstehen liess. Der New Yorker Ron Benvenisti gehört zudem zu einer Generation, die nicht zuletzt durch die bildende Kunst für diese Art des Sehens wach geworden ist.

RON BENVENISTI a su captiver sur notre jaquette les jeux multicolores et formellement fascinants du hasard, empreint de mélancholie face à ces lambeaux d'affiches, ces pittoresques produits de décomposition dénués de tout leur sens. Pour réaliser une série d'études à ce sujet, l'ancien peintre se servait de deux instruments: sa caméra et son œil perceptif formé par l'expérience pratique en tant que photographe et au cours de plusieurs années d'études à une école d'art new-yorkaise. Ron Benvenisti est d'ailleurs un représentant d'une génération dont la nouvelle optique s'inspira des beaux-arts.

Gilles de Bure

The Pedestrian Here and Elsewhere

The journalist GILLES DE BURE expresses here the function of the poster from the pedestrian's point of view. These opinions arose from the changing circumstances in Paris, a city that has perhaps been characterized in its appearance more than any other due to "wild" poster-hanging. Gilles de Bure is co-founder of *Cree* magazine (1969) and has worked for numerous international periodicals as well as for radio and television programmes, above all in the spheres of architecture, design, visual communication and art. In his capacity as manager of the Galerie d'Actualité he worked on the Centre Pompidou project, where he organized more than twenty exhibitions. He is a member of the Board of Advisors of the International Design Conference in Aspen, and is also design consultant for Knoll International. Supported by many artists, he is currently in charge of the *Agence Art+* whose task is to integrate art in all its forms into the environment with paintings, festivals, public events, etc.

It is sometimes said that the best ways to get to know a country are to have breakfast with the local inhabitants and to read the classified advertisements of the regional newspaper with the highest circulation. But while the body and the mind are both excellent collectors of information and transmitters of sensations and intuitions in their own way, the busy eye also has a good deal to be said in its favour.

The pedestrian here and elsewhere leaves his footprints on the tarmac, the pavement and the dust while his eye runs over the walls that are the bearers of images and messages all over the world: painted walls, frescoes, miscellaneous fixtures or supergraphics, all are equally valuable and interesting to him. From the sculpted heads of Mount Rushmore to the gigantic mosaic Lenins of the Gum stores in Alma-Ata or to Picadilly Circus, everything is surprising to him, arresting or emotive. The gradual advance of his journey is thus accompanied by a gradual advance in the knowledge culled by his wandering gaze.

And this gaze skims, skips, skirts and beleaguers the walls of cities with dream-names (Macau, Samarkand, Valparaiso…) or of cities with everyday names (Bielefeld, Pittsburgh, Mulhouse…), discovering on them the sole constant, the true international: the message of the poster, ubiquitous, omnipresent. The poster that is sparkling or flat or marvellous, wild or decorous, a cry of passion or an economic classification, cultural or political, social or commercial, in black and white or in all the colours, giant or pygmy in size. Freshly hung, scintillating with colour, a merry-go-round of images, fitted in the magic frames of professional poster-hangers or flung anarchically here and there in haste and joy or in fear and darkness by militant poster-users of whatever persuasion, the poster seduces us, lures us, embraces us, traps us in all four corners of the globe.

Even in a state of laceration, a sort of mural leprosy, the poster continues to shock us and awakens in us — impenitent adherents of a visual age — a recognition of that form of art that is created by our own cities, places alive with a vibrant bustle and a dazzle of lights....

But these conditions are likely to be less frequent in future. There is more and more talk, in France and elsewhere, of regulating poster-hanging, of specifying official poster sites and of punishing severely all offences against the new code. It is the triumph of the sales spiral over the tree of life, here and elsewhere. It is an eternal game that goes on between regulated and "wild" poster-hanging. The opponents are an institutional economic system claiming the participation of the creative artist in the marketing of its goods, and a parallel, somewhat underground system operating without publicity and trying to upturn this world of pictures and with it this picture of the world.

After the poster, it is now the poster-hanging that is to come in for regulation. The poster has already suffered much insidious damage. The spectacular pieces that hold nothing back are no longer in fashion. As against the humour and strength of the "Mondrian" of the Dutchman Gerd Dumbar or that monument of commercial guile in which the French agency CLM-BBDO showed the Place de la Concorde in Paris transformed into a bucolic meadow to the greater glory of Levi-Strauss, most modern posters are a nexus of dullness, of conformity, of neutralization, of the absence of all argument or shock. For the shock must lie in the concept and the argument, but today, where there is any shock at all, it is only superficial, only a weak formality.

The interest of the reader as he looks through this annual, which brings into focus the best that has been done anywhere in the world in twelve months of intense production, will be concentrated on the virtues of form, for that is how the history of any art is written, whether "major" or "minor", with all its schools, genres and mannerisms.... Yet the field is really wider, more complex, more contradictory and, as a result, richer too. As if the urban environment were not capable of transmitting everything that society may want to say....

The sclerotic tradition of the studios and academies, the banishment of self-contradiction and incongruity, the banalization of photography, the eternal victory of "savoir-faire" over "savoir-être" seem to have destroyed the spirit of derring-do. And the industrial age of the image seems to have led to the extinction of the idea-triggering mechanisms. Yet the role of the poster (if the poster really has a role) is to widen the horizon, and not simply to varnish the surface, a luxury we could surely do without.

The cultural ambiguity that puts the Belgian Folon or the Pole Lenica in the museum but rejects the French Bazooka group out of hand only confirms the ambiguity of the market, which would like advertising to be no more than commercial information. As if the tools of communication were the whole story. Regulations, standards and procedures on the one hand and free expression, wild poster-hanging on the other constitute the dialectic game of a culture and a counter-culture.

A mark on the wall establishes in the eye of the observer, who has looked at the wall before and looks at it now, relations of a new order. Visual relations, perhaps, but also sensual, cultural, emotional relations. Emotion must not be allowed to desert the walls of our towns. Those who are putting up a fight in this cause have already discovered the ruses and the tricks that give back life to posters that are otherwise dead before they are born, and the rightest and most exciting is perhaps diversion from their original purpose.

The idea of alienating things from their original purpose, as practised by the situationists, has enabled the sense of many pictures to be inverted, not by rehabilitation and subsequent sacralization as performed by artists such as La Villéglé, Hains or Rotella, but by spontaneous appropriation by the street, the graffiti, the marking of a thing as part of oneself.... The countries of the Third World have preserved this freshness and "vulgarity" which makes a poster more than a cultural by-product, more than a mere vector of economy.

The poster is part of life. Just as the pedestrian here and elsewhere must get away from the beaten track of the tour operators, the poster must break out of its frame, its boarding, its billboard, its bus shelter, must break away from the norm and the regulation.

Long live, then, the poster-in-the-raw and the wild poster-hanger!

Gilles de Bure

Der Fussgänger, hier und anderswo

Der Journalist GILLES DE BURE äussert sich hier über das Plakat aus der Sicht des Fussgängers in den Städten. Anlass für ihn waren die veränderten Umstände in Paris, einer Stadt, die vielleicht mehr als jede andere durch den freien Plakataushang in ihrem Erscheinungsbild geprägt wurde. Gilles de Bure ist Mitbegründer der Zeitschrift *Cree* (1969), und er hat für zahlreiche internationale Zeitschriften sowie für Radio- und TV-Sendungen gearbeitet, vor allem auf den Gebieten der Architektur, des Designs, der visuellen Kommunikation und der Kunst. Als Verantwortlicher der Galerie d'Actualité hat er an der Eröffnung des Centre Pompidou mitgearbeitet, wo er mehr als zwanzig Ausstellungen organisierte. Er ist Mitglied des Board of Advisors der International Design Conference in Aspen sowie auch Design-Berater für Knoll International. Gegenwärtig leitet er, unterstützt von zahlreichen Künstlern, die *Agence Art+*, eine Agentur, die sich die Integrierung der Kunst in die Umwelt zur Aufgabe macht, in allen ihren Erscheinungsformen (Gemälde, Feste, Veranstaltungen...).

Es gibt, wie man so sagt, zwei einfache Wege, ein Land kennenzulernen: man frühstückt mit den Einheimischen und man liest den Anzeigenteil des auflagestärksten Lokalblattes. Aber während Körper und Geist Informationen über Land und Leute zu Eindrücken und intuitiven Erkenntnissen verarbeiten, darf natürlich auch das Auge als Sinnesempfänger nicht unterschätzt werden.

Hier wie anderswo sind es Betonstrassen, gepflasterte Gassen, staubige Strassenzüge, die der Fussgänger tagtäglich entlanggeht, während sein Auge unablässig die Mauern abtastet, Mauern, die sich auf der ganzen Welt als Träger von Bildern und Botschaften anbieten. Bemalte Wände, Fresken, Leuchtkörper, Supergraphiken ziehen den Vorübergehenden in ihren Bann, als gleichwertige, gleich fesselnde Bilder. Von den in Stein gehauenen Köpfen am Mount Rushmore zu den gigantischen Lenin-Mosaiken im Gum-Warenhaus in Alma-Ata und der Lichterflut des Picadilly Circus, alles bewegt, überrascht und fesselt ihn. Und mit dem Fortschreiten seiner Reise tut sich ihm eine Welt auf, die er durch sein Auge begreifen lernt.

Der Blick, der flüchtig über die Mauern streicht, sie abtastet, sie umschwebt, sie festhält in Städten mit magischen Namen (Macau, Samarkand, Valparaiso...), wie in Städten mit nichtssagenden Namen (Bielefeld, Pittsburgh, Mulhouse...), entdeckt als einzige Konstante das allgegenwärtige, in seiner Aussage internationale Plakat: das ausdruckslose oder faszinierende, das «ausgeflippte» oder fade, das aufrüttelnde oder wirtschaftlichen Gesetzen folgende Plakat, kultureller oder politischer, sozialer oder marktschreierischer Natur, schwarzweiss oder mehrfarbig, grossformatig oder in bescheidener Aufmachung! Diese Plakate, noch feucht vom Kleister, eine Bilderfolge in schillernden Farben, eingefügt in den magischen Rahmen der professionellen Plakataushänger oder hier und da wild an die Wand geklatscht, hastig oder euphorisch, in Nacht und Nebel, in Angst, durch militante Ankleber welcher Überzeugung auch immer, diese Plakate, die uns ergreifen, uns verführen, uns anlocken, uns einfangen, wo immer wir uns befinden.

Selbst in Fetzen herunterhängende Plakate fesseln uns und lassen uns, die wir dem visuellen Zeitalter verschrieben sind, jene Kunstform begreifen, die durch unsere Städte selbst entsteht, jene vibrierenden, schillernden, pulsierenden Orte.

Aber solche «Ungereimtheiten» werden in Zukunft selten sein. Denn in Frankreich wie anderswo spricht man immer häufiger von einer Reglementierung des Plakataushanges, indem bestimmte Flächen zum Aushang freigegeben werden und jedes Zuwiderhandeln streng geahndet wird... Und wieder einmal triumphiert die Verkaufsspirale über den Lebensbaum. Doch dieses Spiel wird sich ewig weiterziehen. Die beiden «Gegenspieler» sind ein institutionalisiertes Wirtschaftssystem, das vom Plakatkünstler die Mitarbeit im Marketing der Artikel verlangt, und ein parallel dazu verlaufendes, fast möchte man sagen Untergrundsystem, das ohne Publizität funktioniert und versucht, diese Welt der Bilder auf den Kopf zu stellen und damit auch das Bild, das wir uns von dieser Welt machen.

So wird nach dem Plakat nun auch der Plakataushang reglementiert. Dem Plakat wurde bereits beträchtlicher Schaden zugefügt. Die spektakulären Aushänge, die alles blosslegten, sind nicht mehr in Mode. Verglichen mit dem Humor und der Schlagkraft von Gerd Dunbars «Mondrian» oder dem als listiger Werbegag getarnten Monument, das die französische Agentur CCM-BBDO zu Ruhm und Ehre von Levi-Strauss errichtete, indem sie die Place de la Concorde in Paris in eine gigantische Alplandschaft verwandelte, bieten die meisten modernen Plakate ein Bild der Langeweile, des Konformismus, der Bedeutungslosigkeit. Soll der Vorübergehende aber aufgerüttelt werden, so muss sich das schon im Konzept, in der herausfordernden Aussage des Plakates manifestieren, aber heute wird dies, wenn überhaupt, auf rein formelle Art und Weise gelöst.

Beim Durchblättern dieses Jahrbuches, das die besten Arbeiten zeigt, die in den vergangenen 12 Monaten intensiven Schaffens auf der ganzen Welt realisiert wurden, wird sich das Interesse des Lesers auf formelle Gesichtspunkte konzentrieren, denn aus diesem Blickwinkel heraus wird heute Kunstgeschichte betrieben, ob es sich nun um bahnbrechende oder eher kurzlebige Tendenzen handelt, mit allen ihren Schulen, Richtungen und Manierismen... Aber dieses ganze Gebiet ist viel weiter, komplexer, widersprüchlicher und daher auch reichhaltiger. Als ob die Stadt selbst nicht dazu beitragen könnte, Aussagen zu unterstützen, sie zu erweitern...

Die verknöcherten Traditionen, die in Ateliers und Akademien noch gepflegt werden, die Verbannung des Widersprüchlichen, Ungereimten, die Banalisierung der Photographie, das ewig über das «savoir-être» triumphierende «savoir-faire» scheint den Mut zum Aussergewöhnlichen zerstört zu haben. Beim industriellen Bildermacher scheint der Mechanismus, der die schlagkräftigen Ideen auslöst, ausgeschaltet zu sein. Die Rolle des Plakates (falls es wirklich noch eine Rolle spielt) ist doch aber, den Horizont zu erweitern und nicht einfach, an der Oberfläche zu glänzen, einen Luxus, auf den wir leicht verzichten können.

Die kulturelle Inkonsequenz, wonach der Belgier Folon und der Pole Lenica im Museum ausgestellt werden, die französische Gruppe Bazooka aber kurzerhand und diskussionslos unter den Tisch gewischt wird, bestätigt, dass nach der vorherrschenden Auffassung Werbung nichts anderes als kommerzielle Information darstellen sollte. Als ob die Kommunikationsmittel an und für sich bereits Kommunikation bedeuteten. Zwischen Reglementierung, Norm und Vorgehen einerseits und freiem Ausdruck und wildem Plakataushang andererseits, spielt sich die dialektische Auseinandersetzung zwischen Kultur und Gegenkultur ab.

Ein Fleck auf der Mauer erweckt im Betrachter, der sie zuvor fleckenlos sah, sofort neue Assoziationen. Visuelle Assoziationen vielleicht, aber auch sinnliche, kulturelle, emotionale. Emotionen dürfen von den Mauern unserer Städte nicht verschwinden. Jene, die darum kämpfen, haben bereits erkannt, mit welchen Schachzügen und Tricks Plakate zu neuem Leben erweckt werden, die sonst, bevor sie überhaupt geboren werden, schon dem Tode geweiht sind, und eines der aufregendsten Mittel ist vielleicht die ironische Umkehrung des ursprünglichen Zweckes.

Die Idee der Verfremdung und Abkehr vom ursprünglichen Zweck, wie sie von Aktionskünstlern zum ersten Mal ausgeführt wurde, erlaubte es, den Sinn einer ganzen Anzahl von Bildern umzukehren, nicht in Form einer Wiederaufnahme oder Sakralisierung, wie es zum Beispiel Künstler vom Range eines La Villéglé, Haines oder Rotella versuchten, sondern durch einen spontanen Bezug zur Strasse, durch Graffiti, durch Zeichen, die einen Teil der eigenen Persönlichkeit ausdrücken. Die Plakatschaffenden in Ländern der Dritten Welt konnten sich diese Frische, Spontaneität und «Vulgarität» erhalten, die das Plakat davor bewahren, ein kulturelles Nebenprodukt oder ein ausschliesslich kommerzielles Ausdrucksmittel zu werden.

Das Plakat ist Teil unseres Lebens. Wie der Mensch hier und anderswo den ausgetretenen Pfaden und vorgegebenen Routen nicht mehr folgen sollte, so muss auch das Plakat aus dem vorgegebenen Rahmen ausbrechen, sich dem Zwang von vorbestimmten Wänden, Normtafeln, Bushaltestellen und Litfasssäulen und damit der Norm und Regel entziehen.

Es lebe das spontan geschaffene Plakat und der freie Plakataushang!

Gilles de Bure

Le Piéton d'ici et d'ailleurs

Le journaliste GILLES DE BURE aborde le sujet du point de vue du «regardeur» de l'affiche à Paris et ailleurs. Ce qui le poussait à choisir ce point de vue c'est surtout l'affichage qui se présente sous un aspect différent à Paris, une ville, où l'affichage sauvage a plus qu'ailleurs donné son empreinte à la physionomie des rues. Gilles de Bure a été cofondateur de la revue *Cree* en 1969 et a collaboré à de nombreux magazines et revues internationaux ainsi qu'à de nombreuses émissions de radio et de télévision, dans les domaines de l'architecture, du design, des communications visuelles et de l'art. En tant que responsable de la Galerie d'Actualité, il a participé à l'ouverture du Centre Georges Pompidou où il a produit plus de vingt expositions. Membre du Board of Advisors de la International Design Conference, Aspen, il est aussi Design Consultant pour Knoll International. Il anime actuellement l'*Agence Art+*, une agence qui a pour objet l'intégration de l'art à l'environnement sous toutes ses formes (œuvres, fêtes, événements...) et a regroupé autour de lui une quinzaine d'artistes, parmi lesquels Kowalski, Malaval, Miralda, Raynaud, Soto, etc.

Les deux meilleures manières de pénétrer un pays sont, dit-on, de prendre son petit déjeuner chez l'habitant et de lire les petites annonces classées du quotidien local au plus fort tirage. Mais si le corps et l'esprit sont bien, chacun à sa manière, deux exceptionnels capteurs d'informations, traducteurs de sensations et d'intuitions, l'œil qui travaille en est un autre et non des moindres.

Le piéton d'ici et d'ailleurs marque de ses pas le macadam, les pavés et la poussière tandis que son œil caresse les murs qui tout autour du monde sont pareillement porteurs d'images et de messages: murs peints et fresques, appareillages de matériaux et monumentalisme graphique, tout est de valeur identique, d'intérêt équivalent. Des visages sculptés du Mount Rushmore aux gigantesques Lénine de mosaïque du Goum d'Alma-Ata en passant par Piccadilly Circus tout lui est de même émotion, de même surprise, de même choc. Les glissements progressifs du voyage aboutissent donc aux glissements progressifs du regard.

Du regard qui lisse, effleure, contourne, investit les murs des villes aux noms de rêve (Macau, Samarkand, Valparaiso...) et aux noms de rien (Bielefeld, Pittsburgh, Mulhouse...) et qui y découvre la seule constante, la véritable internationale, celle de l'affiche, omniprésente, omniparlante. L'affiche lancinante, plate ou merveilleuse, sauvage ou réglementée, jaillissement ou codification économique, culturelle ou politique, sociale ou marchande, en noir et blanc ou en polychromie, en grand format ou en modeste taille. Fraîchement collée, rutilante de couleur, manège ininterrompu d'images, calée dans les cadres magiques des afficheurs professionnels ou encore jetée çà et là anarchiquement dans la hâte et la joie ou dans l'ombre et la peur, par la grâce de l'affichage militant de quelque type qu'il soit, l'affiche, aux quatre coins du monde, nous embrasse, nous séduit, nous attire, nous piège.

Même la lèpre murale et la lacération nous choquent et déclenchent chez nous – visuels impénitents – la reconnaissance de cette forme d'art qu'est la ville qui vibre, qui brille, qui bouge, qui s'anime...

Mais voici que ces «accidents de parcours» risquent de se faire rares. C'est que, de plus en plus fréquemment, on parle, ici et ailleurs, de réglementer l'affichage, d'en réserver les emplacements, de sévèrement punir les contrevenants... C'est le triomphe de la spirale de vente sur l'arbre de vie, ici comme ailleurs. Entre l'affichage sauvage et l'affichage réglementé se joue un jeu éternel. Celui qui oppose un système économique institutionnel réclamant du créateur une participation au conditionnement de la marchandise, à un système parallèle, vaguement souterrain, fonctionnant sans publicité et cherchant à inverser ce monde d'images et, partant, cette image du monde.

Ainsi donc, après l'affiche, c'est l'affichage que l'on va réglementer. Insidieusement l'affiche a déjà subi les pires dommages. Les «pirouettes» qui racontent tout ne sont plus de mode. Pour une merveille d'humour et de force comme le «Mondrian» du Hollandais Gerd Dumbar, pour un monument d'astuce commerciale comme la place de la Concorde à Paris transformée en prairie bucolique à la plus grande gloire de Levi-Strauss par l'agence française CLM-BBDO, quelle masse d'atonie, de conformisme, de neutralisation, de non-discours, de non-choc. Car le choc doit se situer au niveau du concept, donc du discours. Le choc aujourd'hui, quand il existe, n'est plus que formel.

Au fil de cet annuel, qui pourtant regroupe ce qui s'est fait de mieux à travers le monde pendant douze mois d'une production intense, on fondera tout l'intérêt sur les vertus de la forme, car c'est ainsi que l'on écrit l'histoire de tout art, fût-il «majeur», fût-il «mineur»: les écoles, les genres, les manières... pourtant, le champ est plus large, plus complexe, plus contradictoire, et, partant, plus riche. Comme si le support urbain direct n'était pas capable de tout faire passer, de tout expanser?

La sclérosante tradition des ateliers et des académies, le bannissement du contresens et de l'incongruité, la banalisation de la photographie, le savoir-faire sans cesse opposé au savoir-être et éternellement victorieux de lui semblent avoir fait disparaître «l'envie de faire». Et l'industriel de l'image semble avoir éliminé le «déclencheur d'idées». Et pourtant, le rôle de l'affiche (si tant est que l'affiche ait un rôle à jouer), c'est d'élargir l'horizon et non d'apporter un vernis, une éspèce de produit de luxe dont on pourrait faire l'économie.

L'ambiguïté culturelle qui met le Belge Folon et le Polonais Lenica au musée, mais rejette le groupe français Bazooka hors de toute parole, conforte l'ambiguïté marchande qui voudrait que la publicité soit information commerciale. Comme si les outils de la communication étaient toute la communication. Entre la réglementation, la norme, le procédé d'une part, et l'expression, l'affichage sauvage d'autre part, se noue le jeu dialectique d'une culture et d'une contre-culture.

Une tache sur un mur établit chez celui qui regarde le mur, qui l'avait regardé auparavant et qui le regarde maintenant, des relations d'un nouvel ordre. Des relations visuelles soit, mais aussi sensuelles, culturelles, émotionnelles. Il ne faut pas que l'émotion déserte les murs de nos villes. Ceux qui luttent ont déjà découvert les biais et les travers qui donnent la vie à des affiches mortes avant d'être nées et dont le plus marquant, le plus juste est, peut-être, le détournement d'usage.

Le concept du détournement d'usage avancé et pratiqué par les situationnistes a permis d'inverser le sens de bien des images, non pas sous la forme d'une récupération puis d'une sacralisation telles celles pratiquées par des artistes comme La Villéglé, Hains ou Rotella, mais bien sous celles d'une appropriation spontanée par la rue, les graffiti, le marquage d'une part de soi-même... Les pays tiers mondistes ont su garder cette fraîcheur et cette «vulgarité» qui font d'une affiche autre chose qu'un sous-produit culturel, autre chose qu'un seul vecteur économique.

L'affiche fait partie de la vie. Elle doit donc, comme le piéton d'ici et d'ailleurs se doit de sortir des sentiers battus par les «tour-operators», sortir du cadre, du panonceau, du tableau, de l'abri-bus, du billboard, sortir de la norme et de la règle.

Vivent l'affiche brute et l'affichage sauvage.

Index to Artists, Photographers and Designers
Verzeichnis der Künstler, Photographen und Gestalter
Index des artistes, photographes et maquettistes

Index to Art Directors
Verzeichnis der künstlerischen Leiter
Index des directeurs artistiques

Index to Agencies and Studios
Verzeichnis der Agenturen und Studios
Index des agences et studios

Index to Advertisers
Verzeichnis der Auftraggeber
Index des clients

Index to Publishers and Distributors
Verzeichnis der Verleger und Vertriebsstellen
Index des éditeurs et distributeurs

Addresses of Poster Publishers
Adressen von Posterverlegern
Adresses d'éditeurs d'affiches

ATHENA REPRODUCTIONS; Raynham Road, Bishops Stortford, Herts./GBR
CELESTIAL ARTS; 231 Adrian Road, Millbrae, CA 94030/USA
DARIEN HOUSE, INC.; 37 Riverside Drive, New York, NY 10023/USA
DEUTSCHER SPARKASSEN VERLAG GMBH; Postfach 80 03 30, D-7000 Stuttgart 80/GER
DIOGENES VERLAG AG; Sprecherstrasse 8, 8032 Zürich/SWI
FOREIGN TRADE ENTERPRISE; Polish Artistic Posters, Aleje Jerozolimskie 2, 00-374 Warsaw/POL
HALL & CEDERQUIST AB; Strandvägen 5 A, S-11451 Stockholm/SWE
ORANGERIE; Helenenstr. 2, D-5000 Köln 1/GER
SCANDECOR INTERNATIONAL; Box 656, S-751 27 Uppsala/SWE
SCANDECOR PRODUCTION GMBH; Elisabethenstrasse 30, D-6070 Langen/GER
SCHOLASTIC MAGAZINES, INC.; 50 West 44th Street, New York, NY 10036/USA
STALLING VERLAG GMBH; Ammergaustr. 72–78, D-2900 Oldenburg/GER
TAURUS PRESS OF WILLOW DENE; Paul Peter Piech, 2, Willow Dene, Herts WD2 1 PS/GBR
UPSIDE AB; Box 43059, S-10072 Stockholm 3/SWE
VERKERKE REPRODUKTIES BV; Postbus 67, NL-6710 BB Ede/NLD

Editor and Art Director: Walter Herdeg
Assistant Editor: Stanley Mason
Project Manager: Heinke Jenssen
Designers: Martin Byland, Klaus Schröder
Art Assistants: Willy Müller, Peter R. Wittwer

1

Advertising Posters

Werbeplakate

Affiches publicitaires

ARTIST / KÜNSTLER / ARTISTE:

1 Daniel Gendre/Romeo Gross
2, 3 Willi Rieser
4, 5 Tom McCarthy
6 Daniel Gendre

DESIGNER / GESTALTER / MAQUETTISTE:

1 Ernst Herzog
2, 3 Willi Rieser
4, 5 Bob Cargill
6 Daniel Gendre/Urs Glaser

ART DIRECTOR / DIRECTEUR ARTISTIQUE:

1 Ruedi Külling
2, 3, 6 Urs Glaser
4, 5 Bonnie Lovell

AGENCY / AGENTUR / AGENCE-STUDIO:

1 Advico AG
2, 3, 6 McCann-Erickson
4, 5 Cargill and Associates, Inc.

1

2

1 Large-format poster for *Sinalco*, a soft drink. Lettering yellow with green and yellow with red on a dark background. Drink in yellow, clothing in blue shades. (SWI)
2, 3 Complete poster made up of the sections universe, earth and water, with detail of the "earth" section. This poster, specially designed for children, advertises the fruit drink *Fanta* and is available from the manufacturers. (SWI)
4, 5 Two examples from a poster campaign for *Coca-Cola* using the same slogan. Both posters in full colour with the background in green shades. (USA)
6 Three-part poster for *Coca-Cola* from a series of posters using the same slogan. (SWI)

1 Grossformatiges Plakat für das alkoholfreie Getränk *Sinalco*. Buchstaben gelb mit Grün und gelb mit Rot auf dunklem Hintergrund. Getränk gelb, Kleidung in Blautönen. (SWI)
2, 3 Komplettes Plakat, das aus den Teilen Weltall, Erde und Wasser besteht und Detail des Teils «Erde». Das speziell für Kinder konzipierte Plakat wirbt für das Fruchtgetränk *Fanta* und ist beim Hersteller erhältlich. (SWI)
4, 5 Zwei Beispiele aus einer Plakatkampagne für *Coca-Cola* unter dem gleichen Slogan. Beide Plakate mehrfarbig mit Hintergrund in Grüntönen. (USA)
6 Dreiteiliges Plakat für *Coca-Cola* aus einer Serie von Plakaten mit dem gleichen Slogan. (SWI)

1 Affiche grand format pour une boisson de table à plusieurs jus de fruits. Lettres jaunes et verts ou jaunes et rouges sur fond foncé. Boisson jaune, robe en tons bleus. (SWI)
2, 3 Affiche complète présentant la mer, la terre et l'espace et détail de la «terre». Cette affiche, conçue spécialement pour les enfants, fait partie d'une campagne publicitaire pour la boisson *Fanta* et peut être commandée auprès du fabricant. (SWI)
4, 5 Deux exemples d'une campagne de publicité lancée en faveur du *Coca-Cola*. Toutes les affiches portent le même slogan. En polychromie sur fond en vert foncé. (USA)
6 «*Coke*, c'est fait pour ça...» Affiche triple figurant dans une série pour Coca-Cola. (SWI)

4

5

Coke macht mehr draus.

7 Three-part poster for *Jaffa* grapefruit. Yellow fruit on brown background. (SWI)
8 "The small juicy one." Poster for Moroccan oranges. Full colour. (NOR)
9 Poster for *White Label* whisky. (SWI)
10 Full-colour poster for *Mützig*, an Alsatian beer. The slogan reads: "Take the time for a *Mützig*." (FRA)
11 Poster for *Pepita*, a mineral water with grapefruit flavour. As real grapefruit juice is not used for flavouring the drink, it was not permissible for a real grapefruit to be shown on the poster. (SWI)
12 Poster for *Suchard* Swiss chocolate. (SWI)
13 "Midday's better half." Full-colour poster with which a central office for fruit and vegetables advertises its products. (NOR)
14 A further poster from the central office for fruit and vegetables, here for a cider that is supposed to contain the juice of ten apples. Bright red apples, bottle label in red with gold and blue. (NOR)

7 Plakat für *Jaffa*-Pampelmusen. Gelbe Frucht auf braunem Hintergrund. (SWI)
8 «Die kleine Saftige.» Plakatwerbung für marokkanische Orangen. Mehrfarbig. (NOR)
9 Plakat für Whisky der Marke *White Label*. (SWI)
10 Mehrfarbiges Plakat für *Mützig*, eine Elsässer Biermarke. Der Slogan: «Nimm dir Zeit für ein *Mützig*.» (FRA)
11 Plakat für *Pepita*, ein Tafelwasser mit Grapefruit-Geschmack. Da es sich hier nicht um ein reines Fruchtgetränk handelt, durfte aufgrund der amtlichen Bestimmungen keine echte Grapefruit auf dem Plakat gezeigt werden. (SWI)
12 Plakat für Schweizer Schokolade der Marke *Suchard*. (SWI)
13 «Des Mittags bessere Hälfte.» Mehrfarbiges Plakat, mit dem eine Zentralstelle für Obst und Gemüse für ihre Erzeugnisse wirbt. (NOR)
14 Ein weiteres Plakat der Zentralstelle für Obst und Gemüse, hier für einen Apfelmost, der den Saft von 10 Äpfeln enthalten soll. Leuchtend rote Äpfel, Etikette der Flasche rot mit Gold und Blau. (NOR)

ARTIST / KÜNSTLER / ARTISTE:

7 R. Feuz
8 Ragge Strand
9 Atelier tm
10 Luigi Castiglioni
11 René Groebli
12 Daniel Gendre
13, 14 Jon Halvorsen

DESIGNER / GESTALTER / MAQUETTISTE:

7 Ruedi Külling
11 Willi Nydegger
12 Dieter Hofmann

ART DIRECTOR / DIRECTEUR ARTISTIQUE:

7 Ruedi Külling
8, 13, 14 Trygve Foss
9 Stefan Kaister
10 Bruno Sutter
11 H.R. Abächerli
12 Dieter Hofmann

AGENCY / AGENTUR / AGENCE-STUDIO:

7, 12 Advico AG
8, 13, 14 Idé, Reklame & Marketing
9 Urs Tschan AG
10 Feldman et Calleux
11 H.R. Abächerli

8

9

13

12

14

15

16

15 Poster for the red wine *Dôle* from the Valais marketed by the *Provins* wine-growers' association. The stars have been borrowed for this advertisement from the cantonal flag. (SWI)
16 Advertising for a *Suntory* white wine. In full colour. (JPN)
17, 18 Two more posters from *Suntory*, manufacturer of spirits, here for vodka and brandy. Also in full colour. (JPN)
19 "Hi… A brown one, completely *Gauloises*." Three-part poster for a new type of cigarette from *Gauloises*. Brown packet on a dark background. (SWI)
20 "*Carlsberg 25*. Not only because of your thirst." Light beer in front of a blue sky. (DEN)
21 A poster for milk issued by the Canadian milk marketing board. Mostly in black and white. It was displayed primarily in shops and the underground railway. (CAN)

19

15 Plakat für den Walliser Rotwein *Dôle* der Winzergemeinschaft *Provins*. Die Sterne sind der Kantonsfahne entnommen. (SWI)
16 Werbung für einen Weisswein von *Suntory*. In Farbe. (JPN)
17, 18 Zwei weitere Plakate des Spiritu enherstellers *Suntory*, ebenfalls mehrfarbig. Hier für einen Wodka und einen Weinbrand. (JPN)
19 Dreiteiliges Plakat für eine neue So igarettenmarke *Gauloises*. Braune Packung vor dunklem Hintergrund. (SWI)
20 «*Carlsberg 25*. Nicht nur des Durstes wegen.» Helles Bier vor blauem Himmel. (DEN)
21 «Schmeckt so gut.» Vorwiegend in Schwarzweiss gehaltenes Plakat einer kanadischen Marketing-Stelle für Milch. Es wurde hauptsächlich in Läden und der U-Bahn ausgehängt. (CAN)

15 Affiche publiée par la coopérative viticole *Provins* en faveur du *Dôle*, vin du Valais. Les étoiles sont empruntées au drapeau de ce canton suisse. (SWI)
16 Affiche pour un vin blanc de *Suntory*. En polychromie. (JPN)
17, 18 Deux autres affiches de *Suntory*, fabricant de boissons alcooliques, ici pour une vodka et un cognac. En polychromie. (JPN)
19 «Salu. Une brune, tout à fait *Gauloises*.» Affiche triple pour lancer la nouvelle *Gauloises* brune. Paquet brun sur fond foncé. (SWI)
20 «*Carlsberg 25*. Non seulement à cause de la soif.» Bière blonde, ciel bleu. (DEN)
21 «C'est bon.» Affiche d'un centre canadien pour la promotion du lait. Cette affiche est destinée surtout pour les magasins et le métro. Prédominance de noir et blanc. (CAN)

17

18

Carlsberg 25. Ikke kun for tørstens skyld.

20

TASTES SO GOOD

21

22

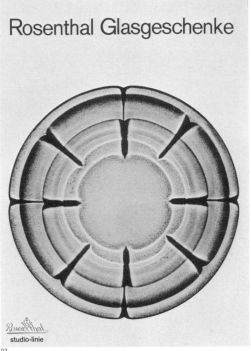

23

24

ARTIST / KÜNSTLER / ARTISTE:

22 Loretta Leiva
23 Gerd Wricke
24 Michael Tessmann/Angela Endress
26 André François
27 Urs Roos
28 Toshiyuki Ohashi
29 Franz Stoffel
30 Almir Mavignier
31 Lea Vähäkuopus

DESIGNER / GESTALTER / MAQUETTISTE:

22 Loretta Leiva
23 Gerd Wricke
24 Klaus Wolowiec
25 Julien van der Wal
27 Urs Derron
28 Shigeo Okamoto/Yukiko Goto
29 Franz Stoffel
30 Almir Mavignier
31 Jorma Hinkka

22 Full-colour poster of a shop advertising house and garden appliances from *Barry-Ware*. (USA)
23 Black-and-white poster for *Rosenthal* glass. (GER)
24 Another poster from the *Rosenthal* studio advertising Finnish kitchen cooking utensils from *Arabia*. (GER)
25 Poster for a boutique. The upper part of the lettering is in yellow, turning into blue, the remaining letters in blue. (SWI)
26 "*Habitat*, the simplest way to feel at home." Full-colour poster for *Habitat* interior decorations. (FRA)
27 Poster advertising *FPS* animal food on the occasion of the *Olma* agricultural exhibition. In full colour. (SWI)
28 Poster for *Moyet* confectionery. In blue and white. (JPN)
29 Poster for *Suchard* chocolate. (SWI)
30 Poster with a colour photograph for the *Brasilia* building housing a Brazilian restaurant with a boutique. (GER)
31 Poster for canned vegetables. (FIN)

22 Plakatwerbung eines Geschäftes für importierte Haushaltgeräte der Marke *Barry-Ware*. Mehrfarbig. (USA)
23 Schwarzweiss-Plakat des Hauses *Rosenthal*. (GER)
24 Ein weiteres Plakat vom *Rosenthal* Studio-Haus, hier für ein Kochgeschirr der finnischen Marke *Arabia*. (GER)
25 Plakat für eine Boutique. Die oberen Buchstabenlängen des Schriftzugs gelb, in Blau übergehend. Die übrige Schrift blau. (SWI)
26 «*Habitat*, die einfachste Art, sich zu Hause wohlzufühlen.» Farbiges Plakat für *Habitat*-Inneneinrichtungen. (FRA)
27 Plakatwerbung für *FPS*-Tiernahrung anlässlich der Landwirtschafts-Ausstellung *Olma*. In Farbe. (SWI)
28 Plakat für *Moyet*-Konfekt, in Blau und Weiss. (JPN)
29 Werbung für *Suchard*-Schokolade. (SWI)
30 Plakat mit Farbaufnahme des Bauwerkes *Brasilia*, das ein brasilianisches Restaurant mit Boutique beherbergt. (GER)
31 Plakat für Gemüsekonserven. (FIN)

22 Affiche d'un magasin en faveur des ustensils de ménage importés. En polychromie. (USA)
23 Affiche noir-blanc de la maison *Rosenthal*. (GER)
24 Une autre affiche de *Rosenthal*, ici pour les casseroles *Arabia* provenant de la Finlande. (GER)
25 Affiche d'une boutique. Les caractères du logo sont en jaune passant au bleu. Le texte est bleu sur un fond foncé. (SWI)
26 «*Habitat*, la plus simple manière d'être bien chez soi.» Affiche polychrome pour une marque d'ameublement. (FRA)
27 Affiche publiée à l'occasion d'une foire-exposition agricole en Suisse pour une marque de nourriture pour animaux. (SWI)
28 Affiche pour une marque de petits-beurre. (JPN)
29 Affiche pour les bonbons de chocolat *Suchard*. (SWI)
30 Affiche avec photo couleur de la construction *Brasilia* où se trouve un restaurant brésilien avec une boutique. (GER)
31 Affiche pour une marque de conserves de légumes. (FIN)

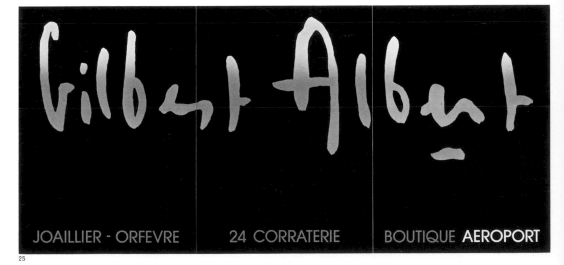

25

26

WIR FÜTTERN IHRE
TIERE MIT ERFOLG.

FPS Der Begriff für moderne Tierernährung.
Feed Production System AG, 9202 Gossau, Friedbergstr. 2, Tel. 071/85 80 81

27

moyet confectionery

28

ART DIRECTOR / DIRECTEUR ARTISTIQUE:

22 Loretta Leiva
23 Gerd Wricke
25 Julien van der Wal
26 Robert Delpire
27 Urs Derron
28 Shigeo Okamoto
29 Franz Stoffel
30 Almir Mavignier
31 Jorma Hinkka

AGENCY / AGENTUR / AGENCE-STUDIO:

22 House & Garden Promotion
23 Gerd Wricke Grafik
24 Rosenthal AG/Verkaufsförderung
25 Julien van der Wal
26 Ideodis
27 Wiederkehr & Derron
28 Shigeo Okamoto Design Center
29 Triplex AG
31 Mainostoimisto Oy Sek Ab

29

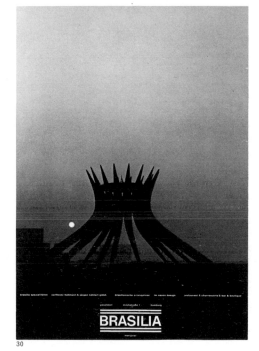

BRASILIA

30

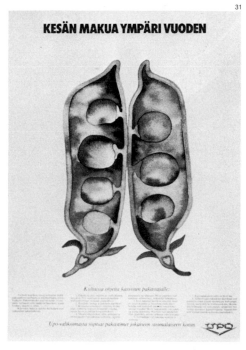

KESÄN MAKUA YMPÄRI VUODEN

31

Varia

33

32

33

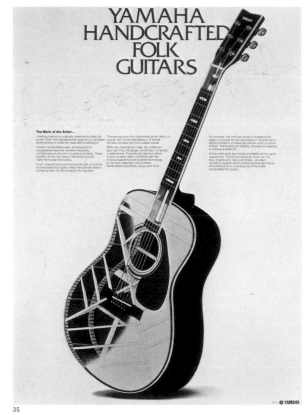

35

36

ARTIST / KÜNSTLER / ARTISTE:

32 Marv Lyons
33 Kishin Shinoyama
34 Kazumasa Nagai
35 Sadahito Mori
36 Ikko Tanaka
38 Poul Ib Henriksen
39 Nobuhiko Yabuki

DESIGNER / GESTALTER / MAQUETTISTE:

33, 36 Ikko Tanaka
34 Kazumasa Nagai
35 Yoshihiro Mizuno
37 Michael Vanderbyl
38 Poul Ib Henriksen
39 Kenichi Samura

ART DIRECTOR / DIRECTEUR ARTISTIQUE:

32 Roger Yost
33, 36 Ikko Tanaka
34 Kazumasa Nagai
35 Satoru Tsurumi
38 Finn Sködt
39 Ikko Tanaka/Kazuko Koike

AGENCY / AGENTUR / AGENCE-STUDIO:

34 Nippon Design Centre
35 Crown Design Center Inc.
37 Vanderbyl Design

Varia

34

32 Large-format poster for *Fieldday* sports clothing manufactured by *Jantzen* for a wide range of sports. The clothes are in full colour and are placed in front of a blue sky. (USA)
33 Poster for the *Seibu* department store referring to a traditional form of the Japanese theatre. Skin and clothing in white, red lips and eyelashes, reddish scarf. (JPN)
34 Poster for a *Prince* cigarette lighter. (JPN)
35 Poster for handmade *Yamaha* guitars. The manufacturing process is described in the text. (JPN)
36 Another poster from the *Seibu* department store (see Fig. 33), here with a cultural announcement. The illustration has a canvas-type structure. Mostly in warm shades of brown. (JPN)
37 Poster of an American association of interior decorators, advertising a sale of home and office furniture. Green sofa with an orange pattern. (USA)
38 Poster for *Kvadrat*, a manufacturer of all kinds of decorating and furniture materials. (DEN)
39 Poster announcing the opening of a new *Seiyu* shop. (JPN)

32 «Wer bringt das beste Sportprogramm? *Jantzen*. Sie wissen wer.» Grossformatiges Plakat für *Fieldday*-Sportbekleidung von *Jantzen*. Kleidungsstücke farbig vor blauem Himmel. (USA)
33 Plakatwerbung des Kaufhauses *Seibu*. Es bezieht sich auf eine traditionelle Form des japanischen Theaters. Haut und Kleidung der Gestalt weiss, Augenumrandung und Mund rot, rötlicher Schal. (JPN)
34 Plakat für ein *Prince*-Feuerzeug. (JPN)
35 Plakatwerbung für handgearbeitete Gitarren von *Yamaha*. Im Text wird der Herstellungsprozess beschrieben. (JPN)
36 Ein weiteres Plakat des Kaufhauses *Seibu* (siehe Abb. 33), das kulturellen Charakter hat. Sichtbare Leinwandstruktur der Illustration; warme, vorwiegend bräunliche Farbtöne. (JPN)
37 Plakat einer amerikanischen Vereinigung von Innenarchitekten, mit dem für eine Ausverkauf von Wohn- und Büromöbeln geworben wird. (USA)
38 Plakatwerbung der Firma *Kvadrat*, Hersteller von Dekorations- und Möbelstoffen aller Art. (DEN)
39 Bekanntmachung der Eröffnung eines neuen *Seiyu*-Geschäftes. (JPN)

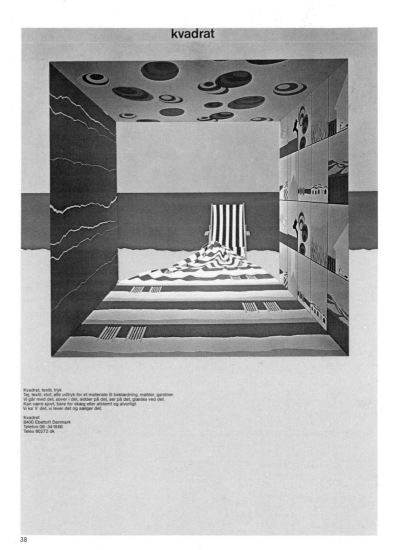

Kvadrat, textil, tryk
Tøj, textil, stof, alle udtryk for et materiale til beklædning, møbler, gardiner.
Vi går med det, sover i det, sidder på det, ser på det, glædes ved det.
Kan være sjovt, bare for skæg eller afstemt og alvorligt.
Vi ka' li' det, vi laver det og sælger det.

Kvadrat
8400 Ebeltoft Danmark
Telefon 06-341866
Telex 60272 dk

34

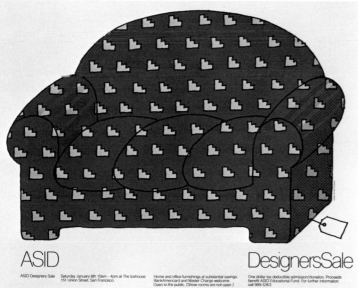

ASID   DesignersSale

ASID Designers Sale   Saturday January 6th 10am—4pm at The Icehouse   Home and office furnishings at substantial savings.   One dollar tax deductible admission/donation. Proceeds
                       151 Union Street, San Francisco.   BankAmericard and Master Charge welcome.   benefit ASID Educational Fund. For further information
                                                                        Open to the public. (Show rooms are not open.)   call 989-5363.

37

32 «Qui présente le meilleur programme sportif? *Jantzen*. Vous le savez.» Affiche grand format pour les vêtements de sport *Fieldday* de *Jantzen*. Vêtements en couleurs vives, ciel bleu. (USA)
33 Affiche d'un grand magasin de Tokyo. Le motif se réfère à un genre théâtral traditionnel du Japon. Visage et robe en blanc, bouche et maquillage des yeux en rouge, écharpe en tons rougeâtres. (JPN)
34 Affiche pour une marque de briquet. (JPN)
35 Affiche en faveur des guitares *Yamaha* faites à la main. Le texte donne des explications concernant la fabrication de guitares. (JPN)
36 Une autre affiche figurant dans la série des grands magasins *Seibu* de Tokyo (voir fig. 33). Celle-ci annonce un événement culturel. L'illustration en prédominance de tons bruns a une structure évoquant une étoffe. (JPN)
37 Affiche publiée par l'Association américaine des architectes-décorateurs. Prédominance de tons bruns. (USA)
38 Affiche pour la promotion du grand choix de tissus d'ameublement de *Kvadrat*, fabricant danois de tissus. (DEN)
39 Affiche annonçant l'ouverture d'un nouveau magasin *Seiyu*. Illustration polychrome ayant une structure de lin. (JPN)

39

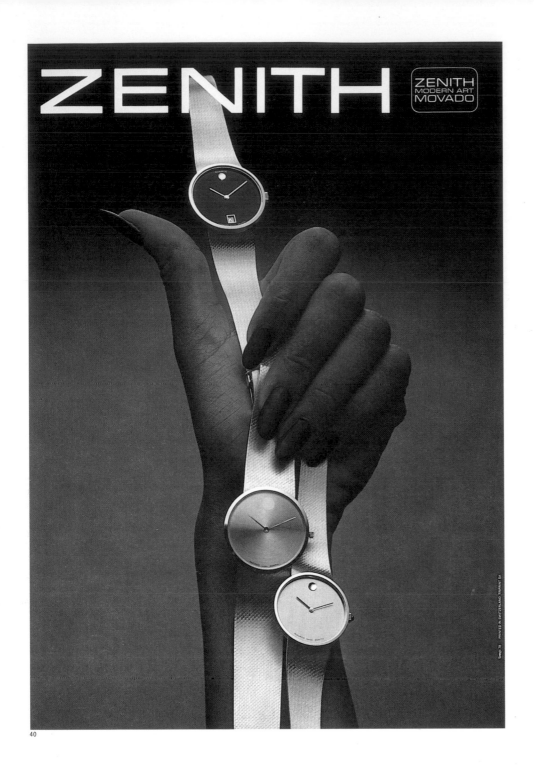

40

41

42

43

36

LUNETTES DE SOLEIL
LE PLUS GRAND CHOIX DE GENEVE
DRUGSTORE
PHARMACIE PRINCIPALE

PHOTO-CINÉ
PHARMACIE PRINCIPALE
Centre ville, Balexert et Aéroport.

44

45

40 Large-format poster for *Zenith* watches. (SWI)
41 Advertisement for *People* magazine, referring to the success of an advertiser who manufactures a special kind of furniture. Red and violet hearts on green background. (USA)
42 Black-and-white poster for a shopping centre. It lists all the services offered by means of symbols and short descriptions. Included in the departments is a medical service centre. (SWI)
43 Full-colour poster advertising an agent for the bleaching out of blue jeans, turning them into "old friends". (USA)
44, 45 Two posters from *Pharmacie Principale*, Geneva. Shown here are sunglasses with polished lenses and the photography and film service of the store. Both in full colour. (SWI)
46, 47 From a series of posters for women's fashions from the *Grieder* fashion store in Zurich. Both posters shown were also used for the *Bon Génie* fashion store in Geneva. Fig. 47 in subdued shades with lettering in pale mauve. (SWI)

40 Grossformatiges Plakat für *Zenith*-Uhren. (SWI)
41 Plakatwerbung der Zeitschrift *People* («Leute») mit Hinweis auf den Werbeerfolg eines ihrer Inserenten, der «Möbel für Liebende» herstellt. Herzen rot und violett auf Grün. (USA)
42 Schwarzweiss-Plakat für ein Einkaufszentrum mit Beschreibung der verschiedenen Dienstleistungen. (SWI)
43 «Mach' aus neuen Jeans alte Freunde.» Mehrfarbiges Plakat für *Old Blue*, ein Mittel zur Behandlung von Blue Jeans, um ihnen ein getragenes Aussehen zu verleihen. (USA)
44, 45 Zwei Plakate der *Pharmacie Principale*, Genf. Hier für Sonnenbrillen mit geschliffenen Gläsern und einen Photo- und Filmdienst. Beide farbig. (SWI)
46, 47 Beispiele aus einer Serie von Plakaten des Modehauses *Grieder* in Zürich. Beide Plakate wurden auch für das Modegeschäft *Bon Génie*, Genf, verwendet. Abb. 47 mit gedämpften Farbtönen, Schal und Schriftzug in einem blassen Mauve-Ton. (SWI)

47

GRIEDER

46

40 Affiche grand format pour les montres *Zenith*. (SWI)
41 Affiche du magazine *People* avec des indications se référant à une campagne publicitaire qu'un fabricant de «meubles pour les amoureux» y a lancée avec succès. Cœurs en rouge et violet sur fond vert. (USA)
42 Affiche noir-blanc pour un supermarché. (SWI)
43 «Soyez de bons amis avec vos nouveaux jeans.» Affiche polychrome pour un produit pour faire pâlir les couleurs. (USA)
44, 45 Deux affiches de la *Pharmacie Principale* de Genève. Ici on fait de la publicité pour des lunettes de soleil optiques et le service photo-ciné. Les deux sont en couleurs. (SWI)
46, 47 Deux affiches figurant dans une longue série pour la confection mode des magasins *Grieder* à Zurich. Fig. 47: tons mats foulard et texte mauve pâle. Les mêmes compositions ont été utilisées pour les grands magasins *Au Bon Génie* de Genève. (SWI)

Varia

48

ARTIST / KÜNSTLER / ARTISTE:

48, 49 Walter Ferrier
50 Jost Wildbolz
51, 52 Francis Delivré
53 Mimmo Francia
54 J.P. Ronzel

DESIGNER / GESTALTER / MAQUETTISTE:

48, 49 Walter Ferrier
50 Franz Merlicek
54 M. Anne

49

50

ART DIRECTOR / DIRECTEUR ARTISTIQUE:

48, 49 Walter Ferrier
51, 52 C. Colin
53 Ghigo Roli
54 J.P. Ronzel

AGENCY / AGENTUR / AGENCE-STUDIO:

48, 49 Walter Ferrier
50 Demner & Merlicek
53 Mimmo Francia
54 J.P. Ronzel & Cie

51

52

53

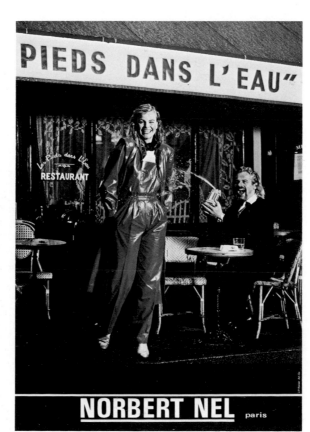

54

48, 49 Two posters advertising *Teeny Tages* children's clothing in shops. Fig. 49 in shades of beige and brown. (SAF)
50 Poster advertising *Lady Manhattan* women's clothes. Beige, pink and white. (AUT)
51, 52 Two posters from *Du Pont* advertising textiles made of *Dacron*, a textured fibre. These posters convey a sense of freedom and ease which the wearer is supposed to feel in clothing manufactured from these fibres. Both posters mainly in blue and yellow. (FRA)
53 Poster advertising *Free Boys* children's clothing. In full colour. (ITA)
54 Poster for *Norbert Nel* fashions. Shown here is a red, lacquered-effect model. (FRA)

48, 49 Zwei Plakate als Werbung für Kindertextilien der Marke *Teeny Tages* in Läden. Abb. 49 in Beige- und Brauntönen. (SAF)
50 Plakatwerbung für Damenbekleidung der Marke *Lady Manhattan*. Beige, Rosa und Weiss. (AUT)
51, 52 Zwei Plakate von *Du Pont*, mit denen für Textilien aus texturiertem *Dacron* geworben wird. Hier soll das Gefühl der Freiheit und Leichtigkeit demonstriert werden, das der Träger von Bekleidung aus dieser Faser empfinden soll. Beide Plakate vorwiegend in Blau und Gelb. (FRA)
53 Plakatwerbung für Kinderbekleidung der Marke *Free Boys*. In Farbe. (ITA)
54 Plakat für Bekleidung von *Norbert Nel*, hier ein rotes lackartiges Modell. (FRA)

48, 49 Deux affiches pour lancer une marque de vêtements pour enfants. Fig. 49 en tons beiges et bruns. (SAF)
50 Affiche pour les vêtements de femme *Lady Manhattan*. Beige, rose et blanc. (AUT)
51, 52 Deux affiches d'une série de la maison *Du Pont de Nemours* vantant le côté naturel et la sensation de liberté qu'on éprouve en portant des costumes en *Dacron*. Prédominance de tons bleus et jaunes. (FRA)
53 Affiche en polychromie en faveur des vêtements pour enfants *Free Boys*. (ITA)
54 Affiche pour les créations de *Norbert Nel*, présentant ici un modèle rouge laqué. (FRA)

明日の女が歩いている。

55

55 Poster advertising *Form Fit Japan*, underwear manufacturers. Models shown here are by the fashion designer *Hanae Mori*. (JPN)
56, 56a, 56b Posters for the *La Rinascente* department stores of Milan. Here for summer and winter fashions and for western-style clothing for children. (ITA)
57 Black-and-white poster for *Marimekko* fabrics showing part of the printing procedure. (FIN)
58 Poster displayed on the occasion of the third anniversary of a fashion centre. In full colour. (JPN)
59 Example from a poster campaign for *Peric* children's spring fashions. Subdued shades of grey and brown. (JPN)

55 Plakatwerbung des Wäsche- und Miederfabrikanten *Form Fit Japan*, hier für Modelle der Mode-Designerin *Hanae Mori*. (JPN)
56, 56a, 56b Plakate des Mailänder Kaufhauses *La Rinascente*. Hier für Sommer- und Wintermode sowie für Kinderbekleidung im Western-Stil. (ITA)
57 Schwarzweiss-Plakat für *Marimekko*-Stoffe. Hier wird ein Teil des Druckvorgangs gezeigt. (FIN)
58 Anlässlich des dreijährigen Bestehens eines Modezentrums veröffentlichtes Plakat. In Farbe. (JPN)
59 Beispiel aus einer Plakatkampagne für Kinder-Frühjahrsmode der Marke *Peric*. Verhaltene Grau- und Brauntöne. (JPN)

55 Affiche de *Form Fit Japan*, fabricant de lingerie. Ici on présente des modèles créés par *Hanae Mori*. (JPN)
56, 56a, 56b Affiches du grand magasin milanais *La Rinascente*, ici pour la collection d'été et d'hiver et pour des vêtements pour enfants style western. (ITA)
57 Affiche noir-blanc pour les tissus *Marimekko*. On montre ici le procédé d'impression. (FIN)
58 Affiche publiée à l'occasion des trois ans d'existence d'un magasin de mode. En polychromie. (JPN)
59 D'une campagne d'affiches en faveur de la collection de printemps pour enfants. Tons gris et bruns. (JPN)

56

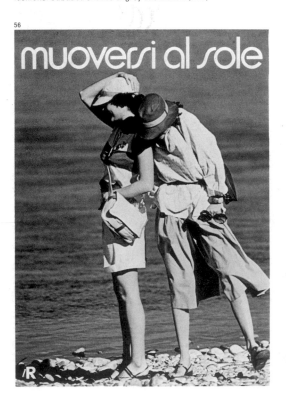

56a

56b

marimekko®

57

FASHION PARK

58

59

41

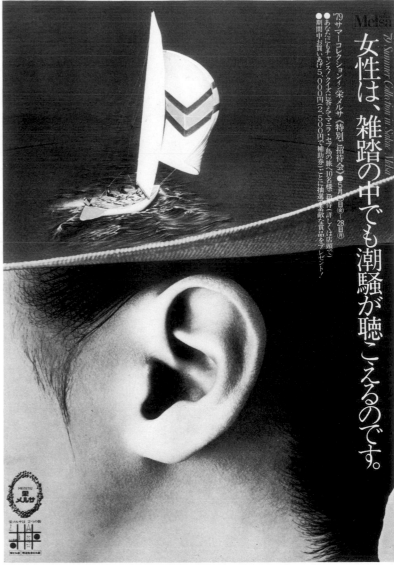

60 Full-colour poster for the Tokyo department store *Matsuya*. (JPN)
61 Advertising for the summer fashion collection of *Sakae-Melsa*. Head and hat in blue, sailboat in white, yellow and blue. (JPN)
62–64 Posters advertising *Bogner* sportswear. White tennis clothing and white lettering on a dark background (Fig. 62), and winter sports clothing in Figs. 63 and 64. (GER)
65, 66 Two more posters, this time for *Bogner* women's fashions. Clothes in Fig. 65 in a warm red, the skirt in Fig. 66 in the same colour as the field. (GER)

60 Mehrfarbiges Plakat des Kaufhauses *Matsuya* in Tokio. (JPN)
61 Plakatwerbung für die Sommermode-Kollektion der Marke *Sakae-Melsa*. Kopf und Hut blau, Segelboot weiss mit Gelb und Blau. (JPN)
62–64 Plakatwerbung für *Bogner*-Sportbekleidung. Hier weisse Tennisausrüstung und weisser Schriftzug vor dunklem Hintergrund (Abb. 62) und Wintersportkleidung (Abb. 63 und 64). (GER)
65, 66 Zwei weitere Plakate des Hauses *Bogner*, hier für Damenmode. Kleidung in Abb. 65 in einem warmen Rot, Rock in Abb. 66 in den Farben der Wiese. (GER)

60 Affiche polychrome pour le grand magasin *Matsuya* de Tokyo. (JPN)
61 Publicité pour la collection d'été présentée par *Sakae-Melsa*. Tête et chapeau bleus, bateau à voiles en bleu, blanc et jaune. (JPN)
62–64 D'une série d'affiches pour les vêtements de sport de la maison *Bogner*. Fig. 62: équipement de tennis (blanc sur fond foncé); fig. 63 et 64: vêtements de sport d'hiver. (GER)
65, 66 Deux autres affiches de *Bogner*, ici pour des articles de mode de femme. En couleurs. (GER)

Fashion/Mode

ARTIST / KÜNSTLER / ARTISTE:

60 Hidesato Iwamura
61 Yoshiro Niwa
62–64 Hans Feurer
65, 66 Rosmarie Bogner

DESIGNER / GESTALTER:

60 Kenji Inoue/Kouji Mizuno
61 Akira Kamesaka

ART DIRECTOR / DIRECTEUR ARTISTIQUE:

60 Hideo Mukai
61 Ken Nishio
62–66 Willy Bogner

AGENCY / AGENTUR / AGENCE-STUDIO:

61 Dentsu Inc.
62–66 Willy Bogner GmbH & Co KG

ARTIST / KÜNSTLER / ARTISTE:
67–71 Noriaki Yokosuka
72, 73 Soumei Kanato

67

68

69

67 Example of a poster advertising products of the Shiseido Cosmetics Co. Here a perfume. (JPN)
68 From a poster campaign for *Shiseido* face treatment products. Red dress. (JPN)
69 Another Shiseido Cosmetics Co. poster advertising liprouge. (JPN)
70, 71 Two examples from a poster campaign for a *Shiseido* nail varnish assortment. (JPN)
72, 73 Full-colour posters for *Pacific* moisturizing creams from *Shiseido*. (JPN)

67 Beispiel der Plakatwerbung für Produkte der Shiseido Cosmetics Co. Hier für ein Parfum. (JPN)
68 Aus einer Plakatkampagne für *Shiseido*-Gesichtspflegeprodukte. Rotes Hemd. (JPN)
69 Ein weiteres Plakat der Shiseido Cosmetics Co. Hier für ein Lippenrouge. (JPN)
70, 71 Zwei Beispiele aus einer Plakatkampagne für die Nagellack-Kollektion von *Shiseido*. (JPN)
72, 73 Farbige Plakate für *Pacific*-Feuchtigkeitscremes von *Shiseido*. (JPN)

67 Exemple d'une série d'affiches pour une marque de produits cosmétiques. (JPN)
68 D'une campagne publicitaire lancée par *Shiseido* en faveur des produits de beauté. (JPN)
69 Une autre affiche pour les produits cosmétiques *Shiseido*, ici pour un rouge à lèvres. (JPN)
70, 71 Exemples d'une campagne d'affiches présentant la collection de vernis à ongles. (JPN)
72, 73 Affiches polychromes pour les lotions hydratantes *Pacific* de *Shiseido*. (JPN)

DESIGNER / GESTALTER / MAQUETTISTE:

67, 69–71 Makoto Nakamura
68 Ikuo Amano
72, 73 Shuji Kawasaki

ART DIRECTOR / DIRECTEUR ARTISTIQUE:

67, 69–71 Makoto Nakamura
68 Ikuo Amano
72, 73 Isamu Hanauchi

74

75

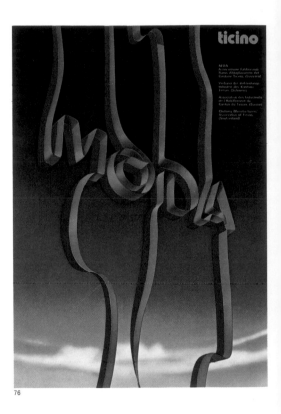

76

そして彼女は、香りのなかのバスタイム。

77

メロウカラー

時間よ止まれ、くちびるに。

78

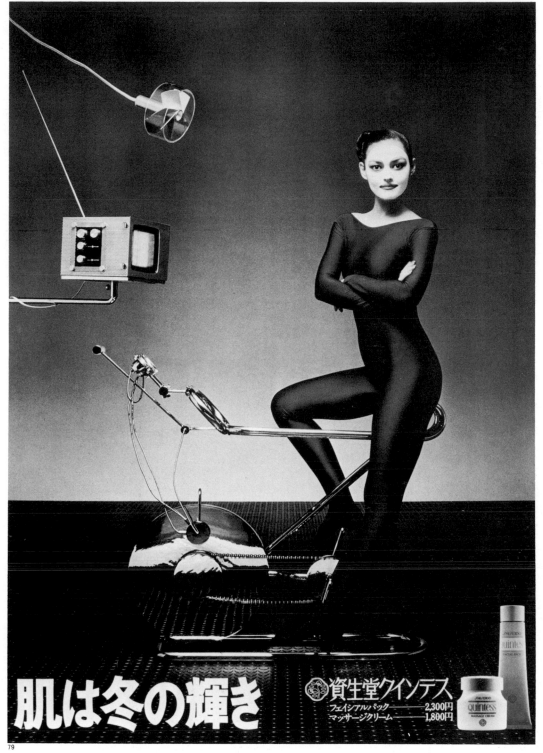

肌は冬の輝き

資生堂クインテス
フェイシァルパック — 2,300円
マッサージクリーム — 1,800円

79

74 Poster advertising *Wrangler* jeans. (USA)
75 Poster for *Skin* ski clothing by Habsburg Sport AG. (SWI)
76 Poster for the Clothing Manufacturers Association of Ticino. Red and blue are the cantonal colours. (SWI)
77 Example from a Shiseido Cosmetics Co. poster campaign, here for bath soap. In full colour. (JPN)
78, 79 Two more posters from the Shiseido Cosmetics Co. Fig. 78: for lipsticks, with the model clothed in blue and a silvery blue lipstick container. Fig. 79: face treatment products with a white pot and violet tube on a dark ground, model in a blue singlet. (JPN)

74 Plakatwerbung für *Wrangler*-Jeans. (USA)
75 Plakat für *Skin*-Skibekleidung, hergestellt von der Firma Habsburg Sport AG. (SWI)
76 Plakat für den Verband der Bekleidungsindustrie des Kantons Tessin. Rot und Blau sind die Kantonsfarben. (SWI)
77 Beispiel aus einer Plakatkampagne der Shiseido Cosmetics Co., hier für Badeseife. In Farbe. (JPN)
78, 79 Zwei weitere Plakate der Kosmetikfirma *Shiseido*, hier für Lippenstifte (Abb. 78) mit Modell in blauer Kleidung, Lippenstifthüllen blau-silbern und Gesichtspflegeprodukte (Abb. 79), weisser Topf und violette Tube vor dunklem Hintergrund, Modell in blauem Trikot. (JPN)

74 Affiche en faveur des jeans *Wrangler*. (USA)
75 Affiche pour les vêtements de ski *Skin* fabriqués par la Habsburg Sport SA. (SWI)
76 Affiche de l'association des industriels de l'habillement du Tessin, canton dont les couleurs sont le rouge et le bleu. (SWI)
77 Exemple d'une campagne publicitaire lancée par *Shiseido* en faveur d'un savon. En polychromie. (JPN)
78, 79 Deux autres affiches figurant dans une campagne publicitaire pour les articles cosmétiques de *Shiseido*, ici pour les rouges à lèvres (fig. 78) – robe bleue, rouges à lèvres en bleu argenté – et des produits de beauté (fig. 79) – pot blanc, tube violet sur un fond de couleur foncée. Tricot bleu. (JPN)

AGENCY / AGENTUR / AGENCE-STUDIO:

74 Altman, Stoller, Weiss
75 H.R. Zimmermann AG
76 Romano Chicherio

Fashion/Mode

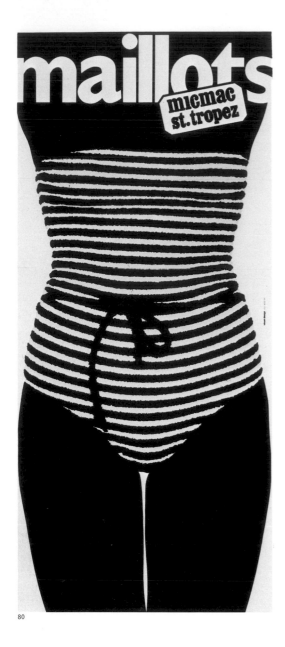

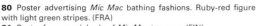

80 Poster advertising *Mic Mac* bathing fashions. Ruby-red figure with light green stripes. (FRA)
81 Poster for a special sale of *Mic Mac* trousers. (FIN)
82 Large-format poster in full colour for the autumn collection of *Rifle* jeans. (SWI)
83 Poster displayed in shops for *Barbados* jeans fashions. Combinations of beige and brown, yellow and blue model. (SWI)
84 Poster for *Mode Avantgarde* fashion magazine. Eyes and mouth in red, greyish-white face, yellow scales. (FRA)
85 Poster for the Japanese fashion designer *Hanae Mori*. Full-colour forms on black. (JPN)
86, 87 Detail and complete black-and-white poster for stockings by *Fogal*. Used as a shop-window decoration. (SWI)

80 Plakatwerbung für Bademode der Marke *Mic Mac*. Weinrote Figur mit hellgrünen Streifen. (FRA)
81 Plakat für einen Ausverkauf von *Mic Mac*-Hosen. (FIN)
82 Grossformatiges Plakat für die Jeans-Herbstkollektion der Marke *Rifle*. Mehrfarbig. (SWI)
83 Ladenplakat für *Barbados*-Jeans-Mode. Kombinationen von Beige und Braun, ein Modell in Gelb und Blau. (SWI)
84 Plakat der Modezeitschrift *Mode Avantgarde*. Augen und Mund rot, weiss-graues Gesicht, gelbe Schuppen. (FRA)
85 Plakatwerbung für die japanische Modeschöpferin *Hanae Mori*. Farbige Formen auf Schwarz. (JPN)
86, 87 Detail und komplettes Schwarzweiss-Plakat für Strümpfe von *Fogal*. Es diente als Schaufensterdekoration. (SWI)

80 Affiche pour les maillots *Mic Mac*. Figure en rouge foncé avec des rayures en vert clair. (FRA)
81 Affiche annonçant les soldes des pantalons *Mic Mac*. (FIN)
82 Affiche grand format en faveur de la nouvelle collection d'automne des jeans *Rifle*. En polychromie. (SWI)
83 Affichette de magasin pour les jeans *Barbados*. Combinaisons de beige et brun, un modèle en jaune et bleu. (SWI)
84 Affiche du magazine de mode *Mode Avantgarde*. Yeux et bouche en rouge, visage blanc-gris, écailles jaunes. (FRA)
85 Affiche autopromotionnelle de la créatrice japonaise de mode *Hanae Mori*. Motifs en couleurs sur fond noir. (JPN)
86, 87 Détail et affiche complète en noir et blanc pour les bas *Fogal*. Elle est utilisée comme décoration de vitrine. (SWI)

ARTIST / KÜNSTLER / ARTISTE:
80 Paolo Roversi
81 Herbie Kastemaa
82 Oliviero Toscani
83 Felix Eidenbenz
84 Beate Brömse
86, 87 Hans Gissinger

ART DIRECTOR / DIRECTEUR ARTISTIQUE:
80 Jean Widmer
82 Peter Marti
83 Christoph Bignens
84 Gunnar Larsen
85 Ikko Tanaka
86, 87 Jean Robert

DESIGNER / GESTALTER / MAQUETTISTE:
80 Jean Widmer
82 Heller & Stillhard
83 Paul A. Widrig
85 Ikko Tanaka
86, 87 Jean Robert/Käti Durrer

AGENCY / AGENTUR / AGENCE-STUDIO:
80 Visual Design
82 Marti Werbung
83 Paul A. Widrig
86, 87 J. Robert/K. Durrer/M. Egli

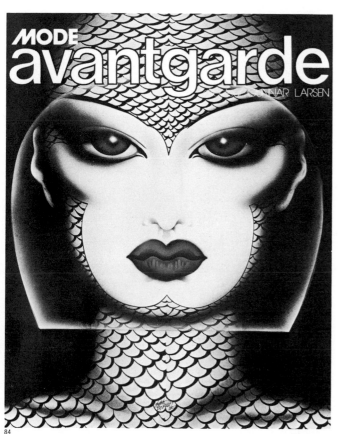

88

89

91

92

90

93

ARTIST / KÜNSTLER / ARTISTE:

88–90 Paul Webb
91 Milou Hermus
92 Jörg Hermle
93 Teruhisa Tajima
94 Klaus Endrikat

DESIGNER / GESTALTER:

88–90 Keith McEwan
91 Milou Hermus
92 Jörg Hermle
93 Tadanori Yokoo
94 Klaus Endrikat

ART DIRECTOR:

88–90 Keith McEwan
92 Philippe Martignoni
93 Tadanori Yokoo
94 Klaus Endrikat

AGENCY / AGENTUR:

88–90 Top Drawers
92 Mandarine
94 Klaus Endrikat

94

88–90 Three examples from a poster campaign for *hij* men's fashions. All three illustrations are mainly in shades of green and brown, the trademark is grey in front of a blue sky. (NLD)
91 Poster advertising *Long Don* shirts. Clothing in gradations of colour ranging from grey to brown; a few strokes of the brush and the trademark are in a bright red. (NLD)
92 Small-format poster for a women's fashion collection from *Cerruti*. The canvas texture of the picture is visible on the poster. Yellow-brown fur in front of a dark green tree. (FRA)
93 Poster advertising *Romance* bedlinen. (JPN)
94 Black-and-white poster for *Joseph Janard* fashions. (GER)

88–90 Drei Beispiele aus einer Plakatkampagne für *hij*-Herrenmode. Alle drei Illustrationen vorwiegend in Grün- und Brauntönen, das Markenzeichen grau vor blauem Himmel. (NLD)
91 Plakatwerbung für Hemden der Marke *Long Don*. Kleidung in Farbabstufungen von Grau bis Braun, einige wenige Pinselstriche und das Markenzeichen in ungebrochenem Rot. (NLD)
92 Kleinformatiges Plakat für die Damenmode-Kollektion von *Cerruti*. Die Leinenstruktur des Bildes wird auf dem Plakat sichtbar. Gelbbraunes Fell vor tiefgrünem Baum. (FRA)
93 Plakatwerbung für Bettwäsche der Marke *Romance*. (JPN)
94 Schwarzweiss-Plakat für Damenmode von *Joseph Janard*. (GER)

88–90 Trois exemples figurant dans une campagne publicitaire lancée en faveur de la mode masculine *hij*. Toutes les illustrations sont en tons verts et bruns prédominant, marque de fabrique en gris sur un ciel bleu. (NLD)
91 Affiche pour les chemises *Long Don*. Chemise en gris passant au brun, marque de fabrique et coups de pinceau en rouge. (NLD)
92 Affichette pour la collection femme créée par *Cerruti*. L'illustration évoque une ancienne peinture à l'huile. Poile en brun jaunâtre, arbre en vert foncé. (FRA)
93 Affiche publiée en faveur de *Romance*, fabricant de literie. En polychromie. (JPN)
94 Affiche noir-blanc pour la mode féminine de *Joseph Janard*. (GER)

Fashion/Mode

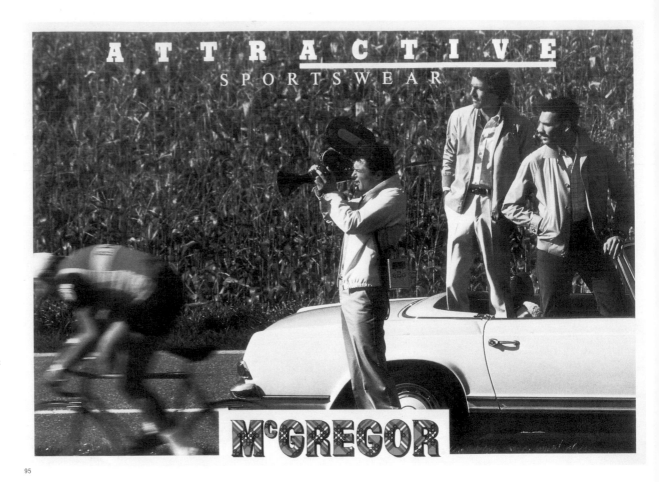

ATTRACTIVE SPORTSWEAR

McGREGOR

ARTIST / KÜNSTLER / ARTISTE:

95 Robert Meier
96 Jost Wildbolz
97 Felix Eidenbenz
98, 99 Hiko Hagiwara
100, 101 Sachiko Kuru
102 Taishi Hirokawa

DESIGNER / GESTALTER / MAQUETTISTE:

95, 96 Paul A. Widrig
97 Dieter Notz
98–101 Hideo Mukai
102 Kenichi Samura

ART DIRECTOR / DIRECTEUR ARTISTIQUE:

95, 96 Jean E. Robert
97 Dieter Notz
98–101 Hideo Makai
102 Kenichi Samura

AGENCY / AGENTUR / AGENCE-STUDIO:

95, 96 Paul A. Widrig
97 Studio Pilone
102 Ikko Tanaka Design Studio

95

"comfortable cover-up"

98

city casual wear by christian aujard

99

100

95, 96 Two examples from a poster campaign for *McGregor* sportswear. Colour photographs with a brilliant yellow border, the trademark in red, green and yellow. (SWI)
97 Poster in brown shades for *Farfalla* leisure clothes. (SWI)
98, 99 Examples from a series of posters for the *Matsuya* department store, here for creations by the fashion designer Christian Aujard. Both in full colour. (JPN)
100, 101 Two more posters for the *Matsuya* department store. Fig. 100 in subdued shades, Fig. 101 in warm autumnal colours bathed in the light of the setting sun. (JPN)
102 Full-colour poster commemorating the six-month existence of a new *Seiyu* store. (JPN)

95, 96 Zwei Beispiele aus einer Plakatkampagne für sportliche Kleidung von *McGregor*. Farbaufnahmen mit leuchtend gelber Umrandung, das Markenzeichen rot, grün und gelb. (SWI)
97 Plakat in Brauntönen für *Farfalla*-Freizeitbekleidung. (SWI)
98, 99 Beispiele aus einer Serie von Plakaten des Kaufhauses *Matsuya*. Hier für Modelle des Modeschöpfers Christian Aujard. Beide mehrfarbig. (JPN)
100, 101 Zwei weitere Plakate des Kaufhauses *Matsuya*. Abb. 100 in gedämpften Tönen, Abb. 101 in warmen Herbstfarben, in das Licht der untergehenden Sonne getaucht. (JPN)
102 Mehrfarbiges Plakat zum sechsmonatigen Bestehen eines neuen *Seiyu*-Geschäftes. (JPN)

95, 96 Deux exemples figurant dans une campagne publicitaire pour les vêtements sportifs *McGregor*. Photo couleurs avec encadrement jaune, marque de fabrique rouge, verte, jaune. (SWI)
97 Pour les modes *Farfalla*. Chauds coloris marron. (SWI)
98, 99 Affiches d'une série publiée par les grands magasins *Matsuya*. Ici on présente des modèles du créateur Christian Aujard. Les deux sont en couleurs. (JPN)
100, 101 Deux autres affiches des grands magasins *Matsuya*. Fig. 100 en tons mats, fig. 101 chauds coloris d'automne au coucher du soleil. (JPN)
102 Affiche polychrome publiée à l'occasion des six mois d'existence d'un nouveau magasin *Seiyu*. (JPN)

96

Farfalla Fashion SA CH 8134 Adliswil-Zürich Telefon 01/710 11 30

97

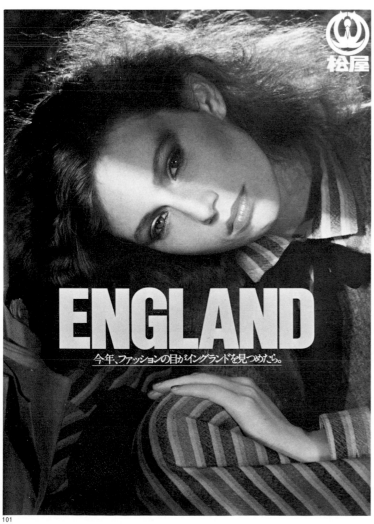

101

102

103 Poster advertising *Bally* products. Red handbag on a white bench and boots in the same colour. (SWI)
104 Poster for fashionable men's shoes by *Bally*. Colour photograph. (SWI)
105 New York poster looking ahead to the 1980 Winter Olympic Games, advertised by the Chamber of Commerce of the state of New York. Girl in red clothing and ski goggles in a shade of yellow. (USA)
106 Poster advertising *Cevre*, a magazine for architecture and applied art. In brown shades. (TUR)
107 Three-part poster for the Swiss fashion house *Au Grenier*. Red with gold, silver and black on white, black lettering. (SWI)
108 Poster for Norand Corporation, issued in association with a drive to upgrade its computer services. (USA)
109 Poster advertising a ski-school in Aspen, Colorado. (USA)

103 Plakatwerbung für *Bally*-Produkte. Hier eine rote Handtasche auf weisser Bank und Stiefel im gleichen Farbton. (SWI)
104 Plakat für modische Herrenschuhe von *Bally*. Farbaufnahme. (SWI)
105 «Ich fahre gern in New York Ski – dem Austragungsort der Olympischen Winterspiele 1980.» Werbeplakat der Handelskammer des amerikanischen Bundesstaates New York. Mädchen in roter Kleidung mit gelblicher Skibrille. (USA)
106 Plakatwerbung für *Cevre*, eine Zeitschrift für Architektur und bildende Kunst. In Brauntönen. (TUR)
107 Dreiteiliges Plakat des Schweizer Modehauses *Au Grenier*. Rot mit Gold, Silber und Schwarz auf Weiss, schwarze Schrift. (SWI)
108 Plakat für Norand Corporation im Zusammenhang mit Bemühungen dieser Firma, ihren Computer-Service zu verbessern. (USA)
109 «Spitzenleistung.» Plakatwerbung einer Ski-Schule in Aspen, einem Ort im amerikanischen Bundesstaat Colorado. (USA)

103 D'une série d'affiches pour les chaussures *Bally*. Sac à main rouge sur un banc blanc, bottes dans le même coloris rouge. (SWI)
104 «*Bally* – le pas vers la mode.» Affiche pour les chaussures messieurs. (SWI)
105 «J'aime beaucoup faire du ski à New York – lieu des Jeux Olympiques d'hiver 1980.» Affiche publiée par la chambre de commerce de l'état de New York. Jeune fille en passe montagne rouge avec des lunettes en jaune. (USA)
106 Affiche en faveur de *Cevre*, magazine d'architecture et de beaux-arts. Prédominance de tons marron. (TUR)
107 Affiche triple pour le magasin suisse de mode *Au Grenier*. Rouge, or, argent et noir sur fond blanc, typographie en noir. (SWI)
108 Affiche de la Norand Corporation publiée dans le cadre du perfectionnement général de ses services dans le domaine des ordinateurs. (USA)
109 «Performance.» Affiche pour une école de ski à Aspen, station d'hiver du Colorado. Dessin à l'aquarelle. (USA)

103

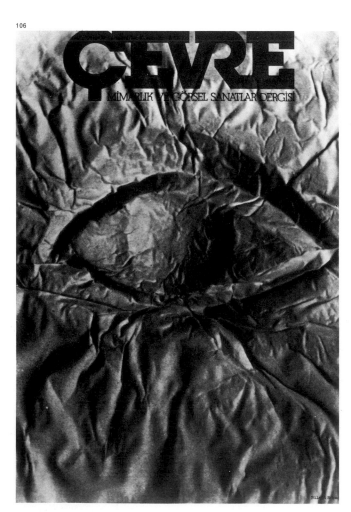
106

107

ARTIST / KÜNSTLER / ARTISTE:

103, 104 Jost Wildbolz
105 Milton Glaser
106 Ayse Erkmen
107 Hans Ulrich
109 Don Weller

DESIGNER / GESTALTER / MAQUETTISTE:

103, 104 Rolf G. Hummel
105 Milton Glaser
106 Bülent Erkmen
107 Kreativ-Team Ulrich & Fehlmann
108 James Potocki
109 Michael Hutchinson

ART DIRECTOR / DIRECTEUR ARTISTIQUE:

103, 104 André Heidelberger
105 Milton Glaser
106 Bülent Erkmen
108 James Potocki
109 Michael Hutchinson

AGENCY / AGENTUR / AGENCE-STUDIO:

103, 104 WDW
105 Milton Glaser, Inc.
106 Reyo
107 Kreativ-Team Ulrich & Fehlmann
108 James Potocki and Associates
109 Tracy Locke

BALLY
Der Schritt zur Mode

104

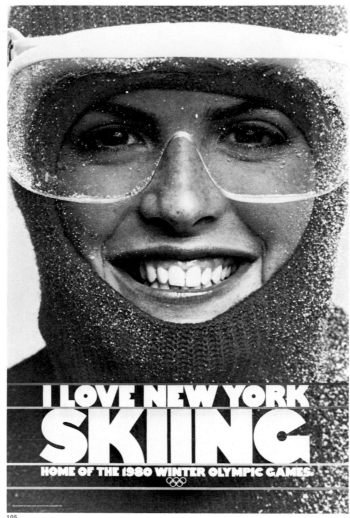

I LOVE NEW YORK
SKIING
HOME OF THE 1980 WINTER OLYMPIC GAMES

105

NORAND
Statement of Design Integrity

108

Peak Performance Aspen Ski School

109

Natürlich Kodak.

110 Three-part poster advertising the *Kodacolor II* colour film. (SWI)
111 Another large-format poster for the *Kodacolor* film made by *Kodak*. (SWI)
112 "*Pentax* is making you an offer you cannot refuse." Black-and-white poster advertising cameras and other photographic equipment made by the Japanese firm *Asahi-Pentax*. (NOR)
113 Poster advertising *Osram* light-bulbs. Packaging in white with red and blue. (GER)
114 "*Hepp*. A durable floor colouring by *Dyrup*. Can be walked on after one to two hours." Red floor beneath the girls' legs, green floor under the soldiers' boots. (DEN)
115 Example from a series of posters advertising *Canon* photographic equipment. (JPN)

110 Affiche triple pour les pellicules *Kodacolor II*. (SWI)
111 Une autre affiche grand format pour les pellicules *Kodacolor II* de *Kodak*. (SWI)
112 «*Pentax* vous fait un offre auquel vous ne résisterez pas.» Affiche en noir et blanc pour les appareils *Asahi-Pentax*. (NOR)
113 Affiche pour les ampoules *Osram*. Emballage en rouge et bleu sur blanc. (GER)
114 Affiche pour un revêtement de sol résistant qui permet de marcher dessus après deux heures. Sol rouge en haut, sol vert en bas. (DEN)
115 Exemple d'une série d'affiches pour les appareils de photo *Canon*. (JPN)

Qualität die einleuchtet

110 Dreiteiliges Plakat für den Farbfilm *Kodacolor II*. (SWI)
111 Ein weiteres grossformatiges Plakat für den Farbfilm *Kodacolor II* von *Kodak*. (SWI)
112 «*Pentax* macht Ihnen ein Angebot, dem Sie nicht widerstehen können.» Schwarzweiss-Plakat für Photoapparate der Marke *Asahi-Pentax*. (NOR)
113 Plakatwerbung für *Osram*-Glühbirnen. Packung weiss mit Rot und Blau. (GER)
114 «*Hepp*. Eine strapazierfähige Bodenfarbe von *Dyrup*. Begehbar in ein bis zwei Stunden.» Roter Boden unter den Mädchenbeinen, grüner Boden unter den Soldatenstiefeln. (DEN)
115 Beispiel aus einer Serie von Plakaten für *Canon*-Photoapparate. (JPN)

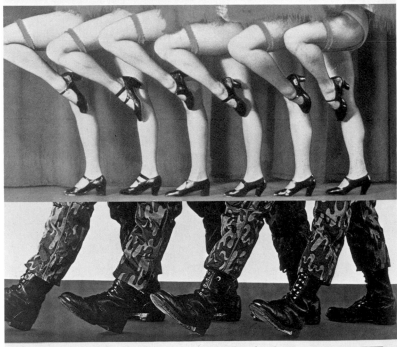

Hepp. En slidstærk gulvmaling fra Dyrup. Gå-klar på 1-2 timer. Hepp.

Hvis der er noget, som stiller krav til styrke, er det gulvmaling. Malingens tykkelse er kun brøkdele af en millimeter, og alligevel skal den lægge ryg til tusindvis af travle fødder.

Malingen, vi lægger navn til, hedder Hepp. Den er nem at arbejde med, fordi både pensler og hænder kan skylles rene under vandhanen. Hepp er alkalibestandig og skaller ikke af.

Når De gi'r Deres gulve en gang Hepp, kan De glemme alt om at male foreløbig. Men hvad gør det? Deres penge har sikkert ben nok at gå på i forvejen.

DYP I DYRUPS. FARVER DER HOLDER.

Industry/Industrie

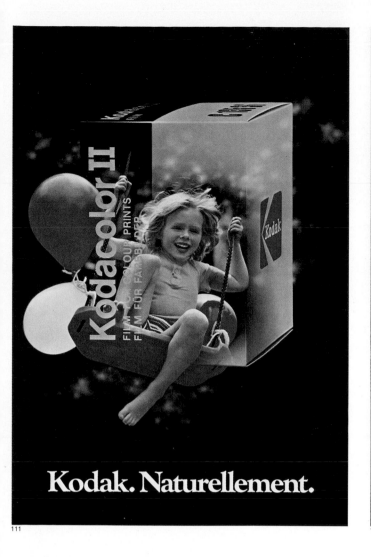

Kodak. Naturellement.

"PENTAX IS GIVING YOU AN OFFER YOU CANNOT REFUSE."

ARTIST / KÜNSTLER:

112 Saeter & Olesen
113 Gerd Hanig
114 Bent Rej
115 Masami Hagiwara/
    Masaru Mera

DESIGNER:

110, 111 Ruedi Külling
112 Per-Charles
    Molkom/
    Tor Kaupang
113 Uwe Stüwe
115 Isao Seki

ART DIRECTOR:

110, 111 Ruedi Külling
112 Per-Charles
    Molkom/
    Tor Kaupang
114 Finn Krob
115 Gan Hosoya

AGENCY / AGENTUR:

110, 111 Advico AG
112 Pepper & Salt
113 Herbert Hecht
114 Lund &
    Lommer A/S

111

112

115

ARTIST / KÜNSTLER / ARTISTE:
116–119 Ron Seymour

DESIGNER / GESTALTER / MAQUETTISTE:
116–119 John Massey
120 Jeff Barnes

ART DIRECTOR / DIRECTEUR ARTISTIQUE:
116–119 John Massey
120 Jeff Barnes

AGENCY / AGENTUR / AGENCE-STUDIO:
116–120 Container Corporation of America

120

116, 117 Detail and complete poster for the Container Corporation, showing a detergent package made from cardboard which has been recycled from old paper. (USA)
118, 119 Two more posters from the Container Corporation advertising cardboard packaging which does no harm to the environment. Also in full colour. (USA)
120 Poster in the form of the top of a can as advertising for cans manufactured by the Container Corporation. (USA)

116, 117 Detail und komplettes Plakat der Container Corporation, hier für eine Seifenpulververpackung aus Pappe, die aus Altpapier hergestellt wurde. (USA)
118, 119 Zwei weitere Beispiele aus der Plakatkampagne der Container Corporation für umweltfreundliche Verpackungen aus Pappe. Ebenfalls farbig. (USA)
120 Plakat in Form des gezeigten Konservendosen-Deckels als Werbung für Dosen von der Container Corporation. (USA)

116, 117 Détail et affiche complète d'un fabricant de conditionnements, ici en faveur d'un emballage pour une lessive en carton recyclé. (USA)
118, 119 Deux autres exemples d'une campagne d'affiches de la Container Corporation lancée en faveur des emballages pour légumes, dont la destruction n'est pas nocive. (USA)
120 Affiche sous forme d'un couvercle d'une boîte. Elément publicitaire pour les boîtes de la Container Corp. (USA)

117

118

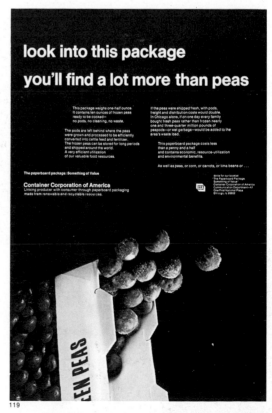

119

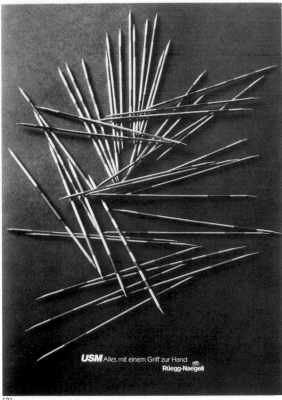

121

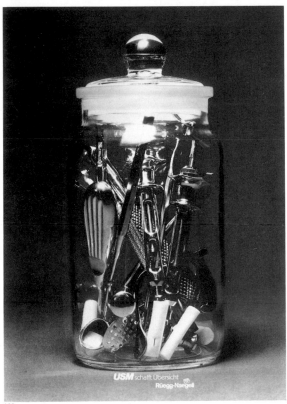

122

123

124

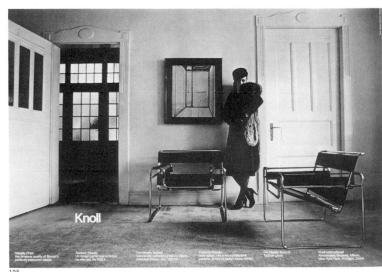

125

ARTIST / KÜNSTLER / ARTISTE:

121, 122 E.T. Werlen
123 Jacques Primois
124 Guy Bourdin
125 Richard Schenkirz
126 Don Kennedy
126a Rolf Rehak
127–130 Earl Woods

DESIGNER / GESTALTER / MAQUFTTISTE:

121, 122 M. + E. Fischer
123–126a Rudolf Beck
127–130 Stephen Frykholm

ART DIRECTOR / DIRECTEUR ARTISTIQUE:

121, 122 M. + E. Fischer
123–126a Wolf Kaiser
127–130 Stephen Frykholm

AGENCY / AGENTUR / AGENCE-STUDIO:

121, 122 Bolleter & Bolleter

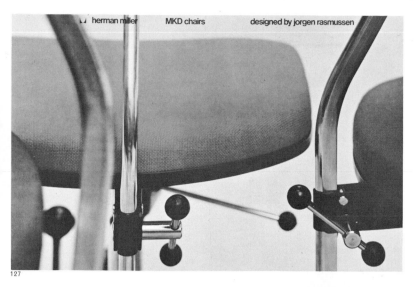

127

128

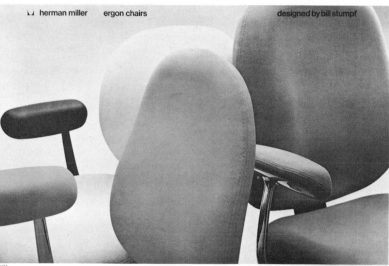

129

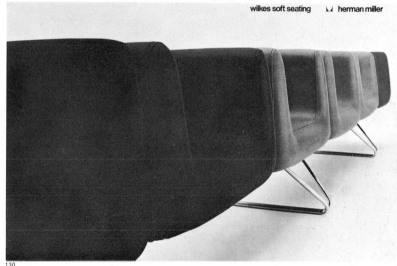

130

121, 122 Examples from a series of posters for the *USM* furnishing system by *Rüegg-Naegeli*. On the back of the posters are lists of application possibilities for the system as regards shops, offices, surgeries, laboratories and other professional uses. In full colour. (SWI)
123–126a Full-colour posters for *Knoll*, furniture manufacturers, for a direct mail campaign as well as for window dressing and exhibition purposes. Text in five languages. (GER)
127–130 Examples from a poster campaign by the *Hermann Miller* furniture manufacturers for furniture by various designers. (USA)

121, 122 Beispiele aus einer Serie von Plakaten für das *USM*-Einrichtungssystem von *Rüegg-Naegeli*. Auf der Rückseite der Plakate werden die Anwendungsmöglichkeiten des Systems für Büros, Läden, Praxisräume, Labors etc. aufgeführt. In Farbe. (SWI)
123–126a Farbige Plakate des Möbelherstellers *Knoll* für eine Direct-Mail-Aktion sowie für Schaufenster- und Ausstellungsgestaltung. Text in fünf Sprachen. (GER)
127–130 Beispiele aus einer Plakatkampagne des Möbelherstellers *Herman Miller* für Möbel von verschiedenen Designern. (USA)

121, 122 Exemples d'une série d'affiches pour un système d'ameublement de *Rüegg-Naegeli*. Au verso de chaque affiche on trouve des indications quant aux maintes possibilités d'utilisation de ce système pour le bureau, le magasin, le labor, le cabinet de consultation. (SWI)
123–126a D'une campagne de publicité directe lancée par *Knoll*, fabricant de meubles. Les affiches sont utilisées aussi pour les vitrines et des salles d'expositions. Texte en cinq langues. (GER)
127–130 Quatre affiches faisant partie d'une campagne publicitaire lancée par *Herman Miller* en faveur de ses meubles créés par divers designers. (USA)

Industry/Industrie

126

126a

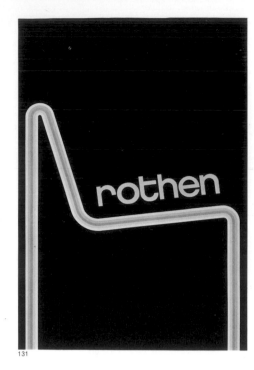

131

The secret of a great table is not why, but Howe.

The Tempest Collection by Howe

132

131 Poster for the *Rothen* furniture shop, Berne. Chair's contours in pastel colours, red name. (SWI)
132 Poster for *Howe* furniture. A red tray in the middle of light furniture, with background in blue tones. (USA)
133, 134 Poster for the Kawakichi Wallpaper Co. Fig. 133 in orange, grey and yellow. (JPN)
135 Black-and-white poster with red lettering for the *Donghia* furniture company. (USA)
136 Poster for *Zanders* quality paper. (GER)
137 From a series of posters for *Sangetsu* wallpaper. Bright blue background. (JPN)

131 Plakat für das Möbelgeschäft *Rothen*, Bern. Konturen des Stuhls in Pastellfarben, roter Name. (SWI)
132 Plakat für *Howe*-Möbel. Eine rote Platte inmitten heller Möbel vor Hintergrund in Blautönen. (USA)
133, 134 Plakatwerbung für Tapeten der Kawakichi Wallpaper Co. Abb. 133 orange, grau und gelb. (JPN)
135 Schwarzweiss-Plakat mit roter Schrift für *Donghia*-Möbel, die auf Bestellung angefertigt werden. (USA)
136 Plakatwerbung für *Zanders*-Feinpapiere. (GER)
137 Aus einer Serie von Plakaten für *Sangetsu*-Tapeten. Leuchtend blauer Untergrund. (JPN)

131 Affiche pour les ameublements *Rothen*. Contour de chaise en tons pastels, nom rouge sur marron foncé. (SWI)
132 Affiche pour les meubles *Howe*. Plaque rouge entourée de meubles clairs, fond en tons bleus. (USA)
133, 134 D'une série d'affiches pour une marque de papiers peints. Fig. 133: orange, gris et jaune. (JPN)
135 Affiche en noir et blanc avec typo rouge pour une marque de meubles fabriqués sur commande. (USA)
136 Affiche pour les papiers couchés *Zanders*. (GER)
137 Affiche figurant dans une série pour une marque de papiers peints. Fond bleu. (JPN)

DONGHIA
THE DONGHIA FURNITURE COMPANY LTD. FURNITURE MADE TO ORDER
LOS ANGELES CHICAGO NEW YORK

135

Industry/Industrie

133

134

V.I.P
VERY IMPORTANT PAPER

136

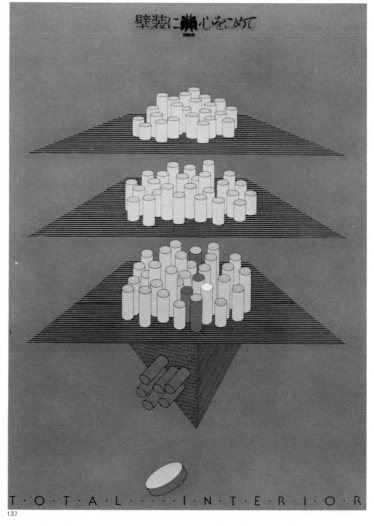

壁装に真心をこめて

T·O·T·A·L·····I·N·T·E·R·I·O·R

137

CB-250

KIA HONDA

138

Genuine Parts give your car a regal bearing

THE PERFECTION PRINCIPLE
GENUINE
TOYOTA PARTS

TOYOTA
GENUINE PARTS

140

Raw power beneath a gentle exterior:
Genuine Parts are the secret.

THE PERFECTION PRINCIPLE
GENUINE
TOYOTA PARTS

TOYOTA
GENUINE PARTS

141

ARTIST / KÜNSTLER / ARTISTE:

138 Young-ki Chun
139 Marv Lyons
140–143 Hiroyuki End

DESIGNER / GESTALTER / MAQUETTISTE:

138 Chang-nam Lee
139 John Lee Wong
140–143 Akira Yamazaki
144 CGSS

ART DIRECTOR / DIRECTEUR ARTISTIQUE:

138 Youn-chong Chung
139 John Lee Wong
140–143 Akira Yamazaki

AGENCY / AGENTUR / AGENCE-STUDIO:

138 Sunkwang Ad. Production
139 Chickering/Howell Advertising
140–143 Yamazaki Design
144 Fiat – Pubblicità e Immagine

139

From a moment of rest, she springs into action:
the smooth precision of Genuine Parts

THE PERFECTION PRINCIPLE
GENUINE
TOYOTA PARTS

TOYOTA
GENUINE PARTS

142

138 Poster advertising a Japanese *Honda* motorbike. (KOR)
139 Poster for *Austro-Daimler* bicycles. The text explains that this model comes from Europe and that not very many are available because of the limited production. (USA)
140–143 Three examples from a poster series for the Toyota Motor Sales Co., and detail of one of the illustrations. All posters are in full colour. The characteristics of the animals portrayed are also attributed to *Toyota Genuine Parts*: the regal stamina of the lion, the horse's tremendous power beneath a placid exterior, and the precision and speed of reaction of an eagle. (JPN)
144 Poster advertising the 238 E, a new *Fiat* transport vehicle. This van is particularly recommended for transporting passengers as well as goods. (ITA)

138 Plakatwerbung für ein Motorrad der Marke *Honda*. (KOR)
139 Plakat für *Austro-Daimler*-Fahrräder. Im Text wird darauf hingewiesen, dass dieses Modell aus Europa stammt und nur in begrenzter Anzahl hergestellt wurde. (USA)
140–143 Drei Beispiele aus einer Plakatserie der Toyota Motor Sales Co. und Detail einer Illustration. Alle Plakate mehrfarbig. Hier werden die Eigenschaften der dargestellten Tiere auf *Toyota Genuine Parts* (*Toyota*-Teile) übertragen: Die königliche Ausdauer des Löwen, des Pferdes grosse Kraft unter einem sanften Äusseren und die Präzision und Reaktionsschnelle des Adlers. (JPN)
144 Plakatwerbung für einen neuen Transporter von *Fiat*, der für die Personen- und Warenbeförderung empfohlen wird. (ITA)

138 Affiche pour les motos *Honda*. (KOR)
139 Affiche pour les bicyclettes *Austro-Daimler*. Dans le texte on mentionne que ce modèle de fabrication limitée provient de l'Europe. (USA)
140–143 Trois exemples d'une série d'affiches de la Toyota Motor Sales Co. et détail d'une illustration. Toutes les affiches sont en couleurs. On compare ici les caractéristiques des animaux représentés aux diverses parties de la *Toyota*: «la constance royale», «la grande puissance sous un extérieur doux» et «la précision et la réaction de l'aigle». (JPN)
144 Affiche pour la nouvelle camionnette de *Fiat*, qui se prête au transport de personnes et de marchandises. (ITA)

144

143

145–147 Advertising for Sharp SA, manufacturer of business machines and computers. Everything begins with the human hand, for counting, pointing and playing. (BRA)
148–150 Small-format posters for *Sharp* computers, radio and television sets. The titles refer to perfect calculation (Fig. 148), colourful tone (Fig. 149) and the miracle of calculating (Fig. 150). The clown portrays Albert Einstein. (BRA)
151–153 "The inner sound", "The better picture" and "The miracle of calculating". Three more examples of posters for the *Sharp* company, for record-players, television sets and computers, with emphasis on the human hand. (BRA)

145–147 Werbung für Sharp SA, Hersteller von Computer und Büromaschinen. Ausgangspunkt ist die menschliche Hand – hier für das Zählen, das Zeigen und das Spielen. (BRA)
148–150 Kleinplakate für *Sharp*-Computer, Radio- und Fernsehgeräte. Die Titel sind: «Die perfekte Kalkulation», «Der farbige Ton», «Das Wunder der Kalkulation». Die Harlekin-Figur stellt Albert Einstein dar. (BRA)
151–153 «Im Innern des Klanges», «Das bessere Bild», «Das Wunder der Kalkulation». Drei weitere Beispiele von Plakaten für *Sharp*, hier für Plattenspieler, Fernsehgeräte und Computer, mit Akzent auf der menschlichen Hand. (BRA)

145–147 Trois exemples figurant dans la campagne publicitaire lancée par un fabricant d'ordinateurs et de machines de bureau. Elles mettent en scène les usages de la main de l'homme – ici, pour compter, désigner, jouer. (BRA)
148–150 Affichettes extraites d'une série pour les ordinateurs, radios et téléviseurs *Sharp*. Leurs titres: fig. 148: le calcul parfait; fig. 149: le son coloré; fig. 150: le miracle du calcul. L'arlequin a les traits d'Albert Einstein. (BRA)
151–153 «A l'intérieur du son.» – «La meilleure image.» – «Le miracle du calcul.» Affiches pour les tourne-disques, téléviseurs et ordinateurs *Sharp*, mettant l'accent sur la main de l'homme. (BRA)

ARTIST / KÜNSTLER / ARTISTE:
145–153 Ziraldo Pinto

AGENCY / AGENTUR / AGENCE-STUDIO:
145–153 Praxis Propaganda Ltda

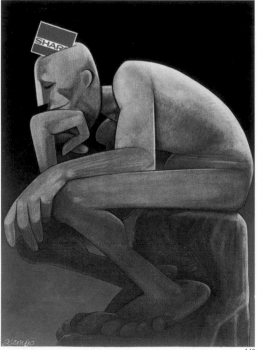

145

146

147

148

149

150

por dentro do som

SHARP

O som colorido

Produtos da Zona Franca de Manaus

151

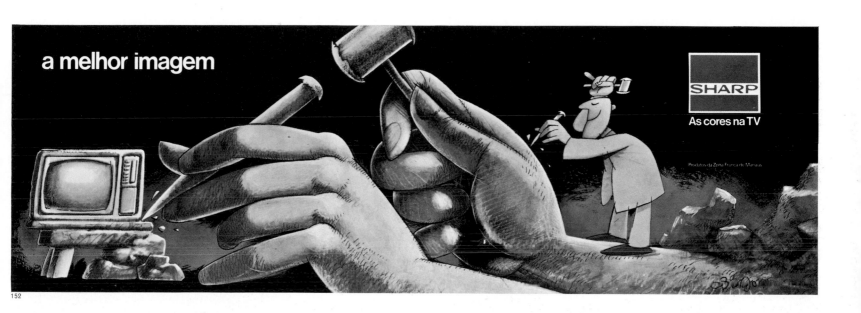

a melhor imagem

SHARP

As cores na TV

Produtos da Zona Franca de Manaus

152

o milagre do cálculo

SHARP

calculadoras
eletrônicas

Produtos
da Zona Franca de Manaus

153

Industry/Industrie

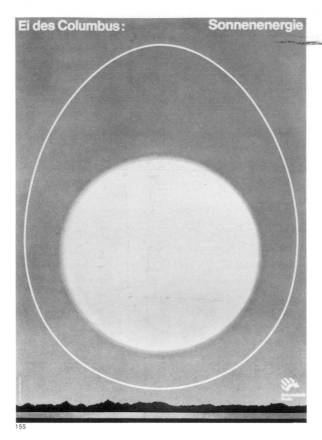

Ei des Columbus: Sonnenenergie

Alô,
torcida brasileira.

Somos amáveis e eficientes, atendendo
o cliente do jeito que ele gosta.

154

155

156

ARTIST / KÜNSTLER / ARTISTE:

154 Garry Morris
155 Reinhart Braun
157 Kenji Ishikawa
158 Tsunao Harada
159 E. Ragazzini
160, 162 S. Libis
161 Ranzini
163 David Spira

DESIGNER / GESTALTER / MAQUETTISTE:

154 Ken White
155 Reinhart Braun
157 Namio Sakamoto/Masunobu Okamoto
158 Yutaka Takama/Takehiko Mikami
159 Giovanni Ferioli
160–162 Walter Ballmer
163 David Spira

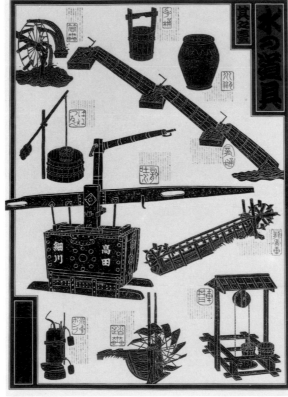

olivetti

158

159

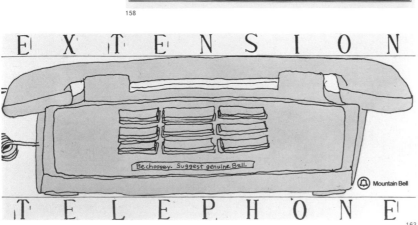

Be choosey. Suggest genuine Bell.

Mountain Bell

163

Industry/Industrie

ART DIRECTOR / DIRECTEUR ARTISTIQUE:

154 Ken White
155 Reinhart Braun
157 Kenji Takahashi/Tsukasa Ishii *String Bikini*
158 Yutaka Takama
159 Giovanni Ferioli
160–162 Walter Ballmer
163 Jerry Murff/David Spira

AGENCY / AGENTUR / AGENCE-STUDIO:

154 IBM Tucson Design Center
155 Reinhart Braun
156 Alcantara Machado, Periscinoto
Comunicações Ltda
158 Diamond Agency Inc.
159 British Olivetti
160–162 Ufficio Pubblicità Olivetti
163 Tracy-Locke

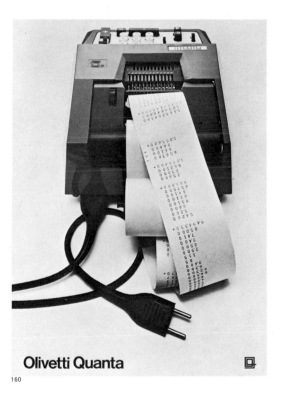

154 Notification of a new IBM factory and laboratory in Tucson, Arizona. Colour photograph. (USA)
155 Poster advertising solar technology in Berlin. Orange sky with yellow sun, blue countryside with violet and green. (GER)
156 Full-colour small-format poster for *Volkswagen*. (BRA)
157 Poster advertising *National* car air-conditioners from the Matsushita Electric Co. (JPN)
158 Poster for the Ebara Corporation, with traditional vessels and equipment powered by water. (JPN)
159–162 Four full-colour examples from a poster campaign for *Olivetti* calculating machines. (ITA)
163 Poster in a striking oblong format for extension telephones from the privately-owned *Mountain Bell* company. (USA)

154 Bekanntmachung eines neuen Herstellungswerkes und Labors von IBM in Tucson, Arizona. Farbaufnahme. (USA)
155 Plakatwerbung der Solartechnik Berlin. Himmel orange mit gelber Sonne, Landschaft blau, violett und grün. (GER)
156 Kleinformatiges Plakat für *Volkswagen*. In Farbe. (BRA)
157 Plakatwerbung der Matsushita Electric Co. für Autoklimaanlagen der Marke *National*. «Küüühl.» (JPN)
158 Plakatwerbung für Ebara Corporation. Hier traditionelle Gefässe und mit Wasser betriebene Einrichtungen. (JPN)
159–162 Vier Beispiele aus einer Plakatkampagne für *Olivetti*-Rechenmaschinen. Alle farbig. (ITA)
163 Plakat in auffälligem Querformat für Zweitapparate der privaten Telephongesellschaft *Mountain Bell*. (USA)

154 Affiche annonçant l'ouverture d'un nouveau centre producteur et d'un labor IBM à Tucson, Arizona. Polychromie. (USA)
155 Affiche en faveur de l'énergie solaire. Ciel orange, soleil jaune, paysage en bleu, violet et vert. (GER)
156 Affichette pour la *Volkswagen*. En polychromie. (BRA)
157 Affiche pour une marque de climatiseurs à utiliser dans les voitures. (JPN)
158 Affiche de l'Ebara Corp. présentant des récipients traditionnels et des installations hydrauliques. (JPN)
159–162 Quatre exemples figurant dans une campagne publicitaire pour les calculatrices *Olivetti*. En polychromie. (ITA)
163 Affiche d'une société de télécommunication en faveur de l'installation d'un deuxième appareil. (USA)

166

167

164

165

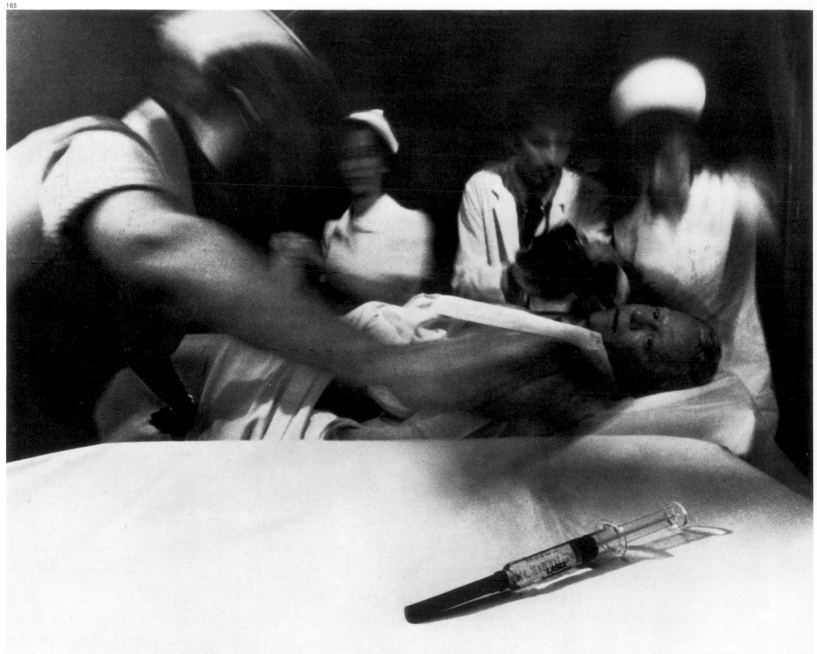

168

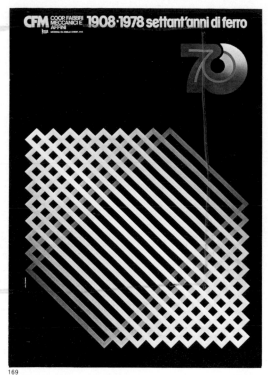

169

170

171

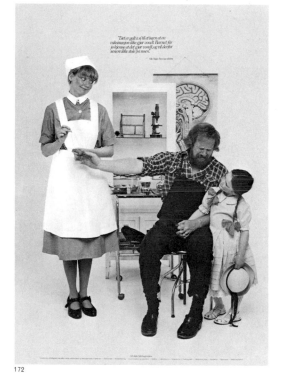

172

173

ART DIRECTOR / DIRECTEUR ARTISTIQUE:

164, 165 Charles Schmalz
168 Pierre Augsburger
169 Lauro Giovanetti
171–173 Per Charles Molkom

AGENCY / AGENTUR / AGENCE-STUDIO:

164, 165 William Douglas McAdams
166, 167 Wolf & Ika Eggers
168 Concepteam
169 Graphic Design Studio
170 Atelier Donald Brun
171–173 Pepper & Salt

Industry/Industrie

164, 165 Complete poster for use in chemists' shops, and detail of the photograph, for a *Hoechst* ready-to-use injection. (USA)
166, 167 Two posters for *Bayer* chemicals, here as components for a plant-protecting agent and a cleaning agent. Fig. 166 in green shades, Fig. 167 blue and white. (GER)
168 "Insulating means saving." Poster for a manufacturer of insulating materials for houses. Magenta, brown shades. (SWI)
169 Poster for the 70th anniversary of an iron and steel company. Yellow, green and blue on a black ground. (ITA)
170 Poster for a chemical marketed by *Sandoz* against scab and mildew on fruit. (SWI)
171–173 Full-colour examples from a series of posters for A/S Saba Sykehusgruppen, producers of hospital furnishings. (NOR)

164, 165 Komplettes Stellplakat für Apotheken und Detail der Aufnahme für eine fertige Spritze von *Hoechst*. (USA)
166, 167 Zwei Plakate für *Bayer*-Chemikalien. Hier als Bestandteile eines Pflanzenschutzmittels und eines Reinigungsmittels. Abb. 166 in Grüntönen, Abb. 167 Blau mit Weiss. (GER)
168 «Isolieren heisst sparen.» Plakat für einen Hersteller von Isolationsmaterial für Häuser. Magenta, Brauntöne. (SWI)
169 Plakat zum 70jährigen Bestehen einer Stahl- und Eisenfirma. Gelb, grün, blau auf schwarzem Untergrund. (ITA)
170 Plakat für das von *Sandoz* hergestellte chemische Mittel *Thiovit* zur Verhütung von Krankheiten an Obstbäumen. (SWI)
171–173 Beispiele aus einer Plakatkampagne für A/S Saba Sykehusgruppen, Hersteller von Spitaleinrichtungen. Farbig. (NOR)

164, 165 Encart utilisé dans les pharmacies et détail de la photo pour une injection *Hoechst*. (USA)
166, 167 Deux affiches pour les produits chimiques de *Bayer*, ici utilisés dans la production d'un produit phytosanitaire et d'un détergent. En polychromie. (GER)
168 Affiche d'un fournisseur de matériaux isolants pour le bâtiment. Magenta et bleu clair sur bleu foncé. (SWI)
169 Affiche publiée à l'occasion des 70 ans d'existence d'une aciérie. Jaune, vert, bleu sur fond noir. (ITA)
170 Pour un produit chimique distribué par *Sandoz*, actif dans la lutte contre la gale et le mildiou. (SWI)
171–173 D'une série d'affiches publiées par un fabricant d'installations pour hôpitaux. En polychromie. (NOR)

174

Big Art

DESIGNER / GESTALTER / MAQUETTISTE:

174 Chris Whorf
175 Tom Wilkes/Lou Adler
176 John Dawson
177 Doug Lew

AGENCY / AGENTUR / AGENCE-STUDIO:

174–177 Foster & Kleiser

ARTIST / KUNSTLER / ARTISTE:

174 Mario Rueda
175, 176 Robert Olson
177 Robert Price

■ Examples of so-called Big Art on walls and billboards are to be seen on this page and the following double spread. The movement was lately accorded recognition when the California Museum of Science and Industry devoted an exhibition to it. The size of these hand-painted giant posters is approximately 4.3×14.6 metres (14×48 ft.). A book on this subject, *The Big Picture* by Henderson and Landau, is being published by Chronicle Books.

■ Auf dieser und der folgenden Doppelseite sind Beispiele sogenannter Grosskunst auf Plakatwänden zu sehen, eine Bewegung, die kürzlich Anerkennung fand, als das kalifornische Museum für Wissenschaft und Industrie ihr eine Ausstellung widmete. Die Ausmasse dieser handgemalten Riesenplakate betragen ca. 4,3×14,6 m. Ein Buch über dieses Thema von Sally Henderson und Robert Landau (*The Big Picture*) ist bei Chronicle Books erschienen.

■ Nous présentons ici et à la double page suivante quelques exemples de peintures sur panneaux d'affichage ou de *Big Art*, phénomène désormais consacré par une exposition au Musée de la Science et de l'Industrie de Californie. Ces œuvres géantes peintes à la main ont une dimension d'environ 4,3×14,6 m. Un livre de Sally Henderson et Robert Landau, *The Big Picture*, est sorti aux Ed. Chronicle Books.

175

178

179

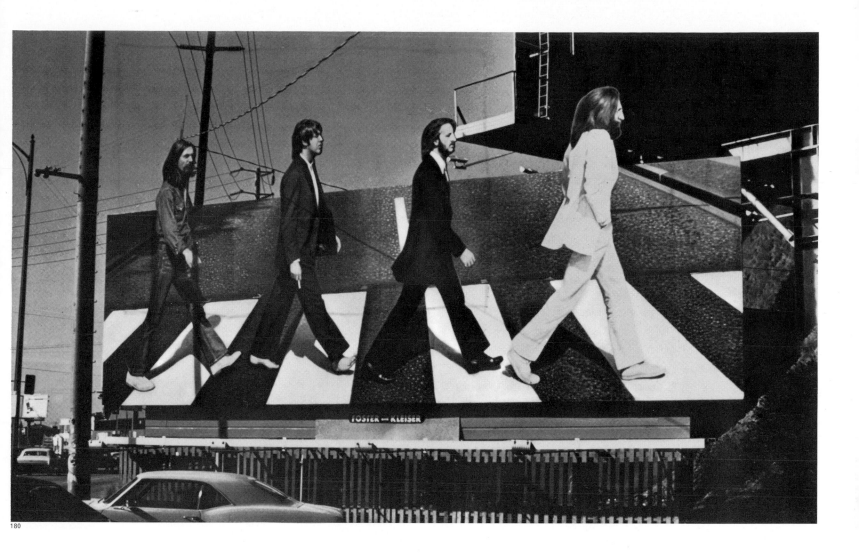

178 Poster advertising a car made by the French *Peugeot* company. (SWI)
179 Example from a series of posters advertising a combined radio-cassette-television set under the name *Jackal* made by the Japanese firm *Sony*. (JPN)
180 Another example of a giant poster as shown on the previous double spread. This one advertises the Beatles' "Abbey Road" album. The obvious danger became reality when, at a later date, Paul McCartney lost his head. (USA)
181 Billboard for an album by Cat Stevens. It is a "sequential" billboard, i.e. it was changed while in use, the cover of the album being replaced by an outsize plywood figure of the star himself as painter. (USA)
182 Poster for a *Mont Blanc* fountain-pen. In blue, white, yellow and black. (JPN)

178 Affiche pour *Peugeot*, une marque de voitures françaises. (SWI)
179 Exemple figurant dans une série d'affiches faisant de la publicité pour un appareil avec radio, magnétophone à cassettes et téléviseur, fabriqué par *Sony*. (JPN)
180 Un autre exemple des panneaux géants présentés à la page double précédente. Celui-ci fait de la publicité pour un album des Beatles. Paul McCartney y a par la suite perdu la tête. (USA)
181 Panneau pour un album par Cat Stevens. Il s'agissait d'un panneau «séquentiel» en ce sens qu'il subit des transformations en cours d'affichage (l'artiste plus grand que nature, en contreplaqué, remplaçant l'album dans le coin de droite, en bas). (USA)
182 Affiche pour les stylos *Mont Blanc*. Bleu, blanc, jaune et noir. (JPN)

178 Plakatwerbung für ein Auto der französischen Marke *Peugeot*. (SWI)
179 Beispiel aus einer Serie von Plakaten für ein kombiniertes Radio-Kassetten-Fernsehgerät der Marke *Jackal* von *Sony*. (JPN)
180 Ein weiteres Beispiel der auf der vorhergehenden Doppelseite gezeigten Riesenplakate. Hier für die Langspielplatte «Abbey Road» von den Beatles. Zu einem späteren Zeitpunkt verlor Paul McCartney seinen Kopf. (USA)
181 Plakatwand für ein Album von Cat Stevens. Es handelt sich hier um eine «sequenzielle» Werbetafel, d.h. sie wurde während des Gebrauchs verändert. (USA)
182 Plakat für Füllfederhalter der Marke *Mont Blanc*. Blau, Weiss, Gelb und Schwarz. (JPN)

Varia

ARTIST / KÜNSTLER / ARTISTE:

183, 184 Tokiyoshi Tsubouchi
185 Jan Tománek
186, 187 G. Rambow/G. Lienemeyer/M. van de Sand
188 Marguerita
189 Uldis Purins

DESIGNER / GESTALTER / MAQUETTISTE:

183, 184 Tokiyoshi Tsubouchi
185 Jan Tománek
186, 187 G. Rambow/G. Lienemeyer/M. van de Sand
188 Marguerita
189 Uldis Purins

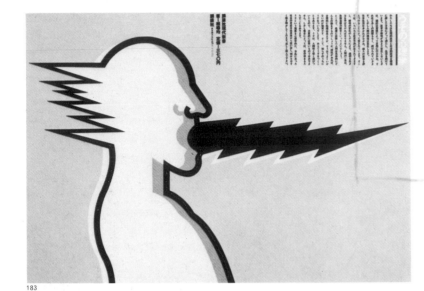

183

185

184

ART DIRECTOR / DIRECTEUR ARTISTIQUE:

183, 184 Tokiyoshi Tsubouchi
185 Jan Tománek
186, 187 G. Rambow/G. Lienemeyer/
         M. van de Sand
188 Arthur Gilmore
189 Uldis Purins

AGENCY / AGENTUR / AGENCE-STUDIO:

188 John Emmerling Inc.
189 Gregory Fossella Associates

188

183, 184 Two posters for a book entitled *Psychology of Lie*. Both are in full colour. (JPN)
185 Poster advertising books recommended by a publisher as holiday reading. Sky and ground green with white, reddish sun. (CSR)
186, 187 Poster announcing the appearance of editions of the magazine *Der neue Egoist* ("The New Egoist") about literature and art in Frankfurt. (GER)
188 From a series of posters for the New York newspaper *The Village Voice*, referring to special ideas for Saturday evenings. Brick-red wall and yellow footpath. (USA)
189 Poster printed on both sides for display in bookshops. Flowers in red, yellow and violet with a green background. (USA)

183, 184 Zwei Plakate für ein Buch mit dem Titel *Psychology of Lie* («Psychologie der Lüge»). Farbig. (JPN)
185 Plakatwerbung eines Verlegers für Bücher, die für die Ferien empfohlen werden. Himmel und Erde grün mit Weiss, rötliche Sonne. (CSR)
186, 187 Plakate zur Bekanntmachung des Erscheinens von Ausgaben der Zeitschrift *Der neue Egoist* über Literatur und Künste in Frankfurt a. M. (GER)
188 Aus einer Serie von Plakaten für die New Yorker Zeitung *The Village Voice*. Hier geht es um ausgefallene Ideen für den Samstagabend: «Sie kommen gerade um die Ecke.» Ziegelrote Mauer, gelber Fussweg. (USA)
189 Beidseitig bedrucktes Ausstellungsplakat für Buchläden. «Frühling für ein Buch.» Blumen rot, gelb und violett vor grünem Hintergrund. (USA)

183, 184 Deux affiches pour un livre intitulé *Psychology of Lie* («Psychologie du mensonge»). En polychromie. (JPN)
185 Avec cette affiche, une maison d'édition recommande des livres de vacances. Ciel et terre en vert et blanc, soleil rougeâtre. (CSR)
186, 187 Affiches annonçant la publication de deux numéros du magazine *Der neue Egoist*, consacré à la littérature et aux beaux-arts. (GER)
188 Affiche d'une série publiée en faveur du magazine newyorkais *The Village Voice*. Celle-ci se réfère à des idées bizarres pour passer samedi soir – «Elles viennent de tourner le coin». (USA)
189 «Printemps pour un livre.» Affiche, imprimée des deux côtés, destinée aux librairies. Fleurs en rouge, jaune et lilas sur fond vert. (USA)

Publishers' Publicity
Verlagswerbung
Publicité d'éditeurs

190

191

192

193

Musik Hug

194

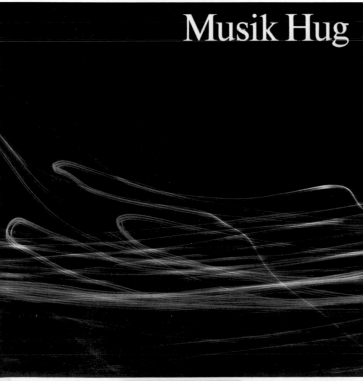

Musik Hug

195

Musik Hug

196

190, 191 Poster for books from a series by the Kadokawa publishers. (JPN)
192 Poster advertising the B.B. King *Midnight Reliever* record. The colours are shades of violet, blue and red. (USA)
193 Poster issued by Tokuma Musical Industries for a record under the title of *Black Saint*. In full colour. (JPN)
194, 195 Two examples from a series of posters for the *Hug* music company with impressions of various instruments. (SWI)
196 Another poster for the *Hug* music company, for electric organs. (SWI)

190, 191 Plakatwerbung für Bücher aus einer Serie des Verlegers Kadokawa. (JPN)
192 Plakatwerbung für die Schallplatte *Midnight Believer* von B.B. King, die bei ABC Records erschienen ist. Violettöne, Blau und Rot. (USA)
193 Plakatwerbung der Tokuma Musical Industries für eine Schallplatte mit dem Titel *Black Saint* («Schwarze Heilige»). Mehrfarbig. (JPN)
194, 195 Zwei Beispiele aus einer Serie von Plakaten für das Musikhaus *Hug* mit Impressionen zu verschiedenen Instrumenten und zum Tonträger (Abb. 194). (SWI)
196 Ein weiteres Plakat für das Musikhaus *Hug*, hier für elektronische Orgeln. (SWI)

190, 191 Affiches d'une maison d'éditions en faveur d'une série de livres. (JPN)
192 Affiche pour le disque *Midnight Believer* de B.B. King. Lilas, bleu et rouge. (USA)
193 Affiche publiée par Tokuma Musical Industries pour un disque intitulé *Black Saint* («Saint noir»). En polychromie. (JPN)
194, 195 Deux exemples d'une série d'affiches de la maison *Hug*. Impressions de divers instruments de musique (et de grammophones, fig. 194). (SWI)
196 Une autre affiche de la maison *Hug*, ici pour les orgues électriques. (SWI)

ARTIST / KÜNSTLER / ARTISTE:

190, 191 Eiichiro Sakata
192 Michael Bryan
193 Atsushi Yoshioka
194–196 E.A. Heiniger/Chr. Küenzi

DESIGNER / GESTALTER:

190, 191 Eiko Ishioka/
Motoko Naruse
193 Katsumi Yamaguchi
194–196 Felix Bader

ART DIRECTOR / DIRECTEUR ARTISTIQUE:

190, 191 Eiko Ishioka
192 Rod Dyer
193 Katsumi Yamaguchi
194–196 Felix Bader

AGENCY / AGENTUR / AGENCE-STUDIO:

192 Rod Dyer, Inc.
194–196 Triplex AG

198

199

197

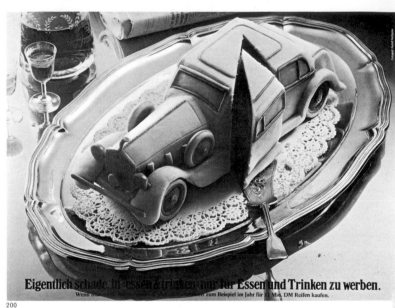

200

201

ARTIST / KÜNSTLER / ARTISTE:

197 John Shaw
198–200 Rudolf Nüttgens
201 Cap Pannell
202 Stanislaw Zagorski
203 Tsutomu Otsuka
204, 205 Jim Adair

DESIGNER / GESTALTER / MAQUETTISTE:

197 Alwyn Clayden
198–200 Michael Borch
201 Glyn Powell
202 Stanislaw Zagorski
203 Tadanori Yokoo
204, 205 Jim Adair

ART DIRECTOR / DIRECTEUR ARTISTIQUE:

197 Alwin Clayden
198–200 Stefan Hagemeister
201 Cap Pannell/Glyn Powell
202 P. Corriston
203 Tadanori Yokoo
204–205 Jim Adair

Guerriera

208

L'imperatore Agramante

209

210

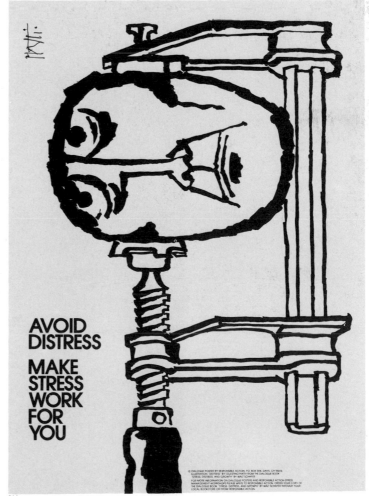

AVOID
DISTRESS

MAKE
STRESS
WORK
FOR
YOU

211

Varia

ARTIST / KÜNSTLER / ARTISTE:

212 Akira Kobayashi
214 Bob Byrd
215 Walter Heckmann
216 Milton Glaser
217 Marjan Vojska

212 Poster for the *Inaba* printing company. Gold with black on a blue background. Green apples, one red apple. (JPN)
213 Poster for the *Haizuka* printing company. A group of people has here been reproduced several times in varying sizes. The T-shirts are in white, red, yellow or blue. The lettering is in yellow and red. (JPN)
214 Poster for the printers Allen, Lane & Scott advertising their services for company brochures. The full-colour illustrations are examples drawn from the Guinness Book of World Records. (USA)
215, 217 Examples of a series of art posters commissioned by the publication agency of West German savings banks for World Savings Day. Fig. 215 is in desert shades with a blue-green sky. Fig. 217 shows a full-colour bullfinch (with "nest-egg") in a light brown tree. (GER)
216 Poster advertising an Elvis Presley book published by *McGraw-Hill*. Full colour. (USA)

212 Plakatwerbung für die Druckerei *Inaba*. Gold mit Schwarz auf blauem Hintergrund. Äpfel grün, einer davon rot. (JPN)
213 Plakat für die Druckerei *Haizuka*. Eine Gruppe von Menschen wurde hier in verschiedenen Grössen wiederholt reproduziert. Die T-Shirts sind weiss, rot, gelb oder blau. Schrift gelb-rot. (JPN)
214 Plakat des Druckers Allen, Lane & Scott, der hier seine Dienste für die Herstellung von Firmenbroschüren anbietet. Die Farbillustrationen zeigen Beispiele aus dem Guinness-Buch der Weltrekorde. (USA)
215, 217 Beispiele aus einer Serie von Künstlerplakaten des Deutschen Sparkassenverlags. Der obere Teil in Abb. 215 in gedämpftem Blaugrün, der untere Teil in erdigen Farben. Abb. 217 in Tönen von Hell- bis Dunkelbraun und Hellgrün; der Dompfaff naturgetreu. (GER)
216 Plakatwerbung für ein Buch über Elvis Presley, das bei *McGraw-Hill* erschienen ist. Mehrfarbig. (USA)

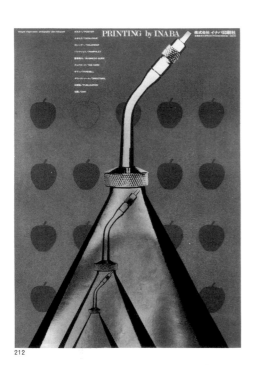

212

DESIGNER / GESTALTER / MAQUETTISTE:

212 Shigeo Asano
213 Tadanori Yokoo
214 The Creative Dept., Inc.
215 Walter Heckmann
216 Milton Glaser
217 Marjan Vojska

ART DIRECTOR / DIRECTEUR ARTISTIQUE:

212 Shigeo Asano
213 Tadanori Yokoo
214 The Creative Dept., Inc.
215, 217 Artur Kulak
216 Kevin Eggers

AGENCY / AGENTUR / AGENCE-STUDIO:

212 Ad Pac
214 The Creative Dept., Inc.
216 Milton Glaser, Inc.

213

212 Affiche d'une imprimerie. Or et noir sur fond bleu. Pommes vertes, l'une d'elles en rouge. (JPN)

213 Affiche pour une imprimerie. Photo d'un groupe de gens prise de différentes distances. T-shirts blancs, rouges, jaunes ou bleus. Typographie en jaune et rouge. (JPN)

214 Affiche de l'imprimerie Allen, Lane & Scott qui offrent leurs services pour la production de brochures de prestige. Les illustrations couleurs présentent quelques exemples du Guinness-Book des records mondiaux (qui ne sont d'ailleurs pas nécessaires pour publier une brochure de prestige). (FRA)

215, 217 Affiches pour la journée mondiale de l'épargne, d'une série réalisée par divers artistes sous le patronat de la Deutsche Sparkassenverlag. Toutes les affiches sont en polychromie. (GER)

216 Affiche annonçant un livre consacré à Elvis Presley. (USA)

Varia

218 Poster from an exhibition staged by a school of designers. White lettering on a black background, doll's clothing in black and white, white face with sea-green eyelids, a blue mouth and a blue tear. (JPN)
219 Poster for the Mitsubishi Shintaku bank. (JPN)
220 Full-colour poster for the Japanese painter Issey Miyake. (JPN)
221 Three famous baseball players of the past symbolize the versatility of a printing and photoengraving company. In full colour. (USA)
222 Poster advertising a school in New York. (USA)
223 Poster advertising *Pantone* paints. (USA)

218 Plakat für eine Ausstellung einer Kunstschule. Weisse Schrift auf schwarzem Hintergrund, Kleidung der Puppe schwarz und weiss, das Gesicht weiss mit blau-grünen Lidern, blauem Mund und blauer Träne. (JPN)
219 Plakatwerbung der Mitsubishi Shintaku Bank. (JPN)
220 Mehrfarbiges Plakat für den japanischen Maler Issey Miyake. (JPN)
221 Drei berühmte Baseballspieler symbolisieren hier die Kapazität eines Unternehmens, das vom Litho bis zum Drucken alles machen kann. In Farbe. (USA)
222 «Für ein Herz, Mut oder ein Gehirn.» Plakatwerbung für eine Schule. (USA)
223 Plakatwerbung für Farben der Marke *Pantone*. (USA)

218 Affiche annonçant l'exposition d'une école d'art. Typographie blanche sur fond noir, robe de la poupée en noir et blanc, visage blanc avec des paupières en bleu-vert, bouche et larme bleues. (JPN)
219 Affiche pour la banque *Mitsubishi Shintaku*. (JPN)
220 Affiche polychrome pour le peintre japonais Issey Miyake. (JPN)
221 Les trois célèbres joueurs de baseball symbolisent ici la capacité d'une entreprise qui offre des services complets de la photolitho à l'impression. En couleurs. (USA)
222 «Pour un cœur, du courage ou un cerveau.» Affiche pour une école. (USA)
223 Affiche pour une marque de peintures. (USA)

218

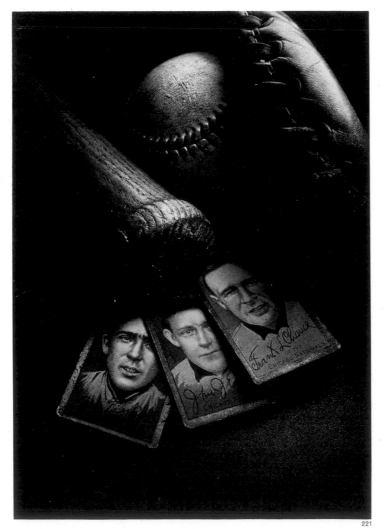

221   222

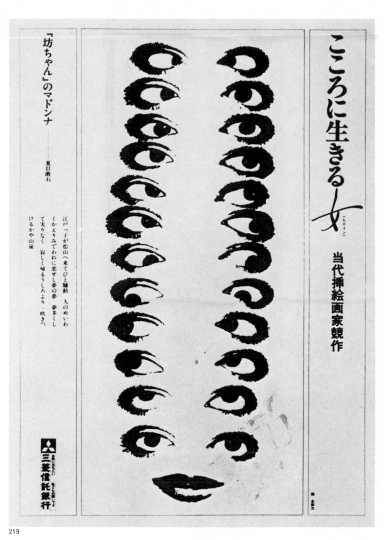

219

220

223

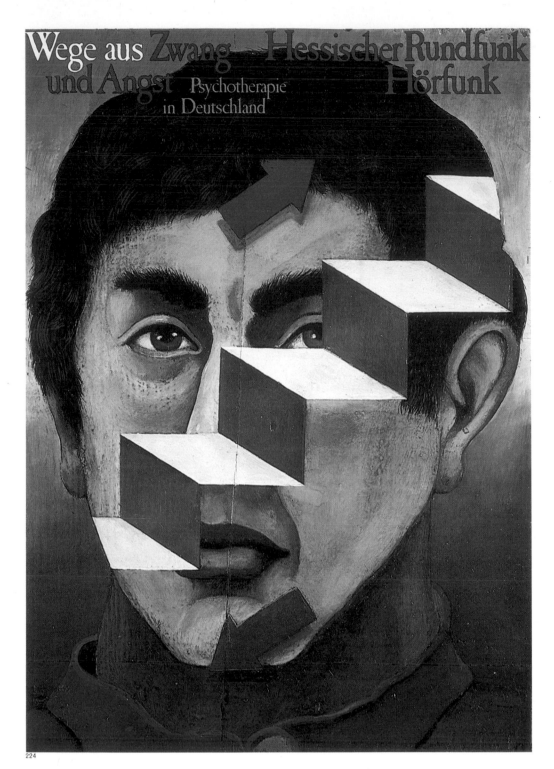

224

225

ARTIST / KÜNSTLER / ARTISTE:

224, 226 Günther Kieser
225 Roswitha + Eberhard Marhold
227 Tony Ynocencio
228 Ivan Chermayeff
229 Phil Marco
230 Hans Hillmann

DESIGNER / GESTALTER / MAQUETTISTE:

224, 226 Günther Kieser
225 Roswitha + Eberhard Marhold
227, 228 Ivan Chermayeff
229 Ivan Chermayeff/Charles Unger
230 Hans Hillmann

ART DIRECTOR / DIRECTEUR ARTISTIQUE:

227–229 Ivan Chermayeff
230 Artur Kulak

AGENCY / AGENTUR / AGENCE-STUDIO:

224–226 Hessischer Rundfunk, Abt. Publizistik
227–229 Chermayeff & Geismar Assoc.

Institutions
Institutionen

224–226 Examples from a series of posters for the Hessian broadcasting authority. Fig. 224 refers to a radio programme about psychotherapy in Germany, Fig. 225, in shades ranging from white to brown, announces a regional television show about graphic artists, and Fig. 226, mainly in shades of green, red, and blue refers to a radio series dealing with children, in this case the child drop-out. (GER)
227–229 Posters for television programmes financed by *Mobil*. Fig. 227 advertises a series about American diplomacy. "Between The Wars", Fig. 228 refers to the play "The Mayor of Casterbridge" starring the British actor Alan Bates, and Fig. 229 advertises a dramatic television series entitled "Edward the King". All posters in full colour. (USA)
230 Examples from a series of art posters distributed by the publishing organization of German savings banks on the occasion of World Savings Day. In full colour. (GER)

224–226 Beispiele aus einer Serie von Plakaten für den Hessischen Rundfunk. Abb. 224 weist auf eine Rundfunksendung über Psychotherapie in Deutschland hin, Abb. 225, in Schattierungen von Weiss bis Braun, kündigt eine regionale Fernsehsendung über bildende Künstler an, Abb. 226, vorwiegend grün, rot und blau, betrifft die Hörfunkreihe «Gebrandmarkte Kinder», bei der es hier um Kinder- und Jugendkriminalität geht. (GER)
227–229 Plakate für Fernsehsendungen, die von *Mobil* finanziert werden. Abb. 227 wirbt für eine Serie über die Geschichte der amerikanischen Diplomatie («Zwischen den Kriegen»), Abb. 228 betrifft ein Stück mit dem Titel «Der Bürgermeister von Casterbridge», Abb. 229 wirbt für eine dramatische Fernsehserie über König Edward. Alle farbig. (USA)
230 Beispiel aus einer Serie von Künstlerplakaten, die vom Deutschen Sparkassenverlag anlässlich des Weltspartags veröffentlicht wurden. In Farbe. (GER)

224–226 Exemples d'une série d'affiches pour la radiodiffusion et télévision de la Hesse. Fig. 224 se réfère à une émission de radio sur la psychothérapie en Allemagne; fig. 225 annonce une émission de TV locale sur sept artistes et sculpteurs – tons blancs passant au marron; fig. 226 pour une série d'émissions intitulée «Les enfants flétris» discutant particulièrement le problème de la délinquance juvénile; prédominance de tons rouges et bleus. (GER)
227–229 Affiches pour une série d'émissions de TV patronnées par *Mobil*. Fig. 227: «Entre les guerres» – une série d'émissions consacrée à la diplomatie américaine; fig. 228 se réfère à une pièce intitulée «Le maire de Casterbridge»; fig. 229 annonce une série d'émissions présentant la pièce «Edward the King», le roi de la paix et le roi playboy. En polychromie. (USA)
230 Exemple d'une longue série d'affiches patronnée par les banques allemandes et publiée à l'occasion de la journée mondiale de l'épargne. Plusieurs artistes ont participé à cette série. (GER)

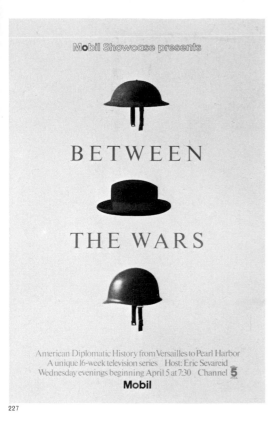

Mobil Showcase presents

BETWEEN THE WARS

American Diplomatic History from Versailles to Pearl Harbor
A unique 16-week television series   Host: Eric Sevareid
Wednesday evenings beginning April 5 at 7:30   Channel **5**

Mobil

227

Masterpiece Theatre presents
The Mayor of Casterbridge
starring Alan Bates

He was invincible—until his past began to haunt him
Sundays at 9pm beginning September 3 Channel 13 PBS

Mobil

228

Edward the King

*Remembered as the Peacemaker King
but not forgotten as the Playboy Prince*

*A 13-week dramatic television series beginning January 1979
Host: Robert MacNeil*

Mobil Showcase

229

**Hessischer
Rundfunk**
Internationale
Rundfunk-
Universität

in der Reihe
"Gebrandmarkte
Kinder"

Kinder auf Abwegen
Hörfunk
Neue Erkenntnisse
in der Kinder- und
Jugendkriminalität

Mittwochs
22.20 Uhr
2. Prog.

2.5.
Kinderdelinquenz
und kriminelle
Karriere
9.5.
Dunkelfeld,
Mädchenkriminalität
und Vandalismus
16.5.
Bandenkriminalität
23.5.
Ursachen,
Vorbeugung und
Behandlung

226

WELTSPARTAG 1978   30. OKTOBER

SPARKASSE

230

Deutsches Fernsehen WDR Kinderprogramm
April, Mai, Juni 1978

Montag, 17. April 1978
17.00–17.50
Mischmasch
Mit Tricks, Gags und einem
Gespenst.
Mit Heinz Bähr und dem Hund
Herzlieb McWau, der
natürlich weiß, wie man
mit Geistern umgeht.

Montag, 1. Mai 1978
15.45–17.15 Uhr
Odysseus und die Sterne
Ein Spielfilm von
Ludvik Raza
Odysseus ist eine Katze.
Sie lebt zweimal – 1976
und im Jahr 2000. Sie
transportiert eine
Botschaft aus dem Weltraum.
Ein Science-Fiction-Film
für Kinder in einer
Co-Produktion Studio
Barrandov, Prag, WDR Köln

Donnerstag, 4. Mai 1978
14.55–16.10 Uhr
**Das Mädchen auf dem
Besenstiel**
Ein Spielfilm von
Vaclav Vorlicek
Buch: Milos Macourek
Saxana hat Ärger in der
Hexenschule. Als sie erfährt,
daß sie 400 Jahre nachsitzen
soll, verschwindet sie zu den
Menschen.
Deshalb steht plötzlich eine
Kuh im Kinderzimmer. Die
Lehrerin läuft mit Nagezähnen
herum. Ein Junge trägt seinen
Kopf unter dem Arm.
Pädagogen werden zu
Kaninchen.
Und das alles nur, weil Saxana
sich verliebt hat und bei den
Menschen bleiben will.

Montag, 29. Mai 1978
17.00–17.50 Uhr
Mischmasch
Mit Tricks, Gags und vielen
Filmen.
Diesmal herrscht Hochbetrieb
im Filmspielautomaten.
Herzlieb McWau hat super-
klotschige Zeichentrickfilme
gefunden. Und die bringt er
gleich an den Mann. Heinz
Bähr macht ihm Konkurrenz
mit einem Gespenst.

Dienstag, 13. Juni 1978
17.00–17.50 Uhr
Die Schatzinsel 1. Teil
Ein Spielfilm nach dem
berühmten Roman von
Robert Louis Stevenson –
mit Orson Welles als
John Silver.

Mittwoch, 14. Juni 1978
17.00–17.50 Uhr
Die Schatzinsel 2. Teil
Wißt Ihr noch, wie der
Junge in der Apfelkiste
hockt und von dem
grimmigen Seeräuber
gesucht wird?

Dienstag, 20. Juni 1978
17.00–17.50 Uhr
**Tschetan, der Indianerjunge
1. Teil**
Ein Spielfilm von Hark Bohm
Alaska, der Schafhirte kommt
gerade noch rechtzeitig.
Der Rancher will Tschetan
verprügeln, weil er ihn für
einen Viehdieb hält.
Alaska befreit den Indianer-
jungen. Aber Tschetan traut
niemanden.
Auch Alaska nicht.

Mittwoch, 21. Juni 1978
17.00–17.50 Uhr
**Tschetan, der Indianerjunge
2. Teil**
Der Rancher will Alaska
und seine Herde vertreiben.
Mit seinen Leuten greift er
die Blockhütte an. Für
Tschetan steht jetzt fest,
daß Alaska ihn wirklich
braucht.

Montag, 26. Juni 1978
17.00–17.50 Uhr
Mischmasch
Mit Tricks, Gags und Herzlieb,
der mal wieder alles besser
kann. Heinz Bähr guckt ganz
gelassen zu. Schließlich
weiß er, daß Hund Herzlieb
eben nur fast alles gelingt.

Und natürlich die
„Sendung mit der Maus"
– Lach- und Sachgeschichten
am Sonntagmorgen
um Viertel
vor Elf.

231

234

235

236

The Channel 2 Auction   June 1-9

233

231 Poster showing children's programmes on West German television. These posters were distributed free of charge to schools and parents' associations to encourage selective viewing. (GER)
232 Illustration from a poster for a jazz concert of the West German broadcasting authority. (GER)
233 Announcement of an auction on American television's Channel 2, in which viewers can participate by telephone. In full colour. (USA)
234–236 Examples from a series of posters for the *Continental* insurance group, here with variations on "C", the symbol of the company. Fig. 234 mostly in green shades, Fig. 235 green landscape with orange, placard in blue and white, Fig. 236 in shades of gold, red and blue. (GER)

231 Plakat mit dem Kinderprogramm des Westdeutschen Rundfunks. Dieses Plakat wird gratis an Schulen und Elternvereinigungen abgegeben, um das selektive Fernsehen zu fördern. (GER)
232 Illustration eines Plakates für ein Jazz-Konzert im Westdeutschen Rundfunk. (GER)
233 Ankündigung einer Wohltätigkeitsversteigerung des amerikanischen Fernsehsenders Kanal 2, an der sich die Zuschauer telephonisch beteiligen konnten. Mehrfarbig. (USA)
234–236 Beispiele aus einer Serie von Plakaten für die Continentale Versicherungsgruppe, hier mit Variationen zum «C», Emblem der Gesellschaft. Abb. 234 vorwiegend in Grüntönen, Abb. 235 grüne Landschaft mit Orange, Schild blau-weiss, Abb. 236 Gold-, Rot- und Blautöne. (GER)

231 Affiche énumérant les programmes d'enfants diffusés par la radio-télévision de l'Ouest de l'Allemagne fédérale pour une période de trois mois en 1978. Ces affiches sont distribuées gracieusement aux écoles et aux associations de parents pour les aider à guider les choix. (GER)
232 Illustration d'une affiche annonçant un concert de jazz de la radio/TV WDR. (GER)
233 Annonce d'une vente aux enchères organisée par la station Chaîne 2 de la TV américaine. Les téléspectateurs qui veulent y participer peuvent appeler par téléphone. En couleurs. (USA)
234–236 Exemples d'une série d'affiches de la compagnie d'assurances *Continentale*, ici avec des variations du «C», le symbole de cette compagnie. En polychromie. (GER)

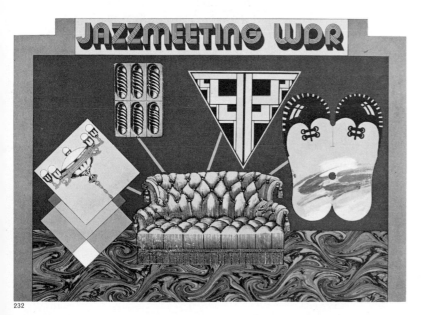

232

ARTIST / KÜNSTLER / ARTISTE:

231, 232 Heinz Edelmann
233 Mark Fisher
234 P. Thoms
235 Shimon Maroz
236 Annette Schwabe

DESIGNER / GESTALTER / MAQUETTISTE:

231, 232 Heinz Edelmann
233 Gaye Korbet
234–236 Coordt von Mannstein

ART DIRECTOR / DIRECTEUR ARTISTIQUE:

233 Gaye Korbet/Mark Fisher
234–236 Coordt von Mannstein

AGENCY / AGENTUR / AGENCE-STUDIO:

233 WGBH Design
234–236 von Mannstein Werbeagentur

Institutions
Institutionen

237

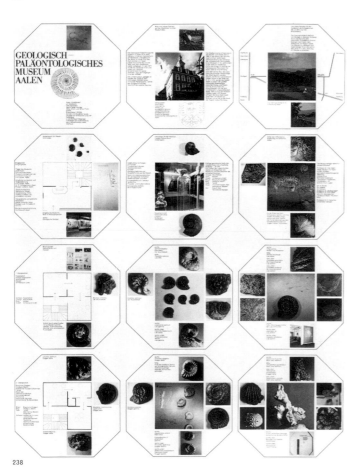

238

239

240

Institutions
Institutionen

241

242

243

237 «Es ist so schön, zu Hause zu sein.» Plakatwerbung der Bank *Crédit Agricole* für Immobilien-Kredite. Schneckenhaus weiss mit gelben, grünen, blauen und roten Tupfen. (FRA)
238 Informationsplakat der Stadt Aalen über das Geologisch-Paläontologische Museum. Alle Abbildungen farbig. (GER)
239 Plakat der Ersten Österreichischen Sparkasse. Mehrfarbig. (AUT)
240 Plakat für das Sommer-Kunststudienprogramm der Portland State University. Es wird hier ein Bild eines der Professoren gezeigt. (USA)
241–243 Plakatwerbung der Tyler-Kunstakademie. Das Plakat in Abb. 241 wird nach Semesterbeginn in einzelne Teile zerschnitten und als Einladung zu den angezeigten Ausstellungen verschickt. Mehrfarbig. (USA)

237 D'une longue série d'affiches du *Crédit Agricole* pour des prêts immobiliers. Coquille de limaçon blanche, taches en jaune, vert, rouge et bleu. (FRA)
238 Affiche d'information de la municipalité d'Aalen pour son Musée de géologie et de paléontologie. Illustrations en couleurs. (GER)
239 Affiche de la Caisse d'épargne de l'Autriche, publiée à l'occasion de la journée d'épargne de la jeunesse. En polychromie. (AUT)
240 Affiche-programme annonçant les cours d'art que la Portland State University organise pendant l'été. (USA)
241–243 Affiches d'une académie des beaux-arts. L'affiche présentée sous fig. 241 sera découpée au début du semestre et les parties individuelles seront distribuées comme invitations pour les expositions indiquées. (USA)

244

Institutions
Institutionen

246

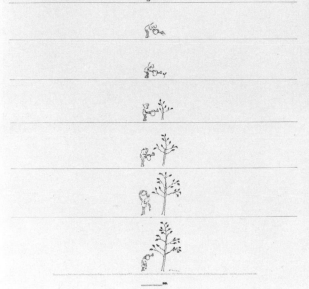

247

94

244 Small-format poster for locations for the sale of lottery tickets in which the lucky winners are paid every Thursday. (USA)
245–247 Poster advertising a special accident and damage insurance for agencies of the Insurance Company of North America. Fig. 245 with full-colour illustration and a black border. Fig. 246 shows in actual size a detail of the illustration of the poster in Fig. 247, with green leaves. (USA)
248 Poster for the *Loterie Romande*, a lottery taking place regularly in French Switzerland. (SWI)
249 Blue-and-white poster with which a system of combined car commuting is propagated for commuters, initiated by the medical faculty of Washington University. (USA)
250 Full-colour poster for modern girl scouts. (USA)
251 Full-colour poster with which *Hungexpo* offers exhibition space. *Hungexpo* is the Hungarian foreign trade organization for trade exhibitions and advertising. (HUN)
252 Poster from a campaign by the Zurich newspaper *Züri Leu* appealing for support for Zurich's zoo in its 50th year. (SWI)

244 Kleinformatiges Plakat für Verkaufsstellen von Lotterielosen. Die Gewinne werden jeden Donnerstag ausbezahlt. (USA)
245–247 Plakatwerbung der Insurance Company of North America für ein spezielles Unfall- und Schadenversicherungsprogramm für Agenturen, unter dem Slogan «Grün und gedeihend». Abb. 245 mit farbiger Illustration in schwarzem Rahmen. Abb. 246 zeigt in Originalgrösse ein Detail der Illustration des Plakates in Abb. 247, mit grünen Blättern. (USA)
248 Plakat für die *Loterie Romande*. (SWI)
249 Blau-weisses Plakat, mit dem ein System für gemeinsame Autofahrten von Pendlern propagiert wird. Auftraggeber ist die Medizinische Fakultät der Washington University. (USA)
250 Farbiges Plakat einer Pfadfinderorganisation für Mädchen, die hier ihr «neues Gesicht» zeigt. (USA)
251 Farbiges Plakat, mit dem Hungexpo, ungarische Aussenhandelsstelle für Messen und Werbung, Messeraum anbietet. (HUN)
252 Plakat aus einer Kampagne der Zürcher Zeitung *Züri Leu* zur Unterstützung des Zürcher Zoos. (SWI)

244 Affichette destinée aux boutiques qui vendent des billets de loterie, dont les gains sont distribués chaque jeudi. (USA)
245–247 Affiches de l'Insurance Company of North America pour un programme d'assurances contre les accidents et les dommages parues avec le même slogan: «Vert et prospérant». Fig. 245: illustration en couleurs, encadrement noir. La fig. 246 montre un détail en grandeur nature de l'illustration présentée sous fig. 247. Feuilles vertes. (USA)
248 Affiche pour la *Loterie Romande*. (SWI)
249 Pour un système de transport en commun pour les personnes qui font la navette entre le domicile et le lieu de travail. De la faculté de médecine de l'Université de Washington. (USA)
250 Affiche en couleurs d'une organisation d'éclaireuses qui présente ici «son nouveau profil». (USA)
251 Le bureau hongrois du commerce extérieur pour les foires et la publicité offre des salles d'exposition. (HUN)
252 Affiche figurant dans la campagne d'un journal zurichois lancée en faveur du jardin zoologique de Zurich. (SWI)

248

249

250

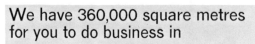

251

252

ART DIRECTOR / DIRECTEUR ARTISTIQUE:

244 Robert Qually
245–247 The Creative Dept., Inc.
249 Barry Tilson
250 Saul Bass
251 Sándor Hemberger
252 Dieter Hofmann

AGENCY / AGENTUR / AGENCE-STUDIO:

244 Lee King & Partners
245–247 The Creative Dept., Inc.
248 Loterie Romande
249 Stangellman Graphic Design
252 Advico AG

95

253

254

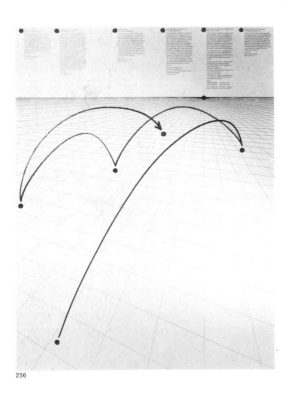

256

257

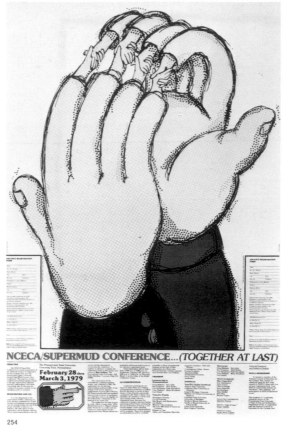

258

Direct Mail
Direktwerbung
Publicité directe

259

255

260

261

ARTIST / KÜNSTLER / ARTISTE:

262, 263 Bruno Garavoglia
264 Joel Naprstek
265 Gebhardt & Lorenz
266 Gian Calvi
267 Ron Hudson
268 Pete Steiner
269, 270 Stephen Graham/
Barbara Marvell

DESIGNER / GESTALTER / MAQUETTISTE:

264 Martha Savitzky
265 Gebhardt & Lorenz
266 Gian Calvi
267 Cap Pannell
268 James L. Selak
269, 270 Barrie Tucker

ART DIRECTOR / DIRECTEUR ARTISTIQUE:

262, 263 Gianni Parlacino
264 Richard Wilde
265 Dieter Gebhardt/Peter Lorenz
266 Gian Calvi
267 Cap Pannell
268 James L. Selak
269, 270 Barrie Tucker

262

263

264

262, 263 Small-format posters by the *Nebiolo* company of typefounders. Dark brown compositors' cases, white lettering. (ITA)
264 Poster by an art school with a white and green tree. Applications are invited for scholarships to the lower classes. (USA)
265 Poster calendar as direct advertising for its producers. (GER)
266 Poster calendar by the *Casa do Desenho* design studio. Head in yellow, red, brown, violet, blue and green stripes. (BRA)
267 Announcement of a meeting of an association for visual communication in Dallas, Texas. Turnip beige and violet with yellow "light". (USA)
268 Poster for the Xerox Corporation's annual sales and service conference. Umbrella in bright red, orange and beige. (USA)
269, 270 Detail of the illustration and complete poster calendar from a series by the Mitchell Press portraying famous men of the same name. (AUS)

262, 263 Kleinformatige Plakate der Firma *Nebiolo*, Ausrüster von Druckereien und Graphikern. Dunkelbraune Setzkästen, weisse Schrift. (ITA)
264 Plakat einer Kunstschule, mit weissem und grünem Baum. Hier wird zur Bewerbung um Stipendien für die untere Studienstufe eingeladen. (USA)
265 Plakatkalender als Direktwerbung der an seiner Herstellung Beteiligten. (GER)
266 Plakatkalender des Design-Studios *Casa do Desenho*. Kopf gelb, rot, braun, violett, blau, grün gestreift. (BRA)
267 Bekanntmachung eines Treffens der Gesellschaft für visuelle Kommunikation in Dallas. Rübe beige und violett mit gelbem «Licht». (USA)
268 Plakat für die Jahresverkaufs- und Service-Konferenz der Xerox Corporation. Schirm leuchtend rot, orange und beige. (USA)
269, 270 Detail der Illustration und komplettes Kalenderplakat aus einer Serie der Druckerei Mitchell Press mit berühmten Männern dieses Namens. (AUS)

262, 263 Affichettes de *Nebiolo*, entreprise qui fabrique des équipements et matériaux graphiques. Casse en brun foncé, typo blanche. (ITA)
264 Affiche d'une école d'art, avec un arbre en blanc, l'autre en vert. On invite les étudiants des premiers semestres de se présenter pour une bourse. (USA)
265 Affiche-calendrier distribuée comme élément de publicité directe par toutes les entreprises qui avaient participé à sa réalisation. (GER)
266 Affiche-calendrier du studio de design *Casa do Desenho*. Tête rayée en jaune, rouge, brun, violet, bleu et vert. (BRA)
267 Affiche annonçant une réunion de la société de communication visuelle de Dallas. Turnep en beige et violet avec «lumière» jaune. (USA)
268 Affiche pour une conférence de la Xerox Corporation sur les chiffres d'affaires annuels et les services rendus. En rouge, orange et beige. (USA)
269, 270 Détail de l'illustration et affiche-calendrier figurant dans une série de l'imprimerie Mitchell, présentant des hommes célèbres portant ce nom. (AUS)

265

266

269

267

268

AGENCY / AGENTUR / AGENCE:

262, 263 Centroune
264 SVA Publications
265 Gebhardt & Lorenz
266 Casa do desenho
267 Eisenberg & Pannell
268 Xerox Corp.
269, 270 Tucker & Kidd

270

Direct Mail
Direktwerbung
Publicité directe

99

271

274

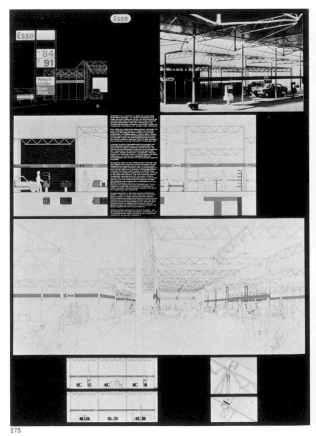

275

271 Self-promotion poster in full colour by a designer. (JPN)
272 Poster aimed at students, issued by the Lincoln Center, New York, with plans of buildings that can be cut out. (USA)
273 Call for entries for suggestions concerning energy saving, initiated by *Owens Corning*. In full colour. (USA)
274 Poster used in a trade fair by the *Owens Corning* company as an invitation to interior decorators to attend a reception on a boat. Illustration mainly in blue and green, red border. (USA)
275 Plan by a design studio and a firm of architects for the carrying out of an improved concept for *Esso* filling stations. Black and white with blue and red elements. (GER)
276 Invitation to an exhibition of the New York Art Directors Club. Red apple on a dark background, brown cardboard. (USA)
277 Poster announcing the change of address of a London firm. (GBR)

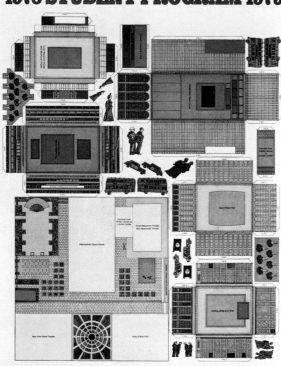

LINCOLN CENTER
1978 STUDENT PROGRAM 1979

LINCOLN CENTER FOR THE PERFORMING ARTS

272

Call for Entries

Owens-Corning Fiberglas

Energy Conservation Awards

273

276

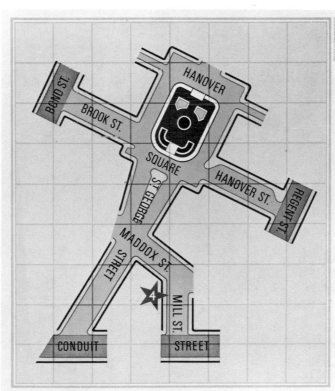

RUCK RYAN LINSELL · ☆ MILL STREET · LONDON WIR9TE · TEL 01-493 8623

277

271 Mehrfarbiges Plakat als Eigenwerbung eines Designers. (JPN)
272 An Studenten gerichtetes Plakat des Lincoln Centers, New York, mit Gebäuden zum Ausschneiden und Nachbauen des Centers. (USA)
273 Einladung zur Einreichung von Vorschlägen zur Energieeinsparung von dem Fiberglas-Hersteller *Owens Corning*. Mehrfarbig. (USA)
274 Anlässlich einer Messe verwendetes Plakat der Firma *Owens Corning* als Einladung zu einem Empfang für Innenarchitekten auf einem Schiff. Illustration vorwiegend blau und grün, mit rotem Rand. (USA)
275 Dokumentation der Ausarbeitung einer verbesserten Konzeption für *Esso*-Tankstellen durch ein Design-Studio und ein Architekturbüro. Schwarzweiss mit blauen und roten Elementen. (GER)
276 Einladung zur Ausstellung des New York Art Directors Club. Roter Apfel auf dunklem Hintergrund, brauner Karton. (USA)
277 Plakatankündigung des Adresswechsels einer Londoner Firma. (GBR)

271 Affiche autopromotionnelle d'un artiste graphique. En polychromie. (JPN)
272 Affiche du Lincoln Center de New York s'adressant aux étudiants. Les différents bâtiments peuvent être découpés pour reconstruire le centre. (USA)
273 Invitation de *Owens Corning*, fabricant de fibres de verre, de soumettre des propositions pour mieux économiser l'énergie. En polychromie. (USA)
274 Affiche que la compagnie *Owens Corning* a publiée à l'occasion d'une foire en tant qu'invitation à une réunion tenue sur un bâteau. à des architectes décorateurs de participer Prédominance de tons bleus et verts, encadrement rouge. (USA)
275 Documentation sur la réalisation d'un projet nouveau pour les postes d'essence *Esso* par un studio de design et d'architecture. Noir-blanc, éléments rouges. (GER)
276 Invitation pour l'exposition annuelle du Club des directeurs artistiques de New York. Pomme rouge sur fond foncé, carton brun. (USA)
277 Affiche annonçant le changement d'adresse d'une entreprise londonienne avec un plan de situation des nouveaux locaux. (GBR)

...GREATway to Europe

Amsterdam Airport Schiphol

278

...GREATway to Europe

Amsterdam Airport Schiphol

279

...GREATway to Europe

Amsterdam Airport Schiphol

280

**Tourism
Tourismus
Tourisme**

102

ARTIST / KÜNSTLER / ARTISTE:

278–280 Brian Shuel
281 Walter Tafelmaier
282 Bernhard Mertens
283 Ewald Becker/Grit von Fransecky

DESIGNER / GESTALTER / MAQUETTISTE:

278–280 Hamper & Purssell
281 Walter Tafelmaier
282 Bernhard Mertens

281

278—280 From a series of gift posters for Schiphol airport, Amsterdam. Photographs in full colour. (NLD)
281 Twenty-four different gables in colour gradations of grey, red and brown advertise the Bavarian university town of Erlangen. (GER)
282 Poster advertising the city of Cologne. (GER)
283 Poster advertising the well-known health resort Baden-Baden. (GER)

278—280 Drei Beispiele aus einer zum Verschenken bestimmten Serie von Plakaten für den Amsterdamer Flughafen Schiphol. Farbaufnahmen. (NLD)
281 Vierundzwanzig verschiedene Giebel in Farbabstufungen von Grau, Rot und Braun werben hier für die bayerische Universitätsstadt Erlangen. (GER)
282 «Overstolzenhaus über blauer Landschaft» ist der Titel des Plakates für die Stadt Köln. (GER)
283 Plakatwerbung für den bekannten Kurort Baden-Baden. (GER)

278—280 Trois exemples d'une série d'affiches-cadeaux publiée en faveur de l'aéroport Schiphol d'Amsterdam. Photos en couleurs. (NLD)
281 Affiche pour la promotion touristique de la ville universitaire Erlangen en Bavière avec vingt-quatre pignons de tons gris, rouges et bruns. (GER)
282 «Overstolzenhaus dans un paysage bleu.» Affiche touristique pour la ville de Cologne. (GER)
283 Affiche pour la promotion touristique de la station thermale Baden-Baden. (GER)

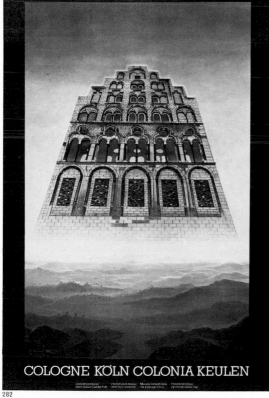

282

ART DIRECTOR / DIRECTEUR ARTISTIQUE:

278—280 Hamper & Purssell
281 Walter Tafelmaier
283 Ewald Becker/Grit von Fransecky

AGENCY / AGENTUR / AGENCE-STUDIO:

278—280 Hamper & Purssell Ltd.
283 Ewald Becker/Grit von Fransecky

283

284

SWITZERLAND *always in sight*

285

288

289

ARTIST / KÜNSTLER / ARTISTE:

284 Hideaki Hiratsuka
285 Beni La Roche
286 Hans Peter Hort
287 Werner E. Grieder
289 Josiane Merz
290 Mitchell Funk/The Image Bank
291 Pete Turner/The Image Bank
292 Bill Carter/The Image Bank

DESIGNER / GESTALTER / MAQUETTISTE:

284 Hideaki Hiratsuka
285 Beni La Roche
286 Hans Peter Hort
287 Werner E. Grieder
288 Atelier Eggmann
289 Peter Merz
290–292 John D. Muller/James D. Bubb/
Janice S. Woo

ART DIRECTOR / DIRECTEUR ARTISTIQUE:

284 Hideaki Hiratsuka
287 Werner E. Grieder
288 Werner Belmont
289 Peter Merz
290–292 John D. Muller

AGENCY / AGENTUR / AGENCE-STUDIO:

284 Dentsu Hakodate Branch
286 Hort Werbung
287 GGK
288 Unternehmenswerbung SBB
289 Publizitätsdienst SBB
290–292 David Pesanelli Assoc.

284 Full-colour poster for a festival town in Japan. (JPN)
285 Tourist poster for Switzerland with full-colour globe on a dark blue sky. (SWI)
286 Poster for Basle. "Basle is fashionable." (SWI)
287 Poster distributed to *Swissair* shareholders. (SWI)
288, 289 Poster advertising the Swiss Federal Railways. "The Swiss Federal Railways for everyone – everyone for the Swiss Federal Railways" is the text in Fig. 288, which is a section of a three-part poster. (SWI)
290 From a series of posters advertising the rediscovery of America by railway travel. Red Capitol for the rediscovery of Washington. The Southwest poster has a red background and the Northeast an orange-coloured sky. (USA)

284 Farbiges Plakat für eine Festspielstadt in Japan. (JPN)
285 «Die Schweiz, immer in Sicht.» Tourismus-Plakat für die Schweiz mit farbiger Weltkugel vor dunkelblauem Himmel. (SWI)
286 Plakatwerbung der Stadt Basel. (SWI)
287 An die Aktionäre verteiltes Plakat der *Swissair*. (SWI)
288, 289 Plakatwerbung der Schweizerischen Bundesbahnen. «Die Schweizerischen Bundesbahnen für alle – alle für die Schweizerischen Bundesbahnen» lautet der Text des dreiteiligen Plakates in Abb. 288. (SWI)
290–292 Aus einer Serie von Plakaten für Eisenbahnreisen in den USA. Hier wird zur Wiederentdeckung von Washington (mit rötlichem Kapitol), des Südwestens (roter Hintergrund) und des Nordostens (rot-gelber Himmel) eingeladen. (USA)

284 Affiche polychrome pour un festival au Japon. (JPN)
285 «La Suisse, toujours en vue.» Affiche touristique pour la Suisse avec globe polychrome sur fond bleu. (SWI)
286 «Bâle est en vogue.» Affiche pour la ville de Bâle avec la crosse qui fait partie des armoiries de ce canton. (SWI)
287 Affiche distribuée aux actionnaires de *Swissair*. (SWI)
288, 289 Affiche triple – «Les CFF pour tous – tous pour les CFF» – et affiche simple – «Par le train à la rencontre de la nature» – des Chemins de fers fédéraux suisses. (SWI)
290–292 D'une série d'affiches pour des voyages en chemin de fer à travers les Etats-Unis. On redécouvre Washington (Capitole en tons rougeâtres), le Sud-Ouest (fond rouge) et le Nord-Est (ciel en rouge et jaune). (USA)

286

287

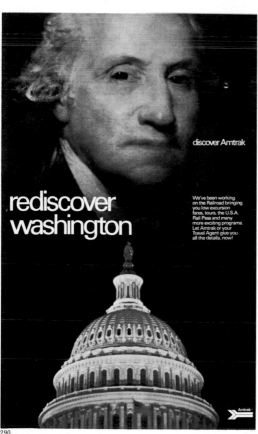

290

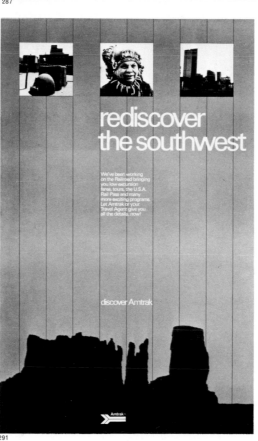

291

292

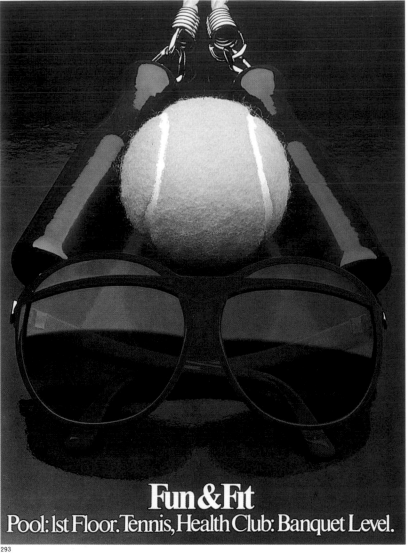

Fun & Fit
Pool: 1st Floor. Tennis, Health Club: Banquet Level.

293

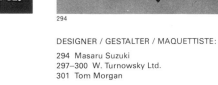

294

ARTIST / KÜNSTLER / ARTISTE:

293 Neal Higgins
294 Masaru Suzuki
295, 296 Gillean Proctor
297 David Sharir
298 Shabtai Tal
299, 300 Marvin E. Newman

DESIGNER / GESTALTER / MAQUETTISTE:

294 Masaru Suzuki
297–300 W. Turnowsky Ltd.
301 Tom Morgan

tel aviv-yafo

297

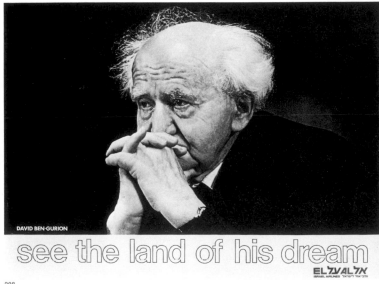

see the land of his dream

298

ART DIRECTOR / DIRECTEUR ARTISTIQUE:

293 Dick Henderson/Bill Sweney
294 Masaru Suzuki
295, 296 Pierre Leduc
297–300 W. Turnowsky Ltd.
301 D.R. Jones

AGENCY / AGENTUR / AGENCE-STUDIO:

293 Cole Henderson Drake, Inc.
294 Media Co., Ltd.
295, 296 Chales & Leduc Ltée
297–300 W. Turnowsky Ltd.
301 Wales Tourist Board

106

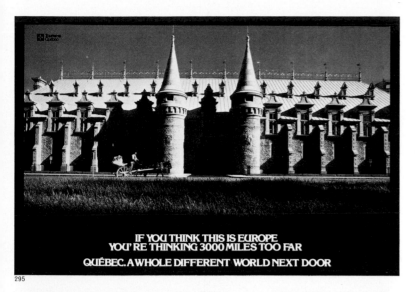

295

296

293 Poster advertising the *Omni International* Hotel in Atlanta, Georgia, referring to various facilities. (USA)
294 Poster for a café, in red and yellow. (JPN)
295, 296 Poster campaign by the Canadian province of Québec underlining in particular its European aspects. (CAN)
297–300 Poster for the Israeli *El Al* airline with an oilpainting by an Israeli artist in Fig. 297, David Ben Gurion in the pose of a philosopher and dreamer in Fig. 298, and photographs of Jerusalem and Tel-Aviv in Figs. 299 and 300. All posters in full colour. (ISR)
301 Poster advertising holidays in Wales with a photograph of a well-known Welsh holiday resort. (GBR)

293 Plakatwerbung des *Omni International* Hotels, Atlanta. Hier wird auf den Swimming-pool, die Tennisanlagen und den Fitness-Club des Hotels hingewiesen. (USA)
294 Gelb-rotes Plakat für ein Kaffeehaus. (JPN)
295, 296 «Wenn Sie glauben, dies sei Europa, denken Sie 3000 Meilen zu weit. Québec, eine ganz andere Welt vor der Tür.» Plakatkampagne der kanadischen Provinz Québec. (CAN)
297–300 Plakatwerbung der israelischen Luftfahrtgesellschaft *El Al*, hier mit einem Ölbild eines israelischen Künstlers (Abb. 297), David Ben Gurion: «Sieh' das Land seiner Träume» (Abb. 298) und Aufnahmen von Jerusalem und Tel-Aviv (Abb. 299 und 300). Alle Plakate mehrfarbig. (ISR)
301 Mit einer Farbaufnahme eines der bekanntesten walisischen Ferienorte wird hier für Wales geworben. (GBR)

293 Affiche pour l'hôtel *Omni International* à Atlanta. Elle se réfère à la piscine, les courts de tennis, et les installations d'exercice physique. (USA)
294 Affiche en jaune et rouge pour un café. (JPN)
295, 296 «Si vous pensez que c'est l'Europe, vous pensez 3000 miles trop loins. Québec. Un monde complètement différent devant la porte.» Campagne d'affiches pour le Québec. (CAN)
297–300 D'une série d'affiches de l'*El Al*, compagnie aérienne israélienne, ici présentant une peinture à l'huile d'un artiste israélien (fig. 297), David Ben Gurion: «Voir le pays de ses rêves» (fig. 298) et des photos de Jérusalem et de Tel Aviv (figs. 299 et 300). En polychromie. (ISR)
301 Affiche touristique pour le pays de Galles avec une prise de vue de l'une des plus célèbres stations balnéaires. (GBR)

299

300

301

2

Cultural Posters

Kulturelle Plakate

Affiches culturelles

302 Small-format poster announcing the performance of a play by Pablo Picasso. Red with black. (SWI)
303 Poster in black and white announcing the performance of a chamber musical by Wolfgang Hildesheimer. (SWI)
304 Poster in soft water-colours for a performance in Poland of a play by Fernando De Royas. (POL)
305 Theatre poster in turquoise and white, black lettering. (SWI)
306 Poster for a performance in Houston, Texas, of *Madame Butterfly*. Butterfly in blue and black. (USA)
307 Announcement of a performance of *Yerma* by Lorca. Blue torso with white clouds and black cord, red title. (GER)
308 Invitation by the Kiel theatre to a youth theatre competition for original ten-minute plays. (GER)
309 Poster for a performance at the Hamburg Thalia Theatre. (GER)

302 Kleinformatiges Plakat für die Aufführung eines Stückes von Pablo Picasso. Rot mit Schwarz. (SWI)
303 Plakat in Schwarzweiss für die Aufführung eines Kammermusicals von Wolfgang Hildesheimer. (SWI)
304 Plakat in zarten Aquarellfarben für die Aufführung eines Stückes von Fernando De Royas in Polen. (POL)
305 Theaterplakat in Türkisblau und Weiss mit schwarzer Schrift. (SWI)
306 Plakat für eine Aufführung von *Madame Butterfly* in Englisch an der Oper von Houston, Texas. Schmetterling blau und schwarz. (USA)
307 Ankündigung einer Aufführung von Lorcas *Yerma*. Torso blau mit weissen Wolken und schwarzer Schnur, Titel rot. (GER)
308 Einladung des Kieler Schauspielhauses zu einem Jugendtheater-Wettbewerb für selbsterfundene 10-Minuten-Spiele. (GER)
309 Plakat für eine Aufführung des Hamburger Thalia Theaters. (GER)

ARTIST / KÜNSTLER / ARTISTE:

302, 303, 305 Stephan Bundi
304 Grzegorz Marszalek
306 John Katz
307 H.H. Palitzsch/Rudolf Keilbach
308, 309 Holger Matthies

DESIGNER / GESTALTER / MAQUETTISTE:

302 303, 305 Stephan Bundi
304 Grzegorz Marszalek
306 David Jenkins
307 H.H. Palitzsch
308, 309 Holger Matthies

ART DIRECTOR / DIRECTEUR ARTISTIQUE:

302, 303, 305 Stephan Bundi
304 Grzegorz Marszalek
306 David Jenkins
307 Günther Zimmermann
308, 309 Holger Matthies

AGENCY / AGENTUR / AGENCE-STUDIO:

302, 303, 305 Atelier Bundi
306 Ogilvy & Mather
308, 309 Holger Matthies

302

303

305

306

302 Affichette pour une représentation de la pièce *Le Désir rattrapé par la queue* par Pablo Picasso. Rouge et noir. (SWI)

303 Affiche en noir et blanc pour la présentation d'une comédie musicale (Helena, le victime). (SWI)

304 Affiche annonçant la représentation d'une pièce de théâtre de Fernando De Royas en Pologne. Aquarelle en tons atténués. (POL)

305 Pour une pièce de théâtre. Turquoise et blanc, typo noire. (SWI)

306 Affiche pour une présentation en langue anglaise de *Madame Butterfly* à l'Opéra de Houston. Papillon en bleu et noir. (USA)

307 Pour une représentation de la pièce *Yerma* de Garcia Lorca. Torse bleu avec des nuages blancs et ficelle noire, titre rouge. (GER)

308 Le Théâtre Municipal de Kiel organise un concours de pièces de théâtre de 10 minutes que les jeunes gens ont écrites eux-mêmes. (GER)

309 Affiche pour une représentation théâtre du Théâtre Thalia. (GER)

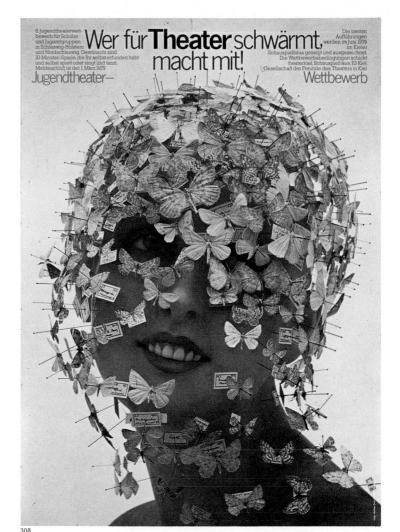

308

304

307

309

111

310 Small-format poster for a play called *Steambath*. Black and white, mouth and small print in red. (USA)
311 Announcement of a month of plays at the Café-Theatre in Tarbes, France. Black and white with red tomatoes. (FRA)
312 Large-format poster announcing the performance of a play by Brecht. Black and white with red. (FRA)
313 "No ship on the horizon." Theatre poster with black-and-white illustration on a beige-green surface, black lettering. (FRA)
314 A cultural centre's announcement of a performance by Czechoslovakian mimic actors at the Alfred Circus. (FRA)
315 Poster displayed on the occasion of a theatre festival. Blue sky, white and pink clouds. (FRA)
316 Poster for a performance by a theatre cooperative. (ITA)
317 Poster for one of the television programmes in the United States which are sponsored by *Mobil*. (USA)

310 Kleinformatiges Plakat für ein Stück mit dem Titel «Dampfbad». Schwarzweiss, Mund und Kleingedrucktes rot. (USA)
311 Plakat für einen in Tarbes, Frankreich, veranstalteten Monat des Café-Theaters. Schwarzweiss mit roten Tomaten. (FRA)
312 Grossformatiges Plakat für die Ankündigung einer Brecht-Aufführung. Schwarzweiss mit Rot. (FRA)
313 «Kein Schiff am Horizont.» Theaterplakat mit schwarzweisser Illustration auf beigegrünem Grund, Schrift schwarz. (FRA)
314 Bekanntmachung eines Kulturzentrums für eine Vorstellung von tschechischen Mimen im Zirkus Alfred. (FRA)
315 Anlässlich eines Theater-Festivals veröffentlichtes Plakat. Blauer Himmel, Wolken weiss und rosa. (FRA)
316 Plakat für die Aufführung einer Theater-Kooperative. (ITA)
317 «Lied für Lied.» Plakat für eine Fernsehsendung, die von *Mobil* finanziert wird. (USA)

310

311

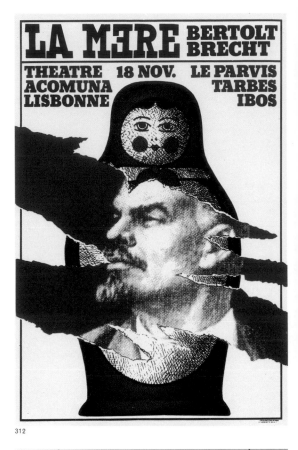

312

314

315

ARTIST / KÜNSTLER / ARTISTE:

310 John Massey
311, 312, 314, 315 Alain Le Quernec
313 André François
316 Giovanni Lussu/Paola Trucco
317 Seymour Chwast

ART DIRECTOR / DIRECTEUR ARTISTIQUE:

310 John Massey
311, 312, 314, 315 Alain Le Quernec
313 Claude Confortés
316 Giovanni Lussu/Paola Trucco
317 Sandra Ruch

310 Affiche pour la représentation d'une pièce intitulée «Bain de vapeur». Noir et blanc, bouche et texte en rouge. (USA)
311 Affiche pour le mois du Café-Théâtre, une manifestation organisée à Tarbes, France. Noir-blanc, tomates rouges. (FRA)
312 Affiche pour la présentation d'une pièce de Bertolt Brecht par une troupe de Lisbonne. Noir-blanc et rouge. (FRA)
313 Affiche annonçant une représentation théâtrale. Illustration en noir et blanc sur fond beige verdâtre, typo noire. (FRA)
314 Affiche annonçant un spectacle de mimes tchécoslovaques par le Cirque Alfred au Centre culturel de Tarbes. (FRA)
315 Affiche pour un festival théâtral. Ciel bleu avec des nuages en blanc et rose. (FRA)
316 Pour une pièce présentée par une coopérative de théâtre. (ITA)
317 «Chanson par chanson.» Affiche pour une émission de TV patronnée par *Mobil*. (USA)

313

316

317

AGENCY / AGENTUR / AGENCE-STUDIO:

311, 312, 314, 315 Kan Ar Mor
316 Fantastici 4
317 Push Pin Studios, Inc.

318

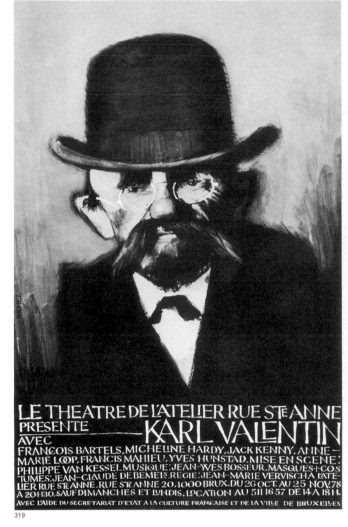

319

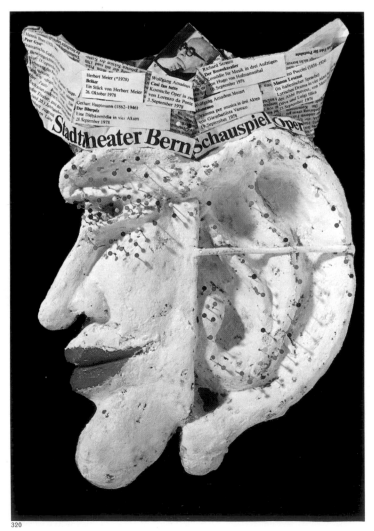

320

321

322

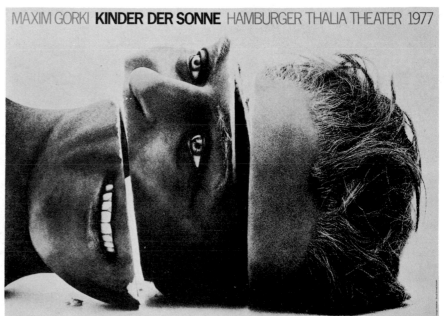

323

ARTIST / KÜNSTLER / ARTISTE:	DESIGNER / GESTALTER / MAQUETTISTE:	ART DIRECTOR / DIRECTEUR ARTISTIQUE:	AGENCY / AGENTUR / AGENCE-STUDIO:
318 Heinz Edelmann	318 Heinz Edelmann	319, 321 Jacques Richez	318 Westdeutscher Rundfunk, Abt.
319, 321 Jacques Richez	319, 321 Jacques Richez	320 Heinz Jost	Publizistik
320 Heinz Jost	320 Heinz Jost	322 Josef Müller-Brockmann	319, 321 Jacques Richez
322 Josef Müller-Brockmann	322 Josef Müller-Brockmann	323 Esko Moilanen	322 Müller-Brockmann & Co.
323 Esko Moilanen	323 Esko Moilanen	324 Holger Matthies	323 Mainosyhtymä Oy
324 Holger Matthies	324 Holger Matthies		

318 Poster for a performance of a musical comedy by Hanns Dieter Hüsch, which was filmed and recorded by the West German radio and television network. (GER)
319 Poster for a Karl Valentin performance. Black and white with red nose. (BEL)
320 Poster announcing performances at the Civic Theatre in Berne. (SWI)
321 Full-colour poster for a performance at an intimate theatre. (BEL)
322 Large-format poster for a performance of the musical *The Man from La Mancha*. Pale shades: green and brown with blue, red and yellow. (SWI)
323 Full-colour poster for an *Andorra* performance in a Finnish theatre. (FIN)
324 Announcement of a Gorki play at the Thalia Theatre in Hamburg. (GER)

318 Plakat für die Aufführung einer musikalischen Komödie von Hanns Dieter Hüsch, die vom Westdeutschen Rundfunk aufgezeichnet wurde. (GER)
319 Plakat für eine Karl-Valentin-Aufführung. Schwarzweiss mit roter Nase. (BEL)
320 Plakat des Stadttheaters Bern für seine Aufführungen. (SWI)
321 Farbiges Plakat für eine Aufführung an einem Kammertheater. (BEL)
322 Grossformatiges Plakat für eine Aufführung des Musicals *Der Mann von La Mancha*. Blasse Farbtöne: Gesichtshälften grün und braun, mit Blau, Rot und Gelb. (SWI)
323 Farbiges Plakat für eine *Andorra*-Aufführung an einem finnischen Theater. (FIN)
324 Ankündigung einer Gorki-Aufführung am Hamburger Thalia Theater. (GER)

318 Affiche annonçant la représentation d'une comédie musicale de Hanns Dieter Hüsch, enregistrée par la radio/TV de l'ouest de l'Allemagne. (GER)
319 Pour une représentation de Karl Valentin qui «n'invente pas des gags» comme le dit Brecht, «il en est un lui-même». Portrait en noir-blanc, nez rouge. (BEL)
320 Affiche pour une série de représentations au Théâtre Municipal de Berne. (SWI)
321 Pour la représentation d'une pièce d'Arrabal au Théâtre de Poche de Bruxelles. (BEL)
322 Affiche pour la présentation de la comédie musicale *L'Homme de La Manche*. Tons atténués: visage en vert et brun avec du bleu, rouge et jaune. (SWI)
323 Pour un représentation de la pièce *Andorra* de Max Frisch en Finlande. (FIN)
324 Pour une pièce basée sur un récit de Maxim Gorki, mise en scène à Hambourg. (GER)

324

325

326

327

328

329

330

ARTIST / KÜNSTLER / ARTISTE:

325, 327–329, 334 Frieder Grindler
326 Klaus Endrikat
330, 332 Holger Matthies
331 Rolf Willimann
333 Richard Müller

DESIGNER / GESTALTER / MAQUETTISTE:

325, 327–329, 334 Frieder Grindler
326 Klaus Endrikat
330, 332 Holger Matthies
331 Eugen Bachmann
333 Richard Müller

ART DIRECTOR / DIRECTEUR ARTISTIQUE:

325, 327–329, 334 Frieder Grindler
326 Klaus Endrikat
330, 332 Holger Matthies
331 Eugen Bachmann
333 Albrecht Ade

AGENCY / AGENTUR / AGENCE-STUDIO:

325, 327–329, 334 Frieder Grindler
326 Klaus Endrikat
330, 332 Holger Matthies

325 Poster for a performance of Harold Pinter's *Old Times* played in Düsseldorf. Silhouettes in rusty red. (GER)
326 Announcement of two Beckett plays at the Civic Theatre in Aachen. (GER)
327 Black-and-white poster for the first performance of Carl Zuckmayer's *Schinderhannes* at the State Theatre, Karlsruhe. (GER)
328 Another poster for the State Theatre, Karlsruhe, for a performance of Leonard Bernstein's successful musical. (GER)
329 Announcement of a farce with music by Nestroy. Black and white. (GER)
330 Poster advertising season tickets for the Wuppertal theatre. (GER)
331 Large black-and-white poster announcing a comedy. (SWI)
332 Announcement of a performance at the Hamburg state opera. Sky in blue, ground and figure bathed in cold moonlight. (GER)
333 Poster in grey shades for a performance of a play. (GER)
334 Full-colour poster for the performance of a play by Martin Sperr at the State Theatre, Karlsruhe. (GER)

325 Plakat für das in Düsseldorf gezeigte Theaterstück «Alte Zeiten» von Harold Pinter. Silhouetten in Rostrot. (GER)
326 Ankündigung einer Beckett-Aufführung des Stadttheaters Aachen. (GER)
327 Schwarzweiss-Plakat für die Uraufführung eines Musicals nach Carl Zuckmayers *Schinderhannes* am Badischen Staatstheater Karlsruhe. (GER)
328 Ein weiteres Plakat des Badischen Staatstheaters Karlsruhe, hier für eine Aufführung von Leonard Bernsteins erfolgreichem Musical. (GER)
329 Ankündigung einer Posse mit Musik von Nestroy. Schwarzweiss. (GER)
330 Plakat für die Abonnentenwerbung der Wuppertaler Bühnen. (GER)
331 Grossformatiges Plakat in Schwarzweiss für eine Komödie. (SWI)
332 Ankündigung einer Aufführung der Hamburger Staatsoper. Der Himmel mittelblau, Erde und Gestalt in kaltes Mondlicht getaucht. (GER)
333 Plakat in Grautönen für eine Theateraufführung. (GER)
334 Farbiges Plakat für die Aufführung eines Stückes von Martin Sperr am Badischen Staatstheater, Karlsruhe. (GER)

325 Affiche pour une représentation de la pièce *Old Times* de Harold Pinter mise en scène par un théâtre à Düsseldorf. Personnages rouille. (GER)
326 Affiche pour deux pièces de Beckett présentées à Aachen. (GER)
327 Affiche en noir et blanc pour la première représentation d'une comédie musicale d'après la pièce *Schinderhannes* de Carl Zuckmayer. (GER)
328 Affiche pour un musical joué à Karlsruhe. (GER)
329 Affiche annonçant une farce musicale de Nestroy. En noir et blanc. (GER)
330 Affiche des théâtres de Wuppertal invitant le public à s'assurer des places en prenant un abonnement. (GER)
331 Affiche du Théâtre Municipal de Lucerne pour une comédie. (SWI)
332 Affiche pour une représentation mise en scène par l'Opéra de Hambourg. Prédominance de tons bleus, froids coloris bleus. (GER)
333 Affiche en tons gris pour la présentation d'une pièce de théâtre. (GER)
334 Affiche annonçant la présentation d'une pièce (Scènes de chasse de la Basse-Bavière) joué par un théâtre de Karlsruhe. (GER)

STADTTHEATER LUZERN
Schönes Weekend Mr. Bennett
Komödie von Arthur Watkyn
Premiere 27.4.1978
Leitung Stöhr
Engler
Tan

331

330

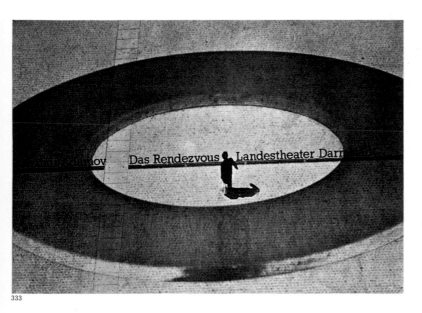

333

334

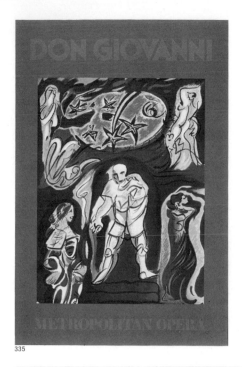

335

336

337

ARTIST / KÜNSTLER / ARTISTE:

335 André Masson
336 Antoni Clavé
337, 339 Marino Marini
338 Richard Lindner

ART DIRECTOR / DIRECTEUR ARTISTIQUE:

335–339 Stephan Lion

338

335–339 Four examples from a series of posters with operatic themes which were designed by well-known artists for the Metropolitan Opera, New York. The posters as well as the original graphic designs were later put on sale by the opera company. The examples shown here are by André Masson, Antonio Clavé, Marino Marini and Richard Lindner. Marino Marini's *La Traviata* (Figs. 337, 339) is an 11-colour lithograph and Richard Lindner's *Der Rosenkavalier* (Fig. 338) is a 22-colour lithograph. There was a limited, numbered and signed edition of 250 of these posters available to the public. (USA)

335–339 Vier Beispiele aus einer Serie von Plakaten mit Opernsujets, die von bekannten Künstlern für die Metropolitan Opera, New York, gestaltet wurden. Die Plakate sowie die ihnen zugrundeliegenden Originalgraphiken werden von der Oper zum Verkauf angeboten. Die hier gezeigten Beispiele sind, der Reihe nach, von André Masson, Antonio Clavé, Marino Marini und Richard Lindner. Marino Marinis *La Traviata* (Abb. 337, 339) ist eine elffarbige Lithographie, Richard Lindners *Der Rosenkavalier* (Abb. 338) ist eine 22farbige Lithographie. Die Auflage dieser Plakate ist auf 250 numerierte und handsignierte Exemplare limitiert. (USA)

335–339 Le Metropolitan Opera de New York a récemment invité huit grands artistes de créer des estampes originales en prenant pour sujet divers opéras. Ces gravures ont été mises en vente en même temps que des affiches les représentant. Nous présentons ici *Don Giovanni* par André Masson (fig. 335), *Carmen* par Antonio Clavé (fig. 336), *La Traviata* par Marino Marini (litho 11 couleurs, fig. 337, 339), *Der Rosenkavalier* par Richard Lindner (litho 22 couleurs, fig. 338). Le tirage fut limité à 250 exemplaires numérotés et signés par l'artiste après quoi les planches et tamis de soie furent détruits. (USA)

MARINO

Paul Wunderlich

342

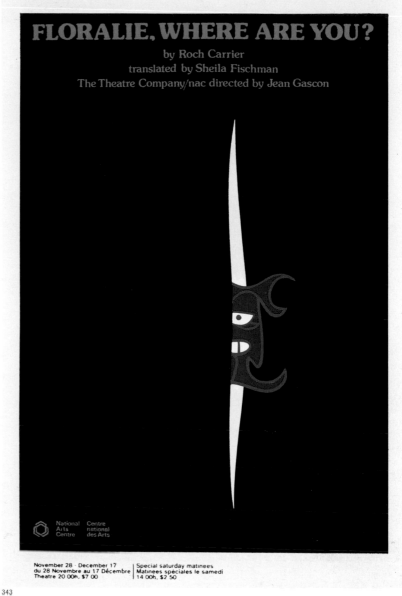

343

Theatre/Theater/Théâtre

ARTIST / KÜNSTLER / ARTISTE:

340, 341 Paul Wunderlich
342 Ivan Chermayeff
343 Vittorio Fiorucci

DESIGNER / GESTALTER / MAQUETTISTE:

342 Ivan Chermayeff
343 Vittorio Fiorucci

ART DIRECTOR / DIRECTEUR ARTISTIQUE:

340, 341 Stephan Lion
342 Ivan Chermayeff
343 Vittorio Fiorucci

AGENCY / AGENTUR / AGENCE-STUDIO:

342 Chermayeff & Geismar Assoc.

340, 341 Another example from the series of art-posters and lithographs shown on the previous double spread for the Metropolitan Opera, New York. Here a five-colour lithograph by Paul Wunderlich for *Aida* (printed in Switzerland by Mathieu), with its poster. (USA)
342 Full-colour poster for a ballet. (USA)
343 Poster for a play performed in Montreal. (CAN)

340, 341 Ein weiteres Beispiel der auf der vorangehenden Doppelseite gezeigten Künstlerplakate für die Metropolitan Opera, New York. Hier *Aida*, eine fünffarbige Lithographie von Paul Wunderlich, gedruckt bei Mathieu, Schweiz, und das entsprechende Plakat. (USA)
342 Farbenfrohes Plakat für eine Ballettaufführung. (USA)
343 Plakat für das in Montreal gezeigte Stück «Floranie, wo bist Du?» (CAN)

340, 341 Voici un autre exemple de la série d'estampes originales et d'affiches du Metropolitan Opera de New York (v. page double précédente). Nous présentons ici la litho 5 couleurs par Paul Wunderlich et l'affiche correspondante pour *Aida*. (USA)
342 Farbenfrohes Plakat für eine Ballettaufführung. (USA)
343 Plakat für das in Montreal gezeigte Stück «Floranie, wo bist Du?». (CAN)

344

344 Poster from a Polish theatrical museum. (POL)
345 Poster in brown shades for a reading from Thomas Mann's *The Magic Mountain*, with old recordings. (GER)
346, 349, 350 Examples from a series of posters for the so-called secondary stage of a Japanese theatre. Fig. 349: black and white with light brown. Fig. 350: the upper part in black turning into white, the lower part green, violet, pink, figures in light brown, black and white lettering. (JPN)
347 Full-colour poster for a musical performance. (JPN)
348 Poster in subdued green with white for a performance of Chekhov's drama *Three Sisters* at the East Berlin Maxim Gorki Theatre. (GDR)

344 Plakat aus einem polnischen Theatermuseum. (POL)
345 In Brauntönen gehaltenes Plakat für eine Lesung aus Thomas Manns *Zauberberg*, mit alten Schallplatten. (GER)
346, 349, 350 Beispiele aus einer Reihe von Plakaten für die sogenannte Nebenbühne eines japanischen Theaters. Abb. 349: Schwarzweiss mit Hellbraun, Abb. 350: Im oberen Teil schwarz in Weiss übergehend, im unteren Teil grün, violett, rosa und Figuren in Hellbraun; Schrift weiss und schwarz. (JPN)
347 Mehrfarbiges Plakat für eine musikalische Darbietung. (JPN)
348 Plakat in gedämpftem Grün mit Weiss für eine Aufführung von Anton Tschechows Drama *Drei Schwestern* am Ostberliner Maxim-Gorki-Theater. (GDR)

344 Affiche d'un musée polonais des spectacles. (POL)
345 Affiche annonçant une soirée de lecture présentant des extraits de la «Montagne magique» de Thomas Mann et de vieux disques. Prédominance de tons bruns. (GER)
346, 349, 350 Exemples d'une série d'affiches publiées par le studio d'un théâtre japonais. Fig. 349: noir et blanc avec brun clair; fig. 350: partie supérieure en noir passant au blanc, partie inférieure en vert, violet, rose, figures en brun clair; typographie en blanc et noir. (JPN)
347 Affiche (en couleurs) pour une représentation musicale. (JPN)
348 Affiche annonçant la représentation du drame «Les Trois Sœurs» d'Anton Tchekhov, mise en scène par le Théâtre Maxim Gorki à Berlin-Est. Tons atténués. (GDR)

ARTIST / KÜNSTLER / ARTISTE:

344 Jan Lenica
345 Otto Kummert
346, 349, 350 Seitaro Kuroda
347 Shinichiro Wakao
348 Erhard Grüttner

DESIGNER / GESTALTER / MAQUETTISTE:

344 Jan Lenica
345 Otto Kummert
346, 349 Keisuke Nagatomo
347 Ikko Tanaka
348 Erhard Grüttner
350 Naohisa Tsuchiya

ART DIRECTOR / DIRECTEUR ARTISTIQUE:

346, 349, 350 Keisuke Nagatomo
347 Ikko Tanaka

AGENCY / AGENTUR / AGENCE-STUDIO:

346, 349, 350 K-Two
347 Ikko Tanaka Design Studio

345

346

越路吹雪ロングリサイタル

リサイタル歴25周年記念

構成・演出＝浅利慶太　音楽監督＝内藤法美
訳詞＝岩谷時子
〈アイデザイン〉音部憲
衣裳＝銀座松坂屋オートクチュール　ニナ・リッチ
演奏＝内藤法美とロイヤルポップスオーケストラ
制作＝日本ゼネラルアーツ

九月一日（金）二十日（水）
十月十八日（水）二十六日（木）

日生劇場

347

348

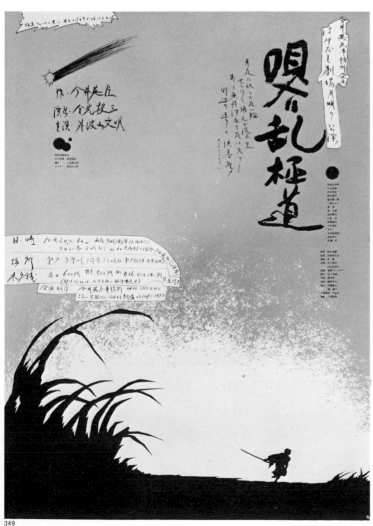

唄・乱・極道

作・今井英丘
演出・金光校三
童謡・外波山文明

349

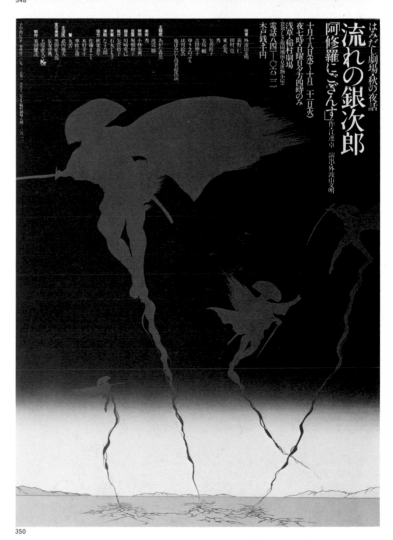

流れの銀次郎

阿修羅にござんす

はみだし劇場・秋の夜話

演出・外波山明

十月十八日（水）〜十月二十一日（水）
夜七時一日曜昼夕方四時のみ

浅草・稲村劇場
電話八四一〜一〇八二
木戸銭全自由

350

123

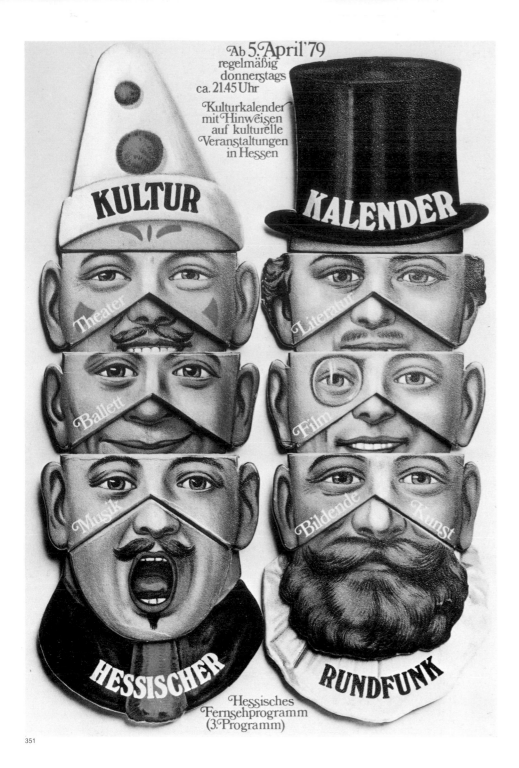

351

352

356

Theatre/Theater/Théâtre

ARTIST / KÜNSTLER / ARTISTE:

351 Günther Kieser
352 Kai Kujasalo
353 Marie Buckley
354 György Kemény
355 Jacques Richez
356 Stephan Bundi
357 Lanny Sommese
358 Heather Cooper

DESIGNER / GESTALTER / MAQUETTISTE:

351 Günther Kieser
352 Kai Kujasalo
353 Marie Buckley
354 György Kemény
355 Jacques Richez
356 Stephan Bundi
357 Lanny Sommese
358 Heather Cooper/Lawrence Finn

353

354

355

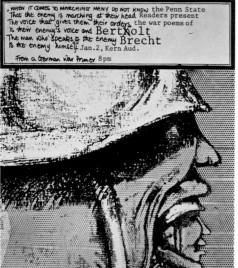

357

ART DIRECTOR / DIRECTEUR ARTISTIQUE:

352 Kai Kujasalo
353 Thomas J. Castle
354 György Kemény
355 Jacques Richez
356 Stephan Bundi
357 Lanny Sommese
358 Heather Cooper

AGENCY / AGENTUR / AGENCE-STUDIO:

351 Hessischer Rundfunk/Abt. Publizistik
353 Media Production Dept., N.T.I.D.
355 Jacques Richez
356 Atelier Bundi
357 Lanny Sommese Design
358 Burns, Cooper, Hynes Ltd.

358

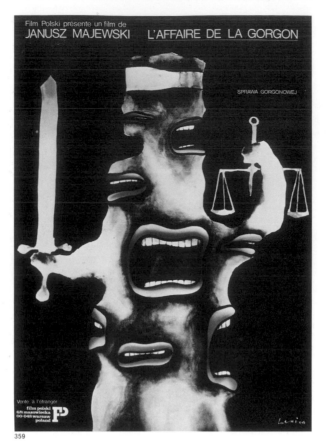

359

360

362

363

ARTIST / KÜNSTLER / ARTISTE:

359 Jan Lenica
360 Vratislav Hlavaty
361 Otto Kummert
362 Thomas Schallnau
363 Karel Vaca
364 István Bakos
365 Tibor Helényi
366 Franciszek Starowieyski

DESIGNER / GESTALTER / MAQUETTISTE:

359 Jan Lenica
360 Vratislav Hlavaty
361 Otto Kummert
362 Thomas Schallnau
363 Karel Vaca
364 István Bakos
365 Tibor Helényi
366 Franciszek Starowieyski

ART DIRECTOR / DIRECTEUR ARTISTIQUE:

360 Hana Kalousová
364 István Bakos
365 Jozsef Adorján

AGENCY / AGENTUR / AGENCE-STUDIO:

363 Filmstudio Prag

359 Poster for a Polish film. "Justitia" white and grey, lips white and violet, dark blue background. (POL)
360 Announcement of a Soviet film. In full colour. (CSR)
361 Poster advertising a documentary film, "Meier's Legacy". (GDR)
362 Announcement of "Unequal Duel", a French detective film. Poster mainly in blue and white, black lettering. (GDR)
363 "Lightning over Mexico" is the title of the film advertised here. Poster in full colour. (CSR)
364 Poster for a showing of a French film. Figures and helmets in khaki colours, blue countryside, violet sky. (HUN)
365 Full-colour poster for the film "Unrestrained Men". (HUN)
366 "Antiques" is the title of the film announced in this poster. Mainly red and brown shades, gold lettering. (POL)

359 Plakat für einen polnischen Film. «Justitia» weiss und grau, Lippen weiss und violett, Hintergrund dunkelblau. (POL)
360 Ankündigung eines sowjetischen Films. In Farbe. (CSR)
361 Plakatwerbung für einen Dokumentarfilm. (GDR)
362 Ankündigung eines französischen Kriminalfilms. Plakat vorwiegend blau und weiss, schwarze Schrift. (GDR)
363 «Blitze über Mexiko» ist der Titel dieses hier angekündigten Films. Mehrfarbiges Plakat. (CSR)
364 Plakat für die Aufführung eines französischen Films. Gestalten und Helm khakifarben, Landschaft blau, Himmel violett. (HUN)
365 Mehrfarbiges Plakat für den Film «Zügellose Männer». (HUN)
366 «Antiquitäten» ist der Titel des hier angekündigten Films. Vorwiegend rote und braune Farbtöne, goldene Schrift. (POL)

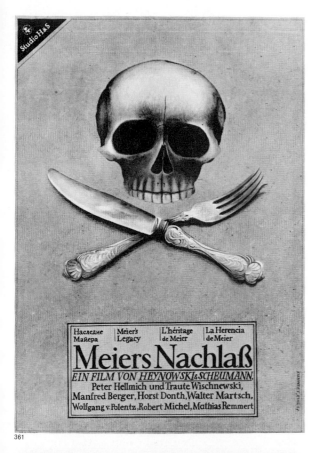

361

365

364

359 Affiche pour un film polonais. «Justice» en blanc et gris, lèvres en blanc et violet, fond en bleu foncé. (POL)
360 Affiche polychrome pour un film sovjétique. (CSR)
361 Affiche annonçant un film documentaire. (GDR)
362 Affiche pour un film policier français. Prédominance de tons bleus et blancs, typographie noire. (GDR)
363 «Eclairs sur le Méxique.» Affiche annonçant un film réalisé par la radio/TV du Nord de l'Allemagne fédérale. En polychromie. (CSR)
364 Affiche pour la présentation d'un film français. Figures et casque kaki, paysage bleu, ciel violet. (HUN)
365 Pour un film intitulé «Des hommes éfrénés». (HUN)
366 Affiche pour un film intitulé «Antiquités». Prédominance de tons rouges et marron, typographie en or. (POL)

366

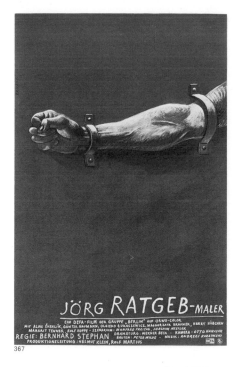

367

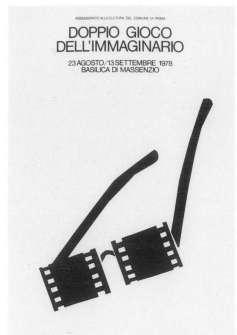

368

369

371

372

373

Films/Filme

367 Film poster in subdued ruby-red with white. (GDR)
368 Poster announcement of a showing with the title "Double play of the Imagination". (ITA)
369 Full-colour poster for a Polish film. (POL)
370 Poster designed for a film festival in Chicago. Black and white, full-colour eye and reel. (USA)
371 Full-colour poster for The Inheritance, a film that won an award at the Cannes Film Festival. (USA)
372 Poster for "K.O.", a Hungarian film. Light grey wall, dark boxing-glove, orange edge to the letters. (HUN)
373 Advertising for the Berlin Film Festival. (GER)
374 Poster advertising special showings of comical graphic design films. The elephant has been designed in blue and the background is in dark pink. (USA)
375 Poster for a typical Andy Warhol film which, apart from the illustration, quotes the excellent review it received in the New York Daily News. (USA)

367 Filmplakat in gedämpftem Bordeauxrot. (GDR)
368 Plakatankündigung einer Vorführung mit dem Titel «Doppeltes Spiel der Imagination». (ITA)
369 Mehrfarbiges Plakat für einen polnischen Film. (POL)
370 Für ein Filmfestival in Chicago gestaltetes Plakat. Schwarzweiss, Auge und Filmstreifen mehrfarbig. (USA)
371 Farbiges Plakat für einen in Cannes ausgezeichneten Film: «Das Vermächtnis». (USA)
372 Plakat für den ungarischen Film «K.O.». Graue Mauer, dunkler Boxhandschuh, Buchstabenrand orange. (HUN)
373 Programm für die Berliner Filmfestspiele. (GER)
374 «Für jene, die eine Spürnase haben» ist die Vorführung von komischen Graphik-Design-Filmen bestimmt. Blauer Elefant, Hintergrund dunkelrosa. (USA)
375 Plakat für einen Film von Andy Warhol. «Ein Film, der für absolut jeden etwas enthält, woran er sich stossen wird» schrieb die Zeitung New York Daily News. (USA)

367 Affiche pour un film. Rouge bordeaux et blanc. (GDR)
368 Affiche annonçant la présentation d'un film intitulé «Le double jeu de l'imagination». (ITA)
369 Affiche polychrome pour un film polonais. (POL)
370 Affiche pour le Festival du film de Chicago. Noir et blanc, œil et pellicules en polychromie. (USA)
371 Affiche pour le film The Inheritance qui a remporté un prix au festival du film de Cannes. Polychromie. (USA)
372 Affiche pour le film hongrois «K.O.». Mur gris, gant de boxe en tons foncés, caractères encadrés d'orange. (HUN)
373 Affiche-programme du Festival du Film de Berlin. (GER)
374 Cette série de films graphiques comiques est destinée à «tous ceux qui ont un bon nez». Eléphant bleu, fond d'un coloris rose foncé. (USA)
375 Affiche pour un film d'Andy Warhol. «C'est un film qui ne manquera pas de choquer chacun d'une façon ou d'une autre» comme le commente le New York Daily News. (USA)

370

374

375

376

377

376 Poster announcing the showing of a film in Sweden with the title "The Long Escape". Mainly in shades of grey and brown. (SWE)
377 Announcement of a film festival for films about mountain expeditions, organized by the Italian Alp Club. Poster in full colour. (ITA)
378 Poster with a programme of French films being shown in Stuttgart. (GER)
379 Full-colour poster for a film comedy. (SWE)
380 Large-format poster for the Swiss film *Les petites fugues* ("The Minor Escapades"). In full colour with a black border. (SWI)
381 Announcement of a film festival dealing with national minority groups. Light brown and black Indian in front of a blue sky. (FRA)
382 Large-format poster for the showing of a film with the title *Port Arthur*. (JPN)
383 Poster for a Polish film. Black and white and blue. (POL)

376 Plakat für die Ankündigung eines Films, der in Schweden unter dem Titel «Die lange Flucht» läuft. Vorwiegend Grau- und Brauntöne. (SWE)
377 Ankündigung eines vom italienischen Alpen-Club veranstalteten Festivals für Filme über Bergexpeditionen. Mehrfarbiges Plakat. (ITA)
378 Programmankündigung für die Aufführung französischer Filme in Stuttgart. (GER)
379 Mehrfarbiges Plakat für die Ankündigung einer Filmkomödie mit Marty Feldmann. (SWE)
380 Grossformatiges Plakat für den Schweizer Film *Les petites fugues* («Die kleinen Eskapaden»). In Farbe, mit schwarzer Umrandung. (SWI)
381 Ankündigung eines Filmfestivals für nationale Minderheiten. Indianer hellbraun und schwarz vor blauem Himmel. (FRA)
382 Grossformatiges Plakat für einen Film mit dem Titel *Port Arthur*. (JPN)
383 Plakat für einen polnischen Film. Schwarzweiss und blau. (POL)

376 Affiche pour un film présenté en Suède sous le titre «La longue fuite». Prédominance de tons gris et bruns. (SWE)
377 Affiche pour un festival de films d'alpinisme organisé par le Club alpin italien. (ITA)
378 Affiche annonçant la présentation d'une série de films français à Stuttgart. Prédominance de tons gris, typo rouge et bleue. (GER)
379 Affiche pour une comédie cinématographique avec Marty Feldmann en vedette. (SWE)
380 Affiche grand format annonçant la présentation du film suisse *Les petites fugues*. Illustration en couleurs, encadrement noir. (SWI)
381 Affiche pour le 2e Festival du cinéma des minorités nationales organisé en France. Indien en brun clair et noir, ciel bleu. (FRA)
382 Affiche grand format annonçant un film intitulé *Port Arthur*. (JPN)
383 Affiche pour la présentation d'un film polonais. Noir et blanc et bleu. (POL)

379

380

ARTIST / KÜNSTLER / ARTISTE:

376, 379 Olle Frankzen
377 Studio Arcoquattro
378 Albrecht Ade
380 Etienne Delessert
381 Alain Le Quernec
382 Tadanori Yokoo
383 Marek Freudenreich

DESIGNER / GESTALTER / MAQUETTISTE:

376, 379 Olle Frankzen
377 Studio Arcoquattro
378 Albrecht Ade
380 Patrick Gaudard
382 Tadanori Yokoo
383 Marek Freudenreich

ART DIRECTOR / DIRECTEUR ARTISTIQUE:

376, 379 Olle Frankzen
378 Albrecht Ade
381 Alain Le Quernec
382 Tadanori Yokoo

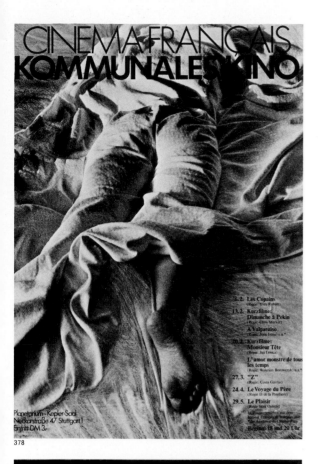

378

381

382

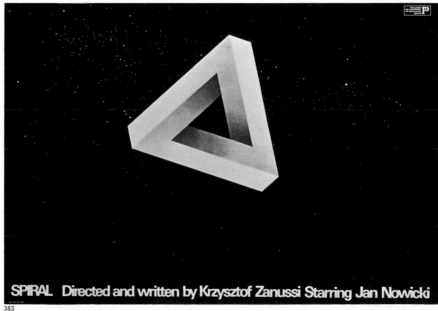

SPIRAL Directed and written by Krzysztof Zanussi Starring Jan Nowicki

383

AGENCY / AGENTUR / AGENCE-STUDIO:

376, 379 Design 2001
377 Studio Arcoquattro
380 Carabosse
381 Kan Ar Mor

384

386

385

389

384 Poster with a list of programmes organized by the cultural administrative authority of Hamburg for free visits to various classical concerts which take place on Sunday mornings. (GER)

385, 386 Two posters for the New York Philharmonic Orchestra referring to programmes on the radio. Fig. 385 blue with a red jug and black-and-white music scores. Fig. 386 with brightly coloured marbles. (USA)

387, 390 Posters for a Jazz Festival in Willisau, Switzerland. Fig. 387: snake and saxophone in green and yellow, magenta tongue; text yellow, white and magenta on a dark blue ground. (SWI)

388 Poster announcing a second evening's entertainment offered by the magazine *People* to the press in Chicago. (USA)

389 Poster for a concert by the Yale Symphony Orchestra. (USA)

391 Large-format poster for the Berlin Jazz festival. Brown shades. (GER)

387

388

390

391

ARTIST / KÜNSTLER / ARTISTE:

384 Angel Medina/Rainer Hansen
385 Arnold Rosenberg
386 Tony Ynocencio
387, 390 Niklaus Troxler
388 Gilbert Lesser
389 Thomas Wedell
391 Volker Hartmann

DESIGNER / GESTALTER / MAQUETTISTE:

385, 486 Ivan Chermayeff
387, 390 Niklaus Troxler
388 Gilbert Lesser
389 Nancy Skolos
391 Günther Kieser

ART DIRECTOR / DIRECTEUR ARTISTIQUE:

385, 386 Ivan Chermayeff
387, 390 Niklaus Troxler
388 Gilbert Lesser
389 Nancy Skolos
391 Günther Kieser

AGENCY / AGENTUR / AGENCE-STUDIO:

385, 386 Chermayeff & Geismar Assoc.
387, 390 Niklaus Troxler
389 Graphic Design Department Yale
 University
391 Günther Kieser

384 Plakat mit dem Veranstaltungsprogramm der Kulturbehörde Hamburg, die hier zum kostenlosen Besuch verschiedener klassischer Konzerte einlädt, die jeweils am Sonntagmorgen stattfinden. (GER)
385, 386 Zwei Plakate der New Yorker Philharmonie. Hier wird auf Philharmonie-Wochen im Radio aufmerksam gemacht. Abb. 385 blau mit rotem Krug und schwarzweissen Notenblättern. Abb. 386 mit bunten Marmeln. (USA)
387, 390 Plakate für das Jazz-Festival in Willisau. Abb. 387: Schlange und Saxophon grün und gelb, Zunge magentafarben; Text gelb, weiss und magenta auf dunkelblauem Grund. (SWI)
388 Einladung der Zeitschrift *People* («Leute») zu einer Pressevorstellung mit dem Titel «Das ist Unterhaltung, Teil 2». (USA)
389 Plakat für ein Konzert des Yale Symphony Orchestra. (USA)
391 Grossformatiges Plakat für die Berliner Jazz-Tage. Brauntöne. (GER)

384 Affiche-programme présentant les différentes manifestations organisées par le département culturel de la ville de Hambourg: on y annonce divers concerts gratuits ayant lieu tous les dimanche matins; (GER)
385, 386 Deux affiches de la Philharmonie de New York. On annonce des semaines philharmoniques à la radio. Fig. 385: pichet rouge sur fond bleu, partitions en noir-blanc; fig. 386: billes de verre en couleurs. (USA)
387, 390 Deux affiches pour le festival annuel de jazz à Willisau. Fig. 387: serpent et instrument vert et jaune, langue magenta, texte jaune, blanc, magenta sur fond bleu foncé. (SWI)
388 Invitation pour une présentation de presse que le magazine *People* a organisée sous le titre «Ça c'est divertissement, 2e partie». (USA)
389 Affiche pour un concert de l'Orchestre symphonique de Yale. (USA)
391 Affiche pour le festival annuel de jazz à Berlin. Tons bruns. (GER)

392

393

397

392 Announcement of radio and television recordings of the 1978 Folk Festival in Cologne. (GER)
393, 399 Announcement of cabaret shows for the West German broadcasting authority. Fig. 393: yellow target, Fig. 399: flesh-coloured figures. (GER)
394 Poster for a musical programme of the West German broadcasting authority. Black and white and yellow. (GER)
395, 396 Two more posters for special West German broadcasting programmes. Both in black and white with one colour. (GER)
397, 398 Programme announcements by the West German broadcasting authority. Fig. 397 black and red, Fig. 398 black and white with an orange number. (GER)

392 Bekanntmachung des von Radio und Fernsehen übertragenen Folk-Festivals 78 in Köln. (GER)
393, 399 Ankündigungen von Kabarett-Sendungen im WDR. Abb. 393: gelbe Zielscheibe, Abb. 399: fleischfarbene Figuren. (GER)
394 Plakat für ein musikalisches Programm im WDR mit Friedrich Gulda und anderen. Schwarzweiss, «Gulda» in Gelb. (GER)
395, 396 Zwei weitere Beispiele von Plakaten für spezielle Programme im WDR. Beide schwarzweiss mit einer Farbe. (GER)
397, 398 Programmankündigungen des WDR. Abb. 397 schwarz und rot, Abb. 398 schwarzweiss mit orangefarbener Zahl. (GER)

392 Affiche annonçant un festival de folk à Cologne destiné à être radiodiffusé et télévisé. (GER)
393, 399 Pour deux programmes de cabaret de la radio/TV WDR. Fig. 393: cible jaune; fig. 399: personnages roses. (GER)
394 «Gulda fait ce qu'il veut.» D'une série de programmes musicaux de la radio/TV WDR. Noir et blanc, nom en jaune. (GER)
395, 396 Pour une série de «musique nocturne» (noir sur mauve) et une émission radio «musique et sport» (noir sur vert). (GER)
397, 398 Pour un oratorio et une chanteuse italienne et un concert du 25e anniversaire d'un orchestre de la radio. (GER)

ARTIST / KÜNSTLER / ARTISTE:
392–399 Heinz Edelmann

DESIGNER / GESTALTER / MAQUETTISTE:
392–399 Heinz Edelmann

394

395

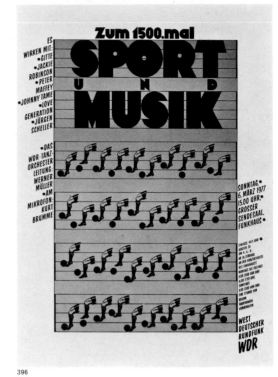

396

398

399

Cultural Events
Veranstaltungen
Evénements culturels

400

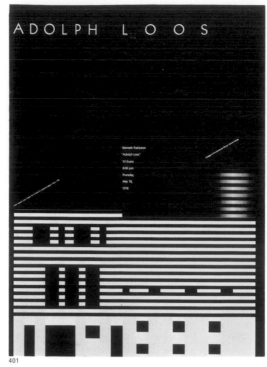

401

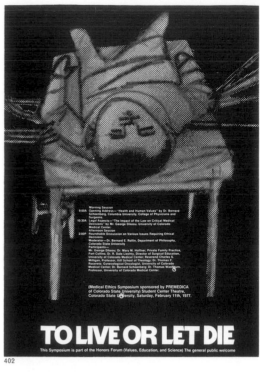

402

404

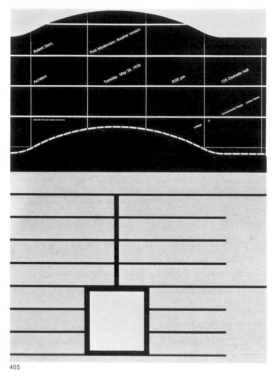

405

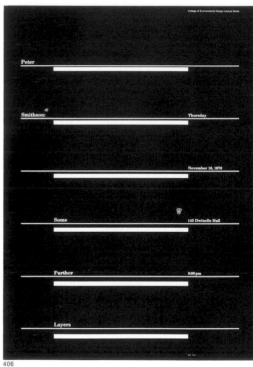

406

Cultural Events
Veranstaltungen
Evénements culturels

400, 401 Posters announcing a series of lectures. Fig. 400 with a stuck-on label ("accepted"). The reference here is to the preservation of historic buildings. Fig. 401: draft of an architectural plan in 1928 for a house for Josephine Baker, in Paris. (USA)
402 Announcement of a symposium dealing with the problems and questions of euthanasia. Black and white. (USA)
403 Announcement of a congress dealing with infectious diseases. Black and white. (USA)
404–406 Examples (see Figs. 400, 401) from a series of posters for lectures about environmental matters. Fig. 404 black and white, Fig. 405 brown and beige, Fig. 406 violet and white. (USA)
407 Poster for an exhibition by Francesco di Giorgio Martini and a subsequent discussion. (ITA)
408 Announcement of an open-air folk festival. (USA)
409 Poster announcing a speech by Richard Schweiker, Senator for Pennsylvania. One colour on tinted paper. (USA)

400, 401 Plakate für die Ankündigung von Vorlesungen. Abb. 400 mit aufgeklebter Etikette («angenommen»). Hier geht es um die Erhaltung historischer Bauten. Abb. 401 zeigt einen Entwurf von 1928 für ein Haus für Josephine Baker in Paris. (USA)
402 Bekanntmachung eines Symposiums, das sich mit der Frage der Sterbehilfe befasst. Schwarzweiss. (USA)
403 Ankündigung eines Kongresses, bei dem es um Infektions-krankheiten geht. Schwarzweiss mit rotem Balken. (ITA)
404–406 Beispiele (siehe Abb. 400, 401) aus einer Serie von Plakaten für Vorlesungen über Umweltgestaltung. Abb. 404 schwarz-weiss, Abb. 405 braun und beige, Abb. 406 violett und weiss. (USA)
407 Plakat für eine Ausstellung von Francesco di Giorgio· Martini und ein Gespräch am runden Tisch. (ITA)
408 Ankündigung eines Folk-Festivals im Freien. (USA)
409 Plakatankündigung einer Rede des Senators von Pennsylva-nien, Richard Schweiker. Einfarbig auf farbigem Papier. (USA)

400, 401 Affiches annonçant divers cours. Fig. 400: ce cours traite de la conservation de bâtiments historiques; étiquette («accepté») collée sur l'affiche. Fig. 401: projet, datant de 1928, pour une maison de Josephine Baker à Paris. (USA)
402 Annonce d'un symposium discutant le problème de l'euthana-sie. En noir et blanc. (USA)
403 Affiche annonçant un congrès sur les maladies infectieuses. Noir et blanc. (USA)
404–406 Exemples d'une série d'affiches annonçant des cours sur la conception de l'environnement (v. aussi figs. 400, 401). Fig. 404 noir-blanc, fig. 405: brun, beige, fig. 406: violet, blanc. (USA)
407 Affiche pour une exposition de l'œuvre de Francesco di Giorgio Martini et une discussion à la table ronde. (ITA)
408 Affiche pour un festival folk de pleine air. (USA)
409 Affiche annonçant un discours de Richard Schweiker, sénateur de la Pennsylvanie. Sur papier coloré. (USA)

OPERATORI
SANITARI
E LOTTA ALLE
MALATTIE
INFETTIVE

CONVEGNO
ORGANIZZATO
DAL PRI
ROMA 18 DICEMBRE
HOTEL
PARCO DEI PRINCIPI
INTERVENGONO
BIAGIO PINTO
MICHELE LA PLACA
FRANCO MINGRINO
GERMANO RICCI

403

La Rampa
di Francesco
Di Giorgio
Martini

Comune di Urbino
Università degli Studi

4 giugno 1977 ore 12
inaugurazione della Rampa e della mostra
di opere di Francesco di Giorgio Martini

4 giugno 1977 ore 16
tavola rotonda con
la partecipazione di
Giulio Carlo Argan
Cesare Brandi
Corrado Maltese
Henry Millon
Pasquale Rotondi
Pietro Zampetti

Saranno presenti
il Comune e
l'Università di Siena
le regioni Marche e Toscana

407

The Second Annual Lehigh Green Grass Folk Festival, sponsored by the Lehigh Student Activities Committee and Sing Out Magazine. Featuring Rosalie Sorrels; the Bottle Hill Boys; Paul Geremia; Martin, Bogen, and Armstrong; Grant Rogers; Alice Gerrard; Honey Boy Edwards. Grace Hall, Lehigh University, Friday and Saturday, April 13 and 14, at 8 p.m. Tickets, $2.50 for each performance, or $4.00 for both, available in Bethlehem at Lehigh Student Activities Desk, Lehigh University Bookstore, and the Renaissance; in Allentown at Upper Story and Music Scene; in Easton at Not Just Another Pretty Face. Free workshops Saturday morning and afternoon in front of the University Center.

408

ARTIST / KÜNSTLER / ARTISTE:

400, 401, 404–406 Marc Treib
402 John J. Sorbie
407 Giancarlo Iliprandi
408, 409 Marvin Simmons

DESIGNER / GESTALTER / MAQUETTISTE:

400, 401, 404–406 Marc Treib
402 John J. Sorbie
403 Michele Spera
407 Giancarlo Iliprandi
408, 409 Marvin Simmons

ART DIRECTOR / DIRECTEUR ARTISTIQUE:

400, 401, 404–406 Marc Treib
402 John J. Sorbie
403 Michele Spera
407 Giancarlo Iliprandi
408, 409 Marvin Simmons

AGENCY / AGENTUR / AGENCE-STUDIO:

400, 401, 404–406 Marc Treib
402 CSU Art Dept.
407 Giancarlo Iliprandi
408, 409 Lehigh University, Office of Publications

409

410

411

412

ARTIST / KÜNSTLER / ARTISTE:

410 Hannes & Barbara Geissler
411 Walt Seng
412 Richard Eckersley
413 Richard Bernstein
414 Lanny Sommese
415 Milton Glaser
416 Karel Mísek
417 R.A. Cooney
418 Susan Slover

DESIGNER / GESTALTER / MAQUETTISTE:

410 Hannes & Barbara Geissler
411 Eddie Byrd
412 Richard Eckersley
413 Richard Seireeni
414 Lanny Sommese
415 Milton Glaser
416 Karel Mísek
417 Robert Cooney
418 Susan Slover

ART DIRECTOR / DIRECTEUR ARTISTIQUE:

410 W. Sien
411 Eddie Byrd
412 Richard Eckersley
413 Richard Seireeni
414 Lanny Sommese
415 Milton Glaser
417 R.A. Cooney
418 Robert E. Cargill

AGENCY / AGENTUR / AGENCE-STUDIO:

410 Geissler Design
411 Byrd Graphic Design, Inc.
412 Kilkenny Design Workshop
413 Warner Bros Records
414 Lanny Sommese Design
415 Milton Glaser, Inc.
417 R.A. Cooney Inc.
418 Cargill & Assoc. Inc.

Cultural Events
Veranstaltungen
Evénements culturels

413

416

414

415

410 Poster for a concert organized by the cultural department of the *Bayer* company. In full colour. (GER)
411 Full-colour poster for a Thanksgiving concert. (USA)
412 Poster announcing cultural events in Kilkenny. (USA)
413 Poster for a performance by the singer Grace Jones. Blue, pink and violet, white lettering. (USA)
414 Invitation to a fancy-dress ball. Black on orange-coloured paper, green lettering. (USA)
415 Poster announcing events in the Catskills, an area where many New Yorkers spend their leisure time. (USA)
416 Poster for an agricultural exhibition: "Bohemia's Garden." Bright colours on a white apple. (CSR)
417 Invitation to a fashion show in the Beverly Hilton Hotel, where French designers displayed their creations. (USA)
418 This poster, which actually has a piece of real rope attached to it, advertises *Coca-Cola's* participation in a movie. (USA)

410 Plakat für ein Konzert, das von der Kulturabteilung der Firma *Bayer* veranstaltet wurde. In Farbe. (GER)
411 Mehrfarbiges Plakat für ein «Erntedank»-Konzert. (USA)
412 Programmankündigung einer Kultur-Woche in Kilkenny. (USA)
413 Plakat für einen Auftritt der Sängerin Grace Jones. Blau, Rosa und Violett, mit weisser Schrift. (USA)
414 Einladung zu einem Kostümfest. Schwarz auf orangefarbigem Papier, grüne Schrift. (USA)
415 Plakat für Veranstaltungen in dem Gebiet der Catskills, einem beliebten Ausflugsziel der New Yorker. (USA)
416 Plakat für eine Landwirtschaftsausstellung: «Der Garten Böhmens.» Leuchtende Farben auf weissem Apfel. (CSR)
417 «Französische Mode kommt nach Californien.» Einladung zu einer Modeschau im Beverly Hilton Hotel. (USA)
418 Thema dieses Plakates (mit echtem Tau) ist die Beteiligung von *Coca Cola* an dem Film «Der weisse Hai». (USA)

410 Affiche pour un concert organisé par le département culturel de *Bayer*. En polychromie. (GER)
411 Pour un concert à l'occasion de la fête d'action de grâces pour la récolte. En polychromie. (USA)
412 Programme pour une semaine culturelle à Kilkenny. (USA)
413 Pour un concert de la cantatrice Grace Jones. (USA)
414 Invitation pour un bal costumé. Noir sur papier orange, typographie en vert. (USA)
415 Affiche pour une manifestation ayant lieu dans la région de Catskills, contrée d'excursion des Newyorkais. (USA)
416 Affiche pour une exposition agricole: «Le jardin de la Bohême.» Couleurs vives sur une pomme blanche. (CSR)
417 «La mode française arrive en Californie.» Invitation pour une présentation des modes à l'hôtel Beverly Hilton. (USA)
418 Cette affiche se réfère à la participation de *Coca Cola* à la réalisation du film «Le requin blanc». Vraie corde. (USA)

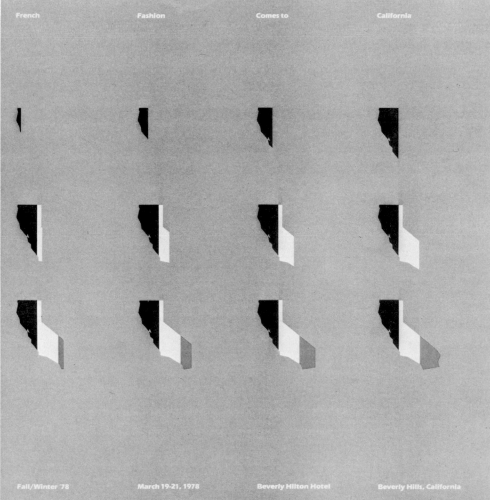

417

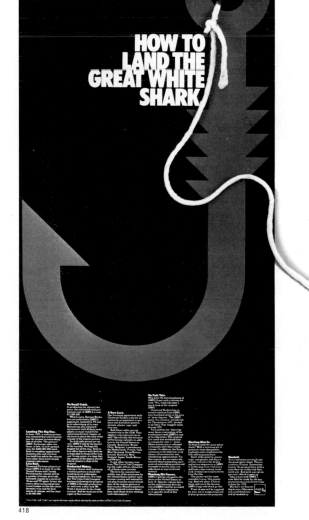

418

419

421

420

422

419, 420 Two examples from a series of circus posters. (POL)
421, 422 Full-colour posters for the *Krone* circus. (GER)
423 Announcement of an exhibition by a Berlin children's publisher. Brown elephant in blue shirt and trousers, bright red background. (GDR)
424 Poster advertising an exhibition. (JPN)
425 Invitation to a disco-dance event. Figures in black, green and red with yellow in front of a blue background. Yellow lettering. (USA)
426 Announcement of a children's and folk festival held at the geographical centre of West Germany. In full colour. (GER)

423

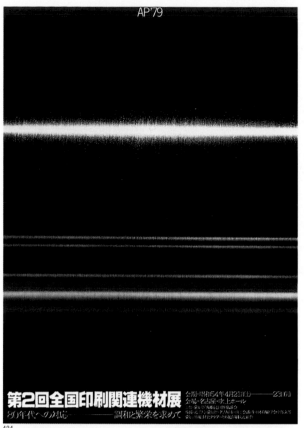

424

425

426

ARTIST / KÜNSTLER / ARTISTE:

419, 420 Hubert Hilscher
421, 422 Dietrich Ebert
423 Manfred Bofinger
424 Toshiyuki Ohashi
425 Marc Gobé
426 Heinz Bähr

DESIGNER / GESTALTER / MAQUETTISTE:

421, 422 Dietrich Ebert
423 Manfred Bofinger
424 Shigeo Okamoto
425 Marc Gobé
426 Heinz Bähr

ART DIRECTOR / DIRECTEUR ARTISTIQUE:

421, 422 Albrecht Ade
424 Shigeo Okamoto
425 Marc Gobé
426 Heinz Bähr

AGENCY / AGENTUR / AGENCE-STUDIO:

424 Shigeo Okamoto Design Center
425 Marc Gobé & Assoc.

419, 420 Zwei Beispiele aus einer Serie von Zirkusplakaten. (POL)
421, 422 Mehrfarbige Plakate für Zirkus Krone. (GER)
423 Ankündigung einer Ausstellung des Kinderbuchverlags Berlin. Brauner Elefant in blauem Hemd und Hose, Hintergrund hellrot. (GDR)
424 Plakat für die Ankündigung einer Ausstellung. (JPN)
425 Einladung zu einer Disco-Tanzveranstaltung. Figuren schwarz, grün und rot mit Gelb vor blauem Hintergrund. Gelbe Schrift. (USA)
426 Bekanntmachung eines Kinder- und Volksfestes am geographischen Mittelpunkt der Bundesrepublik Deutschland. In Farbe. (GER)

419, 420 Affiches d'une longue série pour le cirque national polonais. (POL)
421, 422 Deux affiches polychromes pour le cirque Krone. (GER)
423 Affiche annonçant une exposition organisée par une maison d'édition de livres d'enfant à Berlin. Eléphant brun, chemise et pantalons bleus. (GDR)
424 Affiche pour une exposition. (JPN)
425 Invitation pour une soirée dansante. Figures en noir, vert et rouge avec jaune, fond bleu. Typographie jaune. (USA)
426 Affiche annonçant une fête populaire particulièrement pour enfants au centre géographique de l'Allemagne fédérale. En polychromie. (GER)

Cultural Events

Veranstaltungen

Evénements culturels

141

JAPAN in ASPEN

A SYNTHESIS OF CONTRADICTIONS

THE INTERNATIONAL
DESIGN CONFERENCE IN ASPEN
JUNE 17-22, 1979

427

428

429

Cultural Events
Veranstaltungen
Evénements culturels

427 Poster for the Japanese contribution and participation in a design exhibition in Aspen, Colorado. (USA)
428 Poster for an exhibition in a museum of natural history. The subject is *Kendo*, a Japanese form of fencing (with wooden poles). Originally, the Samurai art of fencing was known by this name. Black and white. (JPN)
429 Announcement of a competition for young people within the framework of certain sciences. White egg on a blue background. (GER)
430 Announcement of an architectural exhibition. (JPN)
431 Poster for a ski week organized by ski instructors. (JPN)
432 Full-colour poster for a congress of a consumer cooperative. (ITA)
433 Full-colour poster for a foodstuffs exhibition. (JPN)

ARTIST / KÜNSTLER / ARTISTE:

427 Heather Cooper
428 Tony Mandarino
429 Holger Matthies
430, 433 Kou Chifusa
432 Gino Cammarota

DESIGNER / GESTALTER / MAQUETTISTE:

427 Lou Dorfsman
428 Tony Mandarino
429 Holger Matthies
430, 433 Yumiko Nishimura
431 Yusaku Kamekura
432 Giulio Cesare Italiani

ART DIRECTOR / DIRECTEUR ARTISTIQUE:

427 Lou Dorfsman
428 Tony Mandarino
429 Holger Matthies
430, 433 Satoru Miyata
431 Yusaku Kamekura
432 Giulio Cesare Italiani

AGENCY / AGENTUR / AGENCE-STUDIO:

427 Lou Dorfsman
430, 433 Miyata Design Office
432 Idea Comunicazione

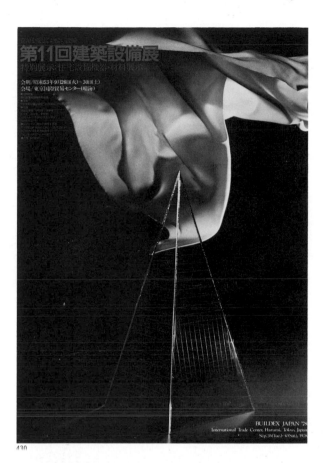

430

431

432

433

R.O. Blechman on film.

434

436

434 Invitation to a speech and film featuring the designer R.O. Blechman. (USA)
435 Announcement of an exhibition by the designer and painter Zélio Alves Pinto. (BRA)
436 Full-colour poster for an international humour and comics exhibition in São Paulo. (BRA)
437, 438 Detail of the illustration and complete poster for a caricature exhibition. (GER)
439 Poster for a slide presentation of graphic design work. Violet and light blue. (USA)
440 Announcement of an exhibition of art at Pennsylvania State University. (USA)

434 Einladung zu einer Ansprache und Vorführung von Filmen des Zeichners R.O. Blechman anlässlich einer Konferenz des Art-Directors/Werbetexter-Clubs von Manhattan. (USA)
435 Bekanntmachung einer Ausstellung des Zeichners und Malers Zélio Alves Pinto. (BRA)
436 Farbiges Plakat für eine internationale Humor- und Comics-Ausstellung in Sao Paulo. (BRA)
437, 438 Detail der Illustration und komplettes Plakat für eine Karikatur-Ausstellung. (GER)
439 Plakat für eine Dia-Vorführung von Graphik-Design-Arbeiten. Violett und Hellblau. (USA)
440 Ankündigung einer Kunstausstellung in der Pennsylvania State University. (USA)

434 Invitation pour un discours et la présentation de films realisés par R.O. Blechman, à l'occasion d'une conférence du club des directeurs artistiques et texters du Manhattan. (USA)
435 Affiche annonçant une exposition de l'œuvre de Zélio Alves Pinto. (BRA)
436 Affiche pour une exposition internationale de dessins animés et de dessins humoristiques. (BRA)
437, 438 Détail de l'illustration et affiche complète pour une exposition de caricatures. (GER)
439 Affiche pour une conférence avec projection de travaux graphiques. Violet et bleu clair. (USA)
440 Affiche pour une exposition d'art à la Pennsylvania State University. (USA)

437

438

439

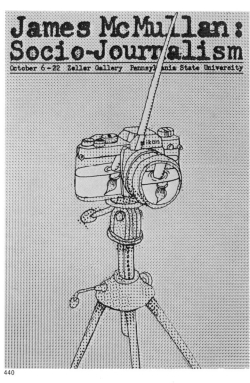

440

AGENCY / AGENTUR

434 Laughing Graphics
439, 440 Lanny Sommese Design

Exhibitions
Ausstellungen
Expositions

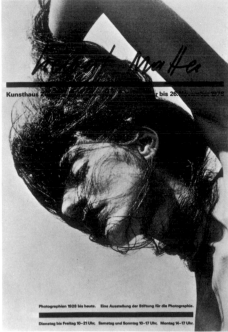

441

Exhibitions
Ausstellungen
Expositions

ARTIST / KÜNSTLER / ARTISTE:

441 Herbert Matter
442 Wettstein & Kauf
443 Balz Baechi
444 Shizuko Müller-Yoshikawa
446 Sigfried Kuhn
447 Paul Brühwiler
448 Vojislav Jakić

DESIGNER / GESTALTER / MAQUETTISTE:

441 Herbert Matter
442, 447 Paul Brühwiler
443 Balz Baechi
445 Paul Leber
446 Herbert Distel
448 Werner Jeker
449 Roger & Elisabeth Pfund

ART DIRECTOR / DIRECTEUR ARTISTIQUE:

441 Herbert Matter
442, 447 Paul Brühwiler
443 Balz Baechi
446 Herbert Distel
448 Werner Jeker
449 Roger Pfund

AGENCY / AGENTUR / AGENCE-STUDIO:

442, 447 Paul Brühwiler
443 Balz Baechi
444 Müller-Brockmann & Co.
446 Herbert Distel
448 Werner Jeker

444

442

443

441 Poster for an exhibition in the Zurich Kunsthaus entitled "1928 until today", with photographs by Herbert Matter. (SWI)
442 Poster for an exhibition in Zurich's Rietberg Museum: Indian playing cards. (SWI)
443 Poster for an exhibition shown simultaneously at a number of venues. (SWI)
444, 445 Two full-colour posters for exhibitions at the Museum of Applied Arts, Zurich. Fig. 444: Japanese posters today. (SWI)
446, 447 Posters for the Zurich Kunsthaus for shows of minute works of art and examples of American culture from 1920 to 1940. (SWI)
448, 449 Posters for exhibitions dealing with *art brut*. Fig. 448 for a collection in Lausanne, Fig. 449 for Adolf Wölfli in Berne. (SWI)

441 Plakat für eine im Kunsthaus Zürich veranstaltete Ausstellung mit Photographien von Herbert Matter, «1928 bis heute». (SWI)
442 Farbiges Plakat für eine Ausstellung im Rietbergmuseum Zürich. (SWI)
443 Plakat für eine an mehreren Orten gleichzeitig gezeigte Kunstausstellung. (SWI)
444, 445 Ausstellungsplakate des Zürcher Kunstgewerbemuseums. Beide farbig. (SWI)
446, 447 Plakate des Kunsthauses Zürich. Hier für das Schubladenmuseum mit Kunstwerken im Kleinstformat und Beispiele amerikanischer Kultur 1920–1940. (SWI)
448, 449 Plakate für Ausstellungen von *art brut*. Hier für die Sammlung in Lausanne und Adolf Wölfli in Bern. (SWI)

441 Affiche pour une exposition des photos d'art de Herbert Matter, 1928–1978, au Musée des Beaux-Arts de Zurich. Gris, noir. (SWI)
442 Pour une exposition de cartes à jouer indiennes à Zurich. En couleurs. (SWI)
443 Pour une exposition bipartite à Zurich d'œuvres d'art basées sur celles du Kunsthaus. Rose, rouge, turquoise, noir. (SWI)
444, 445 Pour des expositions présentées au Musée des Arts Décoratifs de Zurich. (SWI)
446, 447 Deux expositions au Musée des Beaux-Arts de Zurich: «musée à tiroirs» présentant des œuvres d'art en miniature et la culture américaine de 1920–1940. (SWI)
448, 449 Expositions d'Art Brut: collection de Lausanne et d'Adolf Wölfli de Berne. (SWI)

446

RUNNING FENCE - DER LAUFENDE ZAUN IN KALIFORNIEN 1972-76

CHRISTO CHRISTO CHRISTO KUNSTGEWERBEMUSEUM ZUERICH AUSSTELLUNGSSTR. 60 3. JUNI BIS 6. AUGUST 1978 OEFFNUNGSZEITEN DI - FR 10-18 UHR MI 10-21 UHR SA SO 10-12 UHR 14-17 UHR MO GESCHL.

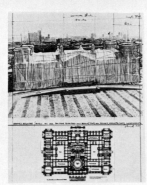

CHRISTO VERPACKTER REICHSTAG PROJEKT FUER BERLIN 1972-

445

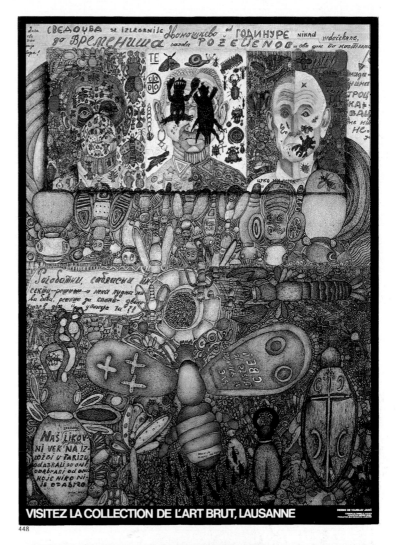

VISITEZ LA COLLECTION DE L'ART BRUT, LAUSANNE

448

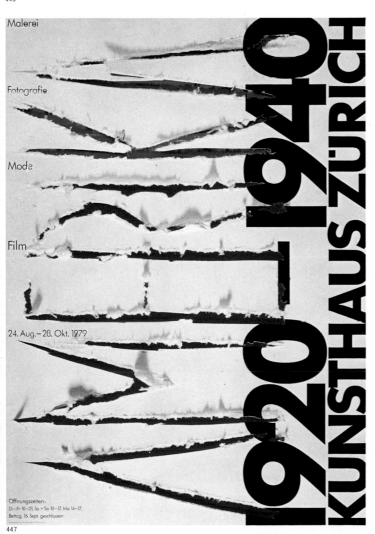

Malerei

Fotografie

Mode

Film

24. Aug. - 28. Okt. 1979

1920-1940 KUNSTHAUS ZÜRICH

447

449

ARTIST / KÜNSTLER / ARTISTE:

450 Kyösti Varis
451, 453 Werner Jeker
452 Roman Cieslewicz
454 Grapus
455 Waldemar Swierzy

DESIGNER / GESTALTER / MAQUETTISTE:

450 Kyösti Varis
451, 453 Werner Jeker
452 Roman Cieslewicz
454 Grapus

450

451

453

ART DIRECTOR / DIRECTEUR ARTISTIQUE:

451, 453 Werner Jeker
452 Georges Ghelbrandt

AGENCY / AGENTUR / AGENCE-STUDIO:

451, 453 Werner Jeker
454 Grapus
455 KAW

450 Announcement of a poster biennale staged in Lahti. (FIN)
451 Poster for the 9th Biennale of tapestry-work at the art museum in Lausanne. (SWI)
452 Poster for an exhibition of work by the artist Roman Cieslewicz. (FRA)
453 Announcement of an exhibition of new Japanese photography in the Museum of Applied Arts, Lausanne. Black-and-white poster. (SWI)
454 Poster announcing an exhibition by the *Grapus* agency. Greetings from Lenin. (FRA)
455 Announcement of an exhibition of award-winning work on the occasion of the VI. International Poster Biennale in Warsaw. (POL)

450 Ankündigung einer im finnischen Ort Lahti veranstalteten Plakat-Biennale. (FIN)
451 Plakat für die 9. Internationale Biennale der Tapisserie im Kunstmuseum Lausanne. (SWI)
452 Plakat für eine Ausstellung der Arbeiten von Roman Cieslewicz. (FRA)
453 Ankündigung einer Ausstellung neuer japanischer Photographie im Kunstgewerbemuseum Lausanne. Plakat in Schwarzweiss. (SWI)
454 Bekanntmachung einer Plakatausstellung der Agentur *Grapus*. Hier grüsst Lenin. (FRA)
455 Ankündigung einer Ausstellung der anlässlich der VI. Internationalen Plakat-Biennale in Warschau ausgezeichneten Arbeiten. (POL)

450 Pour la Biennale Internationale de l'Affiche à Lahti. (FIN)
451 Affiche annonçant la 9e Biennale Internationale de la Tapisserie au Musée des Beaux-Arts de Lausanne. En noir et blanc. (SWI)
452 Affiche pour une exposition présentant les travaux de Roman Cieslewicz. (FRA)
453 Affiche pour une exposition de la nouvelle photographie japonaise présentée au Musée des Arts Décoratifs de Lausanne. En noir et blanc. (SWI)
454 Pour une exposition d'affiches de l'agence *Grapus* à Quimper, ici avec un portrait de Lenin. (FRA)
455 Affiche annonçant une exposition des travaux-lauréats de la 6e Biennale Internationale de l'Affiche à Varsovie. (POL)

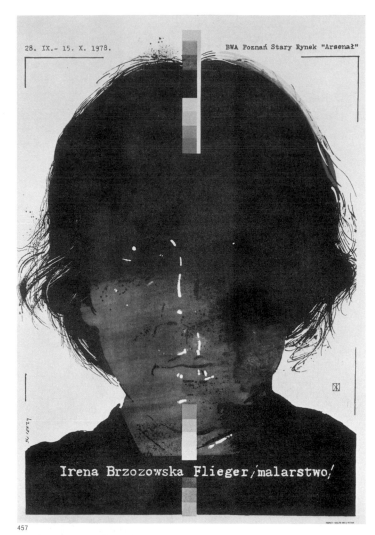

28. IX.– 15. X. 1978. BWA Poznań Stary Rynek "Arsenał"

Irena Brzozowska Flieger /malarstwo/

457

F v B. STAROWIEYSKI

459

BRUSSELS INTERNATIONAL TRADE MART

458

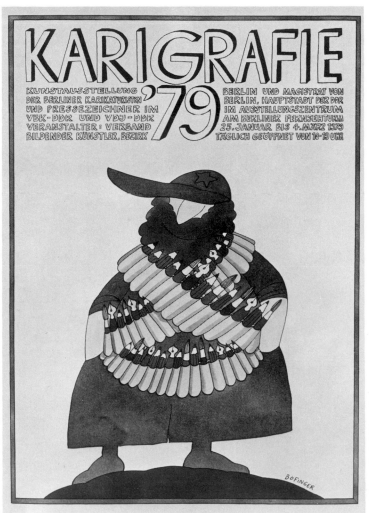

460

457 Poster for an exhibition of art. The colours are black, red and yellow. (POL)
458 Announcement of an exhibition by Serbian artists in Brussels on the occasion of an international trade fair held there. (YUG)
459 For an exhibition of Polish posters. (POL)
460 Poster for an exhibition of Berlin caricaturists and newspaper cartoonists. (GDR)
461 Poster in shades of blue for an exhibition at the Nantes Museum of Applied Arts. (FRA)

457 Plakat für eine Kunstausstellung. Die Farben sind Schwarz, Rot und Gelb. (POL)
458 Ankündigung einer Ausstellung serbischer Künstler in Brüssel anlässlich einer internationalen Messe. (YUG)
459 Ankündigung einer Ausstellung polnischer Plakatkunst. (POL)
460 Plakat für eine Ausstellung von Berliner Karikaturisten und Pressezeichnern. (GDR)
461 Plakat in Blautönen für eine Ausstellung im Kunstgewerbemuseum von Nantes. (FRA)

457 Affiche pour une exposition d'œuvres d'art. En noir, rouge et jaune. (POL)
458 Affiche annonçant une exposition d'artistes serbes à Bruxelles, organisée à l'occasion d'une foire internationale. (YUG)
459 Exposition d'affiches polonaises. (POL)
460 Affiche pour une exposition à Berlin-Est présentant des œuvres de caricaturistes et illustrateurs de presse. (GDR)
461 Pour l'exposition d'un artiste polonais au Musée des Arts Décoratifs de Nantes. (FRA)

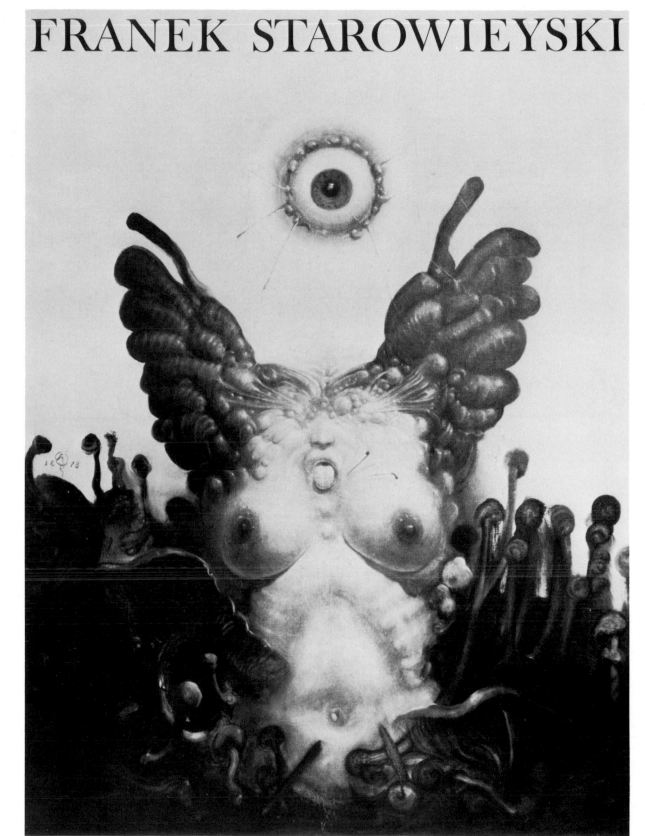

461

Exhibitions

Ausstellungen

Expositions

462

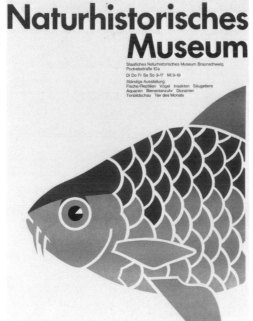

463

ARTIST / KÜNSTLER / ARTISTE:

462, 464 T.A. Lewandowski
466 Holger Matthies
468 Heinz Edelmann
469 Walt Disney
470 David Allen

DESIGNER / GESTALTER / MAQUETTISTE:

462, 464 T.A. Lewandowski
463, 465 Angelika Otte
466 Holger Matthies
467 Jacqueline S. Casey
468 Heinz Edelmann
469 Barbara Balch
470 Jim Donoahue

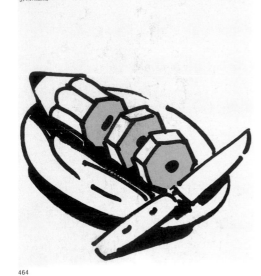

464

465

462, 464 Posters for exhibitions of design and posters by T.A. Lewandowski. Both black and white with one colour. (FRA)
463, 465 Posters for a museum of natural history, with the special attraction of "animal of the month". (GER)
466 Announcement of an exhibition dealing with history and heritage in Hamburg and northern Germany. (GER)
467 Announcement of a Richard Smith exhibition. (USA)
468 Poster for an exhibition in Düsseldorf in 1978 of posters designed by Heinz Edelmann for the West German broadcasting authority. Full colour on grey and white. (GER)
469 Poster for a Mickey Mouse 50th birthday exhibition at the Museum of Modern Art, New York. Mickey Mouse in black and white with red trousers on a yellow background. (Copyright: Walt Disney Productions). (USA)
470 Exhibition in Toronto. Colour photo, white lettering. (CAN)

462, 464 Plakate für Ausstellungen von Zeichnungen und Plakaten von T.A. Lewandowski. Beide schwarzweiss mit einer Farbe. (FRA)
463, 465 Plakate des Naturhistorischen Museums, Braunschweig, mit Informationen über «Das Tier des Monats». (GER)
466 Ankündigung einer Ausstellung über den Historismus in Hamburg und Norddeutschland. (GER)
467 Ankündigung einer Ausstellung von Bildern, Zeichnungen und Graphiken des Künstlers Richard Smith. (GER)
468 Plakat für eine 1978 in Düsseldorf gezeigte Ausstellung der von Heinz Edelmann für den Westdeutschen Rundfunk gestalteten Plakate. Farbig auf Grau und Weiss. (GER)
469 Plakat für eine Ausstellung im Museum of Modern Art, New York, anlässlich des 50. Geburtstages von Mickey Mouse. Mickey schwarzweiss mit roter Hose vor gelbem Hintergrund. (USA)
470 Wood («Holz») ist das Thema der hier angekündigten Ausstellung in Toronto. Farbaufnahme, Schrift weiss. (CAN)

462, 464 Pour des expositions de dessins et d'affiches de T.A. Lewandowski. Les deux sont en noir-blanc avec une couleur. (FRA)
463, 465 Affiches du Musée d'Histoire Naturelle de Braunschweig avec des informations concernant «l'animal du mois». (GER)
466 Affiche pour une exposition sur la période de l'Historisme à Hambourg et en Allemagne du Nord. (GER)
467 Affiche annonçant une exposition de peintures, dessins et travaux graphiques de Richard Smith. (USA)
468 Affiche pour une exposition présentant des affiches réalisées par Heinz Edelmann pour la Radio-Télévision de l'Ouest de l'Allemagne fédérale. Encarts couleurs sur fond gris et blanc. (GER)
469 Pour une exposition du Museum of Modern Art de New York, présentée à l'occasion du 50e anniversaire de Mickey Mouse. Mickey en noir et blanc avec des pantalons rouges, fond jaune. (USA)
470 Le bois c'est le sujet principal de cette exposition à Toronto. Photo couleurs, typographie blanche. (CAN)

466

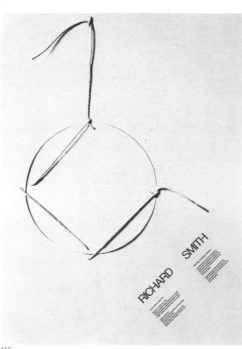

467

468

469

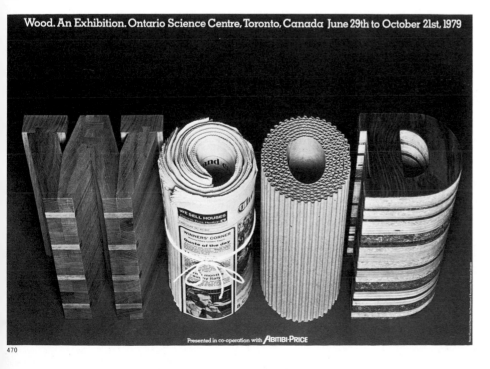

470

ART DIRECTOR / DIRECTEUR ARTISTIQUE:

462, 464 T.A. Lewandowski
463, 465 Klaus Grözinger
466 Holger Matthies
469 Patrick Cunningham
470 Jim Donoahue

AGENCY / AGENTUR / AGENCE-STUDIO:

463, 465 Hochschule für bildende Künste
          Braunschweig
467 MIT Design Services
470 Jim Donoahue & Ass. Ltd.

AVEDON: PHOTOGRAPHS 1947-1977 AN EXHIBITION MADE POSSIBLE BY A GRANT FROM THE SAMUEL I. NEWHOUSE FOUNDATION SEPTEMBER 13-NOVEMBER 5, 1978 THE METROPOLITAN MUSEUM OF ART

471

471 Poster for an exhibition of Richard Avedon's photographs from 1947 to 1977. (USA)
472 "Town planning in the Soviet Union from 1917 until 1978." Exhibition at the Centre Georges Pompidou in Paris. Photomontage in black and white, details on a red ground. (FRA)
473 Poster for an exhibition of photographs by three artists using a new *Polaroid* camera. In full colour, lettering white on black. (USA)
474 Poster for a mobile exhibition dealing with America's architectural heritage. The photograph is a black-and-white print. (USA)
475 Full-colour poster for an exhibition in a newly opened wing of the Metropolitan Museum of Art, New York. Shown here is the Temple of Dendur, one of the best preserved temples in Egypt. (USA)

471 Plakat für eine Ausstellung von Richard Avedons Photographien von 1947 bis 1977. (USA)
472 «Städteplanung in der UdSSR von 1917 bis 1978» ist das Thema der hier angekündigten Ausstellung im Pariser Centre Georges Pompidou. Photomontage schwarzweiss, Angaben auf rotem Grund. (FRA)
473 «Gesichter im Brennpunkt.» Ankündigung einer Ausstellung von Photographien, die von drei Künstlern mit einer neuen *Polaroid*-Kamera aufgenommen wurden. Farbig, Schrift weiss auf Schwarz. (USA)
474 Plakat für eine Wanderausstellung, deren Thema Amerikas architektonisches Erbe ist. Schwarzweiss-Aufnahme. (USA)
475 Farbiges Plakat für eine Ausstellung in einem neueröffneten Flügel des Metropolitan Museum. Thema ist der Tempel von Dendera, der besterhaltenen Tempel Ägyptens. (USA)

471 Affiche pour une exposition des photos de Richard Avedon de 1947 à 1977. (USA)
472 Affiche annonçant une exposition au Centre Georges Pompidou à Paris sur l'urbanisme en URSS. Photomontage en noir-blanc. (FRA)
473 «Visant les visages.» Affiche annonçant une exposition de photos prises par trois artistes avec un nouvel appareil *Polaroid*. En polychromie, typographie blanche sur fond noir. (USA)
474 Affiche pour une exposition itinérante sur l'architecture américaine comme patrimoine national. Photo en noir et blanc. (USA)
475 Pour une exposition présentée dans une aile nouvelle du Metropolitan Museum of Art. Elle est consacrée au temple de Dendérah, l'un des temples les mieux conservés de l'Egypte. (USA)

Exhibitions
Ausstellungen
Expositions

ARTIST / KÜNSTLER / ARTISTE:

471 Richard Avedon
472 Alexandre Rodtchenko
474 G. E. Kidder Smith
475 Malcolm Varon

DESIGNER / GESTALTER / MAQUETTISTE:

471 Elizabeth Paul
472 Roman Cieslewicz
473 Jacqueline S. Casey
474 James Morrison
475 Ivan Chermayeff

ART DIRECTOR / DIRECTEUR ARTISTIQUE:

471 Elizabeth Paul
472 Pontus Hulten
474 James Morrison
475 Ivan Chermayeff

AGENCY / AGENTUR / AGENCE-STUDIO:

472 Centre Georges Pompidou
473 MIT Design Services
475 Chermayeff & Geismar Assoc.

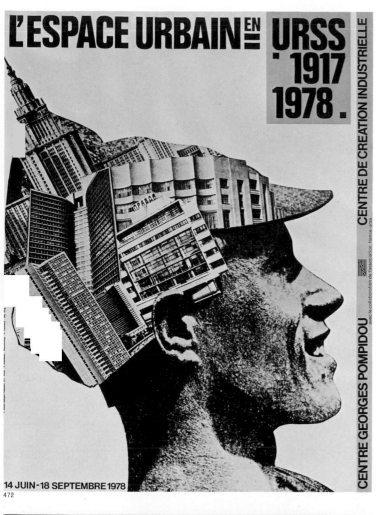

L'ESPACE URBAIN EN URSS 1917 1978.

CENTRE DE CREATION INDUSTRIELLE

avec la collaboration de l'association, france-urss

CENTRE GEORGES POMPIDOU

14 JUIN-18 SEPTEMBRE 1978

472

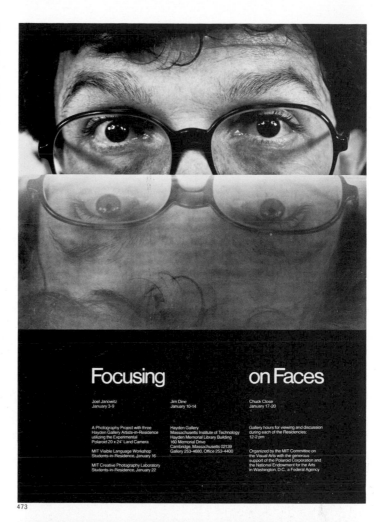

Focusing on Faces

Joel Janowetz
January 3-9

Jim Dine
January 10-14

Chuck Close
January 17-20

A Photography Project with three
Hayden Gallery Artists-in-Residence
utilizing the Experimental
Polaroid 20 x 24" Land Camera

MIT Visible Language Workshop
Students-in-Residence, January 16

MIT Creative Photography Laboratory
Students-in-Residence, January 22

Hayden Gallery
Massachusetts Institute of Technology
Hayden Memorial Library Building
160 Memorial Drive
Cambridge, Massachusetts 02139
Gallery 253-4680, Office 253-4400

Gallery hours for viewing and discussion
during each of the Residencies:
12-2 pm

Organized by the MIT Committee on
the Visual Arts with the generous
support of the Polaroid Corporation and
the National Endowment for the Arts
in Washington, D.C., a Federal Agency

473

AMERICA'S ARCHITECTURAL HERITAGE

474

The Temple
of Dendur
in the new
Sackler Wing
will be open
to the public
Thursday evenings
Sept 28-Nov 16
The Metropolitan
Museum of Art
Fifth Ave & 82nd St
Made possible
by a grant
from Mobil

475

ARTIST / KÜNSTLER / ARTISTE:

476 Luis Alonso
479 Seymoour Chwast
480 Ken Thompson
481 Anne Wood/Kristi Mathias
482 Marlen Perez

DESIGNER / GESTALTER

477 Terrence Westmacott
478 Kurt Meinecke
479 Seymour Chwast
480 Ken Thompson
481 Anne Wood/Kristi Mathias
482 René Gauch
483 Jacqueline S. Casey

ART DIRECTOR / DIRECTEUR ARTISTIQUE:

478 Kurt Meinecke
479 Seymour Chwast
480 Ken Thompson
482 René Gauch

AGENCY / AGENTUR / AGENCE-STUDIO:

476 Taller Grafico I.C.P.
478 Stan Gellman Graphic Design
479 Push Pin Studios, Inc.
480 Ken Thompson
482 René Gauch
483 MIT Design Services

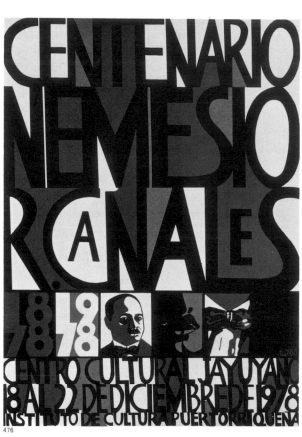

476

477

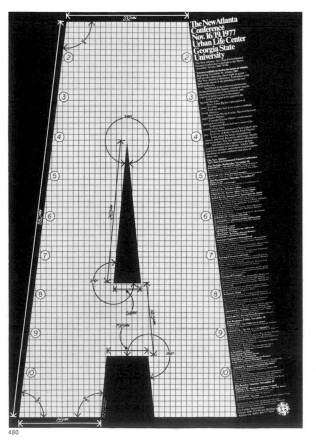

480

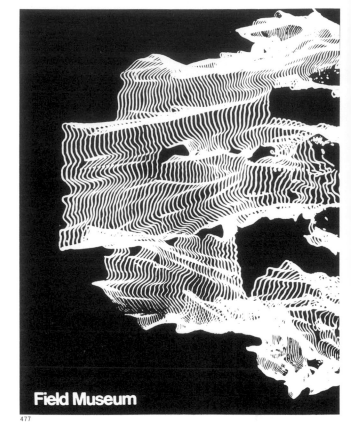

481

Exhibitions
Ausstellungen
Expositions

476 Pour une manifestation organisée en honneur de l'écrivain puertoricain Nemesio Canales, mort il y a cent ans. Gris, noir et rouge. (USA)

477 Affiche pour le Field Museum. (USA)

478 Affiche pour une exposition d'art contemporain américain. (USA)

479 «Les femmes et les arts dans les années 20 – Paris et New York.» Pour une exposition présentée à la State University de New Jersey. (USA)

480 Affiche-programme annonçant une conférence discutant les problèmes urbains de la ville d'Atlanta. Bleu et blanc. (USA)

481 Pour une exposition du Musée d'Art contemporain de Washington au sujet de la pollution. Brun foncé sur papier d'emballage. (USA)

482 Affiche pour une exposition présentant l'œuvre de William Morris, au Musée Bellerive de Zurich. Tons atténués. (SWI)

483 Invitation pour une exposition de dessins de sculptures de pleine air des années 1946 à 1977. En noir et blanc. (USA)

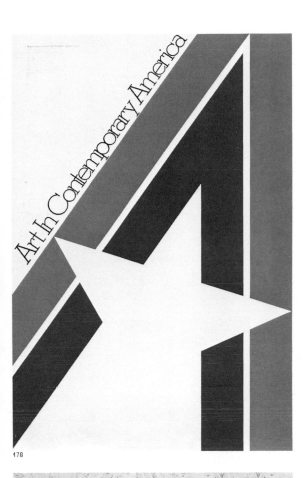

478

479

482

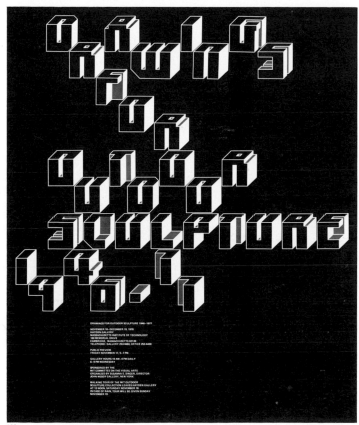

483

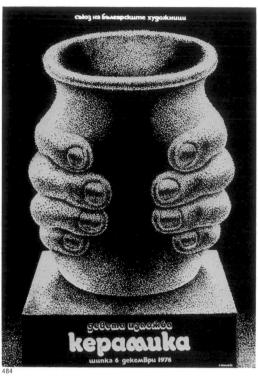

484

485

486

488

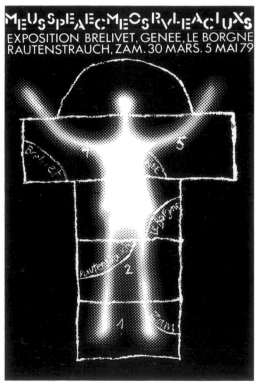

489

490

487

SCANDINAVIAN SCULPTURE
SCANDINAVIAN ART CENTER · SUOMENLINNA

28.7 - 10.9 1979

491

484 Poster for an exhibition of ceramics. (BUL)
485 Poster recruiting members for the Poldi Pezzoli Museum in Milan. (ITA)
486 Announcement of an exhibition of the college of art and design in Offenbach. (GER)
487 Invitation to a poster and postcard exhibition and sale. The oilpainting has been reproduced in full colour. Light green border. (CAN)
488 Exhibition of French theatre posters featuring Josephine Baker and the Folies Bergères. Full-colour poster. (USA)
489 Poster for a joint exhibition of five artists. Yellow, white and black. (FRA)
490 Full-colour poster for an exhibition of photography by Fulvio Roiter. (SWI)
491 Announcement of an exhibition of Scandinavian sculpture. (FIN)
492 Poster for an exhibition of art at the Slovakian Museum. (CSR)

484 Plakat für eine Keramikausstellung. (BUL)
485 Plakat für die Mitgliederwerbung des Museums Poldi Pezzoli, Mailand. (ITA)
486 Plakat in Schwarzweiss für die Ankündigung einer Ausstellung aus dem Fachbereich «Visuelle Kommunikation» der Hochschule für Gestaltung, Offenbach. (GER)
487 Einladung zu einer Plakat- und Postkarten-Verkaufsausstellung. Der Titel des farbig reproduzierten Ölbildes ist «Pflanzenmusik». Hellgrüne Umrandung. (CAN)
488 «Josephine Baker und die Folies Bergères» ist der Titel einer Ausstellung französischer Theaterplakate. Mehrfarbiges Plakat. (USA)
489 Plakat für eine Gruppenausstellung von fünf Künstlern. Gelb, Weiss und Schwarz. (FRA)
490 Farbiges Plakat für eine Photographie-Ausstellung. (SWI)
491 Ankündigung einer Ausstellung skandinavischer Skulptur. (FIN)
492 Plakat des Slowakischen Museums für eine Kunstausstellung. (CSR)

484 Affiche pour une exposition de poterie. (BUL)
485 Affiche autopromotionnelle du Musée Poldi Pezzoli de Milan. (ITA)
486 Affiche en noir et blanc annonçant une exposition que la faculté de «Communication Visuelle» de la Hochschule für Gestaltung, Offenbach, a organisée. (GER)
487 Invitation pour une vente-exposition d'affiches et de cartes postales. La peinture à l'huile reproduite en couleurs est intitulée «musique des plantes». Cadre vert clair. (CAN)
488 Affiche pour une exposition d'affiches françaises de théâtre, présentée sous le titre «Josephine Baker et les Folies Bergères». En polychromie. (USA)
489 Affiche pour une exposition collective de cinq artistes. Jaune, blanc et noir. (FRA)
490 Affiche pour une exposition des photos de Fulvio Roiter. (SWI)
491 Affiche annonçant une exposition de sculptures scandinaves. (FIN)
492 Affiche du Musée Slovaque pour une exposition d'œuvres d'art. (CSR)

AGENCY / AGENTUR / AGENCE-STUDIO:

485 Studio Iliprandi
488 Stan Gellman Graphic Design
489 Kan Ar Mor
490 Portfolio
492 Josef Flejsar

492

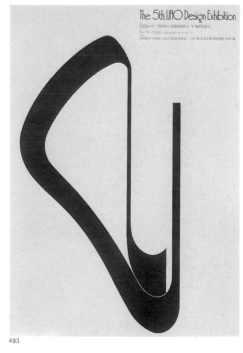

493

ARTIST / KÜNSTLER / ARTISTE:

493–495 Yukihisa Takakita
496 Joe A. Goulait
497 Masaru Suzuki
498 Yutaka Takama
499 Yoshiro Katoh
500, 501 Shigeo Fukuda

DESIGNER / GESTALTER / MAQUETTISTE:

493–495 Yukihisa Takakita
496 Bill Caldwell
497 Masaru Suzuki
498 Yutaka Takama
499 Yoshiro Katoh
500, 501 Shigeo Fukuda

ART DIRECTOR / DIRECTEUR ARTISTIQUE:

493–495 Yukihisa Takakita
496 Bill Caldwell
497 Masaru Suzuki
498 Yutaka Takama
499 Yoshiro Katoh
500, 501 Shigeo Fukuda

AGENCY / AGENTUR / AGENCE-STUDIO:

493–495 Takakita Design Institute
497 Media Co., Ltd.
499 Katoh Design

496

493, 494 Silk-screen posters for a graphic design group exhibition (Fig. 493) and a one-man show (Fig. 494). Both red and grey on white. (JPN)
495 Poster specially designed for an exhibition of work done for exams at a school of design and art. Red, blue and white. (JPN)
496 Announcement of a mobile exhibition of Latin American graphic design. In full colour. (USA)
497 Black-and-white poster for an exhibition of graphic design by Masaru Suzuki. (JPN)
498 Full-colour poster for an exhibition of art. Red, blue, yellow and black. (JPN)
499 Exhibition poster for an advertisers' club. Blue on pink, red lettering. (JPN)
500, 501 Posters announcing an exhibition by the artist Shigeo Fukuda. (JPN)

493 Siebdruckplakat für eine Gruppenausstellung von Graphik-Designern. Rot auf Weiss. (JPN)
494 Ankündigung einer Graphik-Design-Einzelausstellung. Siebdruck, Rot und Grau auf Weiss. (JPN)
495 Plakat für eine Ausstellung von Abschlussarbeiten einer Kunstschule. Rot, Blau, Weiss. (JPN)
496 Ankündigung einer Wanderausstellung lateinamerikanischer Graphik. Mehrfarbig. (USA)
497 Plakat in Schwarzweiss für eine Graphik-Design-Ausstellung von Masaru Suzuki. (JPN)
498 Plakat für eine Kunstausstellung. Die Farben: Gelb, Schwarz, Blau und Rot. (JPN)
499 Ausstellungsplakat für einen Werbe-Club. Blau auf Rosa, rote Schrift. (JPN)
500, 501 Zwei Plakate für die Ankündigung einer Ausstellung des Künstlers Shigeo Fukuda. (JPN)

493 Affiche sérigraphique annonçant une exposition collective de graphistes. Rouge sur blanc. (JPN)
494 Affiche pour une exposition de travaux graphiques. Sérigraphie en rouge et gris sur blanc. (JPN)
495 Affiche pour une exposition présentant les travaux de fin d'études d'une école d'art. (JPN)
496 Pour une exposition itinérante d'art graphique latino-américain. En polychromie. (USA)
497 Affiche pour une exposition des travaux graphiques de Masaru Suzuki. En noir et blanc. (JPN)
498 Affiche pour une exposition d'œuvres d'art. Jaune, noir, bleu et rouge. (JPN)
499 Affiche d'exposition d'un club publicitaire. Bleu sur rose, typographie rouge. (JPN)
500, 501 Deux affiches annonçant une exposition des œuvres de Shigeo Fukuda. (JPN)

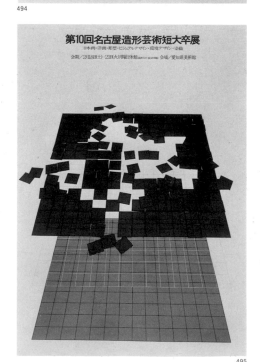

494

495

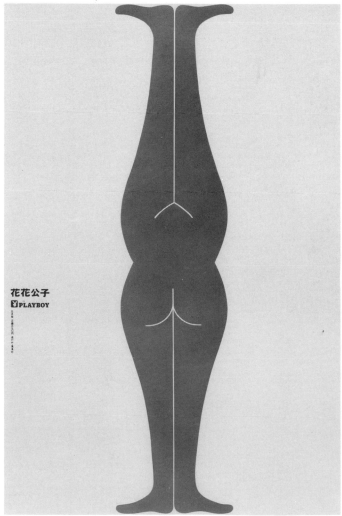

花花公子

499

MASARU SUZUKI GRAPHIC DESIGN IMAGINATION 1979

鈴木勝イメージ展
1979年5月15日(火)−5月21日(月)
午前10時−午後6時
ギャラリー タケガ
名古屋市中区錦3丁目5−32 電話/052・961・1871

497

TA KA MA

498

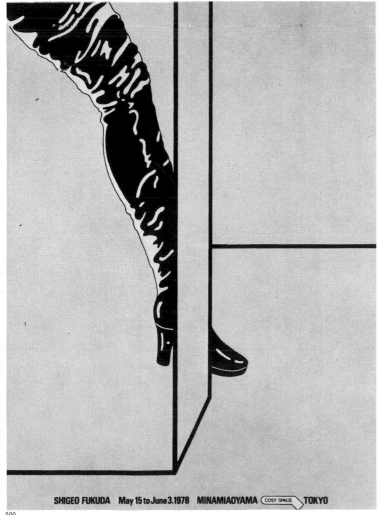

SHIGEO FUKUDA   May 15 to June 3.1978   MINAMIAOYAMA   COSY SPACE   TOKYO

500

SHIGEO FUKUDA   May 15 to June 3.1978   MINAMIAOYAMA   COSY SPACE   TOKYO

501

3

Social Posters

Soziale Plakate

Affiches sociales

502

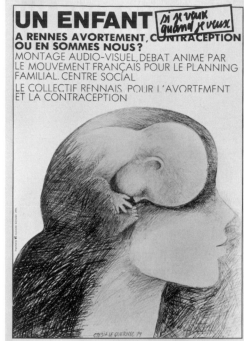

503

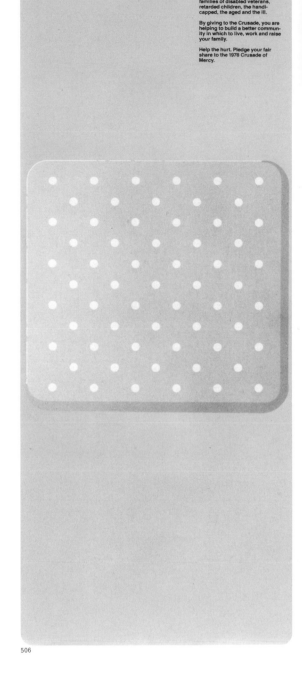

504

505

506

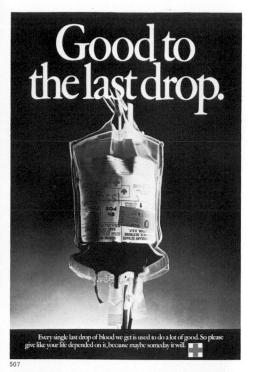

507

508

509

510

511

512

ARTIST / KÜNSTLER / ARTISTE:

502 L. Toivanen
503 Czesia Le Quernec
505 Reinhart Braun/
    Harry Suchland
507, 511 Terry Collier
508 Pio Corradi
509 Ibid
510 Thomas Pratt
512 Fred Bird

DESIGNER / GESTALTER:

502 Leif Tallqvist
503 Czesia & Alain Le Quernec
504 Georg Erhardt
505 Reinhart Braun
506 Jeff A. Barnes
507, 511, 512 Joe Shyllit
508 Fred Bauer
509 Larry Smith
510 Thomas Pratt

ART DIRECTOR:

502 Leif Tallqvist
503 Alain Le Quernec
504 Georg Erhardt
505 Reinhart Braun
506 Jeff A. Barnes
507, 511, 512 Joe Shyllit
508 Fred Bauer
509 Larry Smith
510 Thomas Pratt

AGENCY / AGENTUR / AGENCE:

502 Turkama & Kumppanit
504 Studio Erhardt
505 Reinhart Braun
506 Container Corporation of
    America
507, 512 Kuleba & Shyllit
    Creative Services
508 G. Tscharner AG
509 Luckie & Fornie
510 Graphic Communications
511 McConnell Advertising

513

514

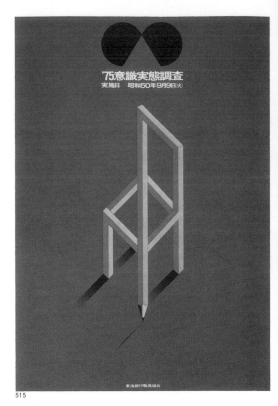

515

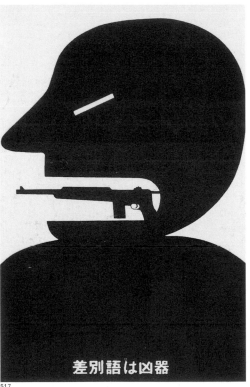

517

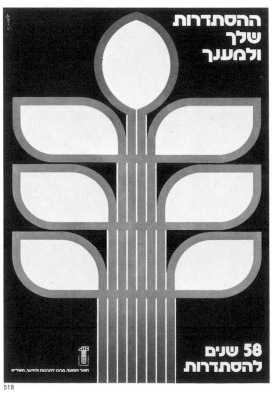

518

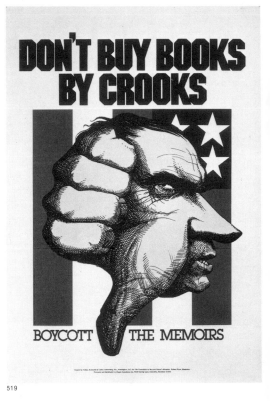

519

513 Poster demonstrating for the freedom of the Third World. Two colours on wrapping paper. (USA)
514 Poster for 1st May. Red flower, lettering and border. (HUN)
515 Poster displayed on the occasion of a union-organized investigation into the economic situation of bank employees. Illustration in garish green and red. (JPN)
516 "For the defence of human rights." Poster issued by the prisoners' aid organization *Amnesty International*. The figure is in red. (ITA)
517 "Discriminating words are a dangerous weapon" is the title given to this poster. (JPN)
518 "The union is there for you." Red and white illustration on a green background. (ISR)
519 Anti-Nixon poster. The United States flag is shown in its actual colours, black and pink head. (USA)
520 Poster displayed for European Day. One figure is in black, the other in full colour with the European flag. (SWI)
521 Poster in opposition to the death penalty. (FRA)

513 Plakat, das für die Befreiung der Dritten Welt plädiert. Zweifarbig auf Packpapier. (USA)
514 Plakat zum 1. Mai. Nelke, Schrift und Rand rot. (HUN)
515 Von der Gewerkschaft im Rahmen einer Untersuchung der wirtschaftlichen Situation von Bankangestellten veröffentlichtes Plakat. Illustration in grellem Grün und Rot. (JPN)
516 «Für die Verteidigung der Menschenrechte.» Von der Gefangenenhilfsorganisation *Amnesty International* herausgegebenes Plakat. Schwarzweiss mit roter Gestalt. (ITA)
517 «Diskriminierende Worte sind eine gefährliche Waffe» ist der Titel dieses Plakates. (JPN)
518 «Die Gewerkschaft ist für Sie da.» Illustration rot und weiss auf grünem Hintergrund. (ISR)
519 Aufruf zum Boykott der Nixon-Memoiren. Flagge der USA in den Originalfarben, Kopf schwarz und rosa. (USA)
520 Anlässlich des Europatages veröffentlichtes Plakat. Eine Gestalt schwarz, die andere mehrfarbig mit Europaflagge. (SWI)
521 Von Gegnern der Todesstrafe veröffentlichtes Plakat. (FRA)

513 Appel lancé en faveur de la libération du Tiers Monde. Deux couleurs sur papier d'emballage. (USA)
514 Pour le 1er mai. Œillet, typo, et encadrement rouges. (HUN)
515 Affiche d'un syndicat publiée dans le cadre d'une enquête concernant la situation économique des employés de banque. Illustration en vert et rouge vif. (JPN)
516 «Pour la défense des droits de l'homme.» Affiche de l'organisation d'aide aux prisonniers d'opinion, *Amnesty International*. Noir et blanc, figure rouge. (ITA)
517 Affiche intitulée «Des mots discriminatoires sont des fois des armes dangereuses.» (JPN)
518 «Le syndicat est là pour vous.» Illustration en rouge et blanc sur fond vert. (ISR)
519 Ici on fait appel au public de ne pas acheter les mémoires de Nixon. Drapeau en bleu-blanc-rouge, tête noire et rose. (USA)
520 Affiche publiée à l'occasion de la journée européenne. L'une des figures en noir, l'autre en couleurs. (SWI)
521 De l'Association française contre la peine de mort. (FRA)

516

520

Solidarity Posters
Solidaritätsplakate
Affiches de solidarité

521

167

522

523

524

522 Linocut poster for the Third World. Green and red on brown paper. (GBR)
523 Poster quoting Martin Luther King. Linocut, red and blue. (GBR)
524 Poster for *Amnesty International* advertising one of its exhibitions. (GBR)
525, 526 "The right to education." Two full-colour posters for the seventh film festival organized by the International Human Rights Committee in Strasbourg. (FRA)
527 Poster dealing with the subjects of freedom and truth, quoting John F. Kennedy. (GBR)
528 Poster by a women's movement for peace in Northern Ireland. (GBR)

522 Linolschnitt-Plakat für die Dritte Welt. Grün und rot auf braunem Papier. (GBR)
523 Plakat mit Worten von Martin Luther King. Linolschnitt, rot und blau. (GBR)
524 Plakat für eine Ausstellung der Gefangenenhilfsorganisation *Amnesty International*. (GBR)
525, 526 «Das Recht auf Ausbildung.» Plakate, beide zweifarbig, für das 7. Filmfestival, das von der internationalen Menschenrechtskommission in Strassburg veranstaltet wurde. (FRA)
527 Freiheit und Wahrheit sind das Thema des Plakates. Mit Worten von John F. Kennedy. (GBR)
528 «Brich das Schweigen.» Plakat einer Frauenbewegung für Frieden in Nordirland. (GBR)

522 Affiche en linogravure. Soleil rouge, bras verts, fond ocre. (GBR)
523 Affiche avec une citation de Martin Luther King. Linogravure en rouge et bleu. (GBR)
524 Pour une exposition d'*Amnesty International*, organisation d'aide aux prisonniers politiques. (GBR)
525, 526 Affiches, en deux couleurs, annonçant le 7e Festival international du film organisé par l'Institut international des droits de l'homme à Strasbourg. (FRA)
527 Affiche avec une citation de John F. Kennedy au sujet de la liberté et la vérité. (GBR)
528 Un mouvement pour la libération de la femme plaide pour la paix en Irlande du Nord. (GBR)

Solidarity Posters
Solidaritätsplakate
Affiches de solidarité

ARTIST / KÜNSTLER / ARTISTE:
522–528 Paul Peter Piech

DESIGNER / GESTALTER / MAQUETTISTE:
522–528 Paul Peter Piech

ART DIRECTOR / DIRECTEUR ARTISTIQUE:
522–528 Paul Peter Piech

LE DROIT À l'EDUCATION
7e Festival International du Films des DROITS de l'HOMME — STRASBOURG
Institute International des Droits de l'Homme

525

527

LE DROIT À l'EDUCATION

7e Festival International du Films des DROITS de l'HOMME — STRASBOURG
Institute International des Droits de l'Homme

526

528

ARTIST / KÜNSTLER / ARTISTE:

529 Marian Nowinski
530 Jean-Pierre Ader
531 Reijo Kalevi Ström
532 Jozef-Rafal Olbinski
533 Simon Koppany
534 Thomas Kruse

529

530

531

529 This poster deals with the suppression of the works of the Chilean poet and writer Pablo Neruda. The designer was awarded a prize in the Third World category. (POL)
530 Original poster in black, blue and white. Clenched fists here make up a dove. (FRA)
531 Photo-poster referring to resistance movements. Black-and-white rectangle on a light blue surface. (FIN)
532 Original poster with black face, a white wing and a red and yellow ground. (POL)
533 Original poster for Palestine. Grey barbed wire and white lettering on a yellow background. (HUN)
534 Linocut poster, black and white. "Recognize the PLO." One of the special awards, here in the Palestine category. (DEN)

529 Die Unterdrückung der Werke des chilenischen Dichters und Schriftstellers Pablo Neruda sind das Thema dieses Plakates. Es wurde mit einem Preis ausgezeichnet. (POL)
530 Originalplakat in Schwarz, Blau und Weiss. Die geballten Fäuste ergeben hier die Umrisse einer Taube. (FRA)
531 Photoplakat zum Thema Widerstandsbewegung. Schwarzweisses Rechteck auf hellblauem Grund. (FIN)
532 «Wach auf, Dritte Welt.» Schwarzes Gesicht, weisser Flügel, Grund rot und gelb. Originalplakat. (POL)
533 Originalplakat zum Thema Palästina. Davidstern aus grauem Stacheldraht und weisse Schrift auf Gelb. (HUN)
534 «Anerkennt die PLO.» Schwarzweisses Linolschnitt-Plakat. Es erhielt eine Spezialauszeichnung. (DEN)

529 Cette affiche se réfère à l'interdiction des œuvres du poète et écrivain chilien Pablo Neruda, prix Nobel. Elle a remporté un prix dans la catégorie Tiers Monde. (POL)
530 Les poings serrés dessinent ici le profil d'une colombe. Affiche originale en noir, bleu et blanc. (FRA)
531 Affiche-photo dédiée à la résistance. Rectangle noir et blanc sur fond en bleu pâle. (FIN)
532 «Réveille-toi, Tiers Monde!» Visage noir, aile blanche, fond rouge, jaune. Affiche originale. (POL)
533 Etoile de David comme sujet d'une affiche originale pour la Palestine. Barbelés gris, text blanc sur fond jaune. (HUN)
534 «Reconnaissez l'OLP!» Affiche en linogravure, noir-blanc. Cette affiche a été attribuée une mention spéciale. (DEN)

Third World Posters
Plakate der Dritten Welt
Affiches du Tiers Monde

■ The Baghdad International Poster Exhibition was staged by the Iraqi Cultural Centre in March/April 1979 in London and in May in Baghdad, and combined the best work of a competition in two categories: *The Third World's Struggle for Liberation* and *Palestine – a Homeland Denied*. Prior to this political posters were almost unknown in the Third World, and many of the entries reveal artists learning a new language. A small selection of these posters is shown on this double spread.

■ Die internationale Plakatausstellung Bagdad, vom irakischen Kulturzentrum im März/April 1979 in London und im Mai in Bagdad gezeigt, vereinigte die besten Arbeiten eines Wettbewerbs zu den Themen *Der Kampf der Dritten Welt für die Befreiung* und *Palästina – verweigertes Heimatland*. Politische Plakate waren bis dahin in der Dritten Welt praktisch unbekannt, und zahlreiche Einsendungen dokumentieren das Erlernen einer neuen Sprache. Auf dieser Doppelseite wird eine kleine Auswahl der Plakate gezeigt.

■ L'exposition internationale d'affiches de Bagdad, organisée par le Centre culturel irakien à Londres en mars/avril 1979 et à Bagdad en mai, réunissait les meilleurs travaux d'un concours où deux sujets étaient à traiter: *La lutte du Tiers Monde pour sa libération* et *La Palestine – une patrie refusée*. Jusqu'alors, les affiches de caractère politique étaient presque inconnues du Tiers Monde, et nombre de travaux révèlent l'apprentissage d'un langage nouveau. On trouvera sur cette page double une sélection de ces œuvres.

533

532

534

171

no pasaran

our future is where our past is

ISRAEL

535

536

537

IL DISSENSO CULTURALE

NEI PAESI DELL'EST

538

539

535 Poster for a Free Spain movement. (SPA)
536 From a series of anti-Apartheid posters. (GBR)
537 A test tube with blue liquid in an earthen vessel reminds Israelis of their heritage and future. (ISR)
538 Comment on the situation of artists and cultural workers in countries behind the Iron Curtain. White, red and black. (ITA)
539 Poster referring to Palestine, showing the number of villages that existed before 1948, those ruined by warfare or the like, and those existing today. (YUG)
540 Poster for the *Junge Union* party, Lower Saxony. (GER)
541 The Third World behind bars. Special award of The National Museum of Modern Art, Baghdad. (CHI)

535 Plakat einer Bewegung für ein freies Spanien. (SPA)
536 Aus einer Serie von Plakaten, die sich gegen die Apartheids-Politik in Südafrika richten. (GBR)
537 «Unsere Zukunft liegt in unserer Vergangenheit.» Glasflasche mit blauer Flüssigkeit in Tongefäss. (ISR)
538 Kommentar zur Situation der Kulturschaffenden in den Ostblockstaaten. Weiss, Rot und Schwarz. (ITA)
539 Plakat zum Thema Palästina. Hier werden die vor 1948 existierenden Dörfer aufgeführt, die Anzahl der zerstörten und die der heute noch vorhandenen Dörfer. (YUG)
540 Farbiges Plakat der *Jungen Union*, Niedersachsen. (GER)
541 Die Dritte Welt hinter Gittern. Dieses Plakat wurde vom Nationalmuseum für moderne Kunst, Bagdad, ausgezeichnet. (CHI)

535 Affiche d'un mouvement pour une Espagne libre. (SPA)
536 Affiche extraite d'une série militant contre l'apartheid sudafricaine. (GBR)
537 «Notre avenir c'est notre passé.» Flacon avec liquide bleu dans un vase de terre. (ISR)
538 «La dissension culturelle.» Référence à la situation des créateurs culturels dans les pays de l'Europe orientale. (ITA)
539 Affiche au sujet de la Palestine. On y énumère les villages palestiniens qui existaient avant 1948, ceux qui ont été détruits et ceux qui existent encore aujourd'hui. (YUG)
540 Affiche polychrome d'un parti politique allemand. (GER)
541 Le Tiers Monde derrière les barreaux. Prix spécial du Musée d'art moderne de Bagdad. (CHI)

541

540

ARTIST / KÜNSTLER / ARTISTE:

535 Giancarlo Iliprandi
536 David King
537 Koren
538 Folon
539 Vladimir Bonacic
541 R.A.S. Matta

DESIGNER / GESTALTER / MAQUETTISTE:

535 Giancarlo Iliprandi
536 David King
537 Koren
540 Steffen Jünger

ART DIRECTOR / DIRECTEUR ARTISTIQUE:

535 Giancarlo Iliprandi
536 David King
537 Ran Caspi/Benny Ribatzky
540 Coordt von Mannstein

AGENCY / AGENTUR / AGENCE-STUDIO:

535 Studio Iliprandi
536 David King
537 R. Rolnik Ltd.
538 Futura
540 von Mannstein Werbeagentur

Political Posters
Politische Plakate
Affiches politiques

542

543

■ As part of a campaign for the election of the first European parliament, Jack Lang, national delegate of the French Socialist party, asked François Barré and Gilles de Bure to produce a collection of posters illustrating the principal issues involved. Acting in the capacity of art directors and consultants, they called upon eight of the leading French graphic designers and entrusted the mise-en-pages of the whole collection to Roman Cieslewicz. Seven posters and a portrait are shown here.

■ Im Rahmen einer Wahlkampagne für das erste Europäische Parlament beauftragte der nationale Delegierte der sozialistischen Partei Frankreichs, Jack Lang, François Barré und Gilles de Bure mit einer Serie von Plakaten, die die Hauptthemen der Kampagne illustrieren. Als Art Directors und Berater wandten sich diese an acht führende Graphik-Designer Frankreichs und betrauten Roman Cieslewicz mit der Realisation der gesamten Serie. Hier sieben Plakate und ein zusätzliches Porträt.

544

547

■ Dans le cadre de la campagne pour les élections au premier Parlement européen, Jack Lang, délégué national au Parti socialiste français, a chargé François Barré et Gilles de Bure de réaliser une collection de posters illustrant les grands thèmes de la campagne. Agissant en tant que directeurs artistiques et conseillers, ceux-ci ont fait appel à huit grands créateurs français, en confiant la mise en pages de l'ensemble à Roman Cieslewicz. Nous reproduisons ici sept posters et un portrait.

ARTIST / KÜNSTLER / ARTISTE:

542 Roman Cieslewicz
543 Topor
544 Avoine
545 Corentin
546 Jean Lagarrigue
547 Paul Davis
548 Alain Le Saux
549 André François

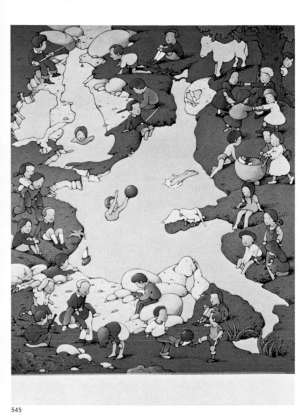

545

546

merci Giscard

PARTI SOCIALISTE, 7 bis, PLACE DU PALAIS-BOURBON, 75007 PARIS.

548

549

542 *Woman is the future of Europe.*
543 *Inflation, recession, pollution, denunciation... everything is fine!*
544, 545 *Change life, change the town* and *A Europe one would like to grow up in.*
546 *For a Socialist Europe.*
547 Portrait of François Mitterrand.
548 *Thank you, Giscard.* Poster dealing with the problem of unemployment.
549 *Is there no way to escape, then, from the fatality of history?*

542 *Die Frau ist Europas Zukunft.*
543 *Inflation, Rezession, Umweltverschmutzung, Verrat... Alles in Ordnung!*
544, 545 *Änder' das Leben, änder' die Stadt* und *Ein Europa, in dem man aufwachsen möchte* sind hier die Themen.
546 *Für ein sozialistisches Europa.*
547 Porträt von François Mitterrand.
548 *Danke Giscard.* Plakat zum Thema der Arbeitslosigkeit.
549 *Gibt es also keinen Weg, um der Fatalität der Geschichte zu entkommen?*

542 Affiche se référant au rôle de la femme en Europe.
543 *Inflation, récession, pollution, délation... Tout va très bien Mme la Marquise.*
544, 545 *Changer la vie, changer la ville,* et *Une Europe qui donne envie de grandir.*
546 *Pour une Europe socialiste.* La rose, emblème du socialisme européen.
547 Portrait de François Mitterrand.
548 Affiche au sujet du chômage.
549 *N'y a-t-il donc aucun moyen d'échapper à la fatalité de l'histoire?*

175

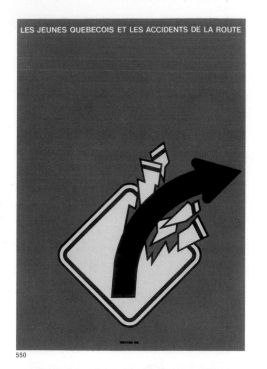

550

551

552

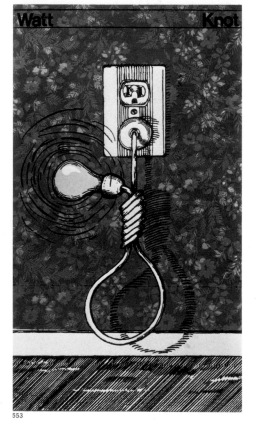

553

554

550 Poster dealing with road safety for youngsters. (CAN)
551, 552 Two posters on the subject of better leadership for employees. Full-colour illustrations. (GER)
553 Energy supply. Black-and-white drawing with a yellow lightbulb and wallpaper in grey shades. (USA)
554 Poster by the German Foreign Academic Service for scholarships awarded for studies in France. (GER)
555 Full-colour poster with advice and suggestions on how to avoid accidents in swimming pools. (USA)
556 Poster urging people to learn Hebrew. (ISR)
557 Poster in favour of a nuclear energy protection law. (SWI)
558 Informative poster dealing with ancient Peru. (USA)

550 Plakat im Zusammenhang mit einer offiziellen Studie der Unfälle von Jugendlichen auf der Strasse. (CAN)
551, 552 Zwei Plakate zum Thema der besseren Mitarbeiterführung. Illustrationen in Farbe. (GER)
553 Schwarzweiss-Zeichnung mit gelber Glühbirne auf Tapete in Grautönen. Thema des Plakates ist die Energieversorgung. (USA)
554 Plakat des Deutschen Akademischen Auslandsdienstes für Stipendien zum Studium in Frankreich. (GER)
555 Ratschläge des Roten Kreuzes zur Verhinderung von Unfällen in Swimming-pools. Mehrfarbiges Plakat. (USA)
556 Plakat zum Erlernen der hebräischen Sprache. (ISR)
557 Plakat zugunsten eines Atomschutzgesetzes. (SWI)
558 Informatives Plakat über das alte Peru. (USA)

550 Affiche figurant dans une campagne de sécurité routière de la jeunesse québécoise. (CAN)
551, 552 Deux affiches extraites d'une campagne lancée pour améliorer l'atmosphère dans l'entreprise. En polychromie. (GER)
553 Affiche au sujet de l'alimentation en énergie. Dessin noir-blanc, ampoule jaune, papier peint en gris. (USA)
554 Affiche du service universitaire allemand se référant ici aux bourses d'étude en France. (GER)
555 Cette affiche contient des conseils du Croix-Rouge concernant la prévention d'accident dans la piscine. En couleurs. (USA)
556 Affiche pour apprendre la langue hébreu. (ISR)
557 «Oui à la protection contre les radiations atomiques.» (SWI)
558 Affiche contenant des informations sur le Pérou. (USA)

Educative Posters
Erzieherische Plakate
Affiches éducatives

ARTIST / KÜNSTLER / ARTISTE:

550 Alain Le Quernec
551, 552 Theo Kerb
553 Lanny Sommese
554 Heinz Bähr
555 Tony Kew
556 Avner Katz

DESIGNER / GESTALTER / MAQUETTISTE:

550 Alain Le Quernec
553 Lanny Sommese
554 Heinz Bähr
555 Joe Shyllit
556 Avner Katz
557 Pierre Brauchli
558 Elizabeth Shepard

ART DIRECTOR / DIRECTEUR ARTISTIQUE:

550 Jacques Nadeau
551, 552 Graphicteam H. Lippert/R. Richter
553 Lanny Sommese
554 Heinz Bähr
555 Joe Shyllit
556 Avner Katz
557 Pierre Brauchli
558 Larry Klein

AGENCY / AGENTUR / AGENCE-STUDIO:

550 Ideacom Inc.
551, 552 Graphicteam
553 Lanny Sommese Design
555 Kuleba & Shyllit Creative Services
556 R. Rolnik Ltd.
557 Pierre Brauchli
558 Field Museum

555

556

557

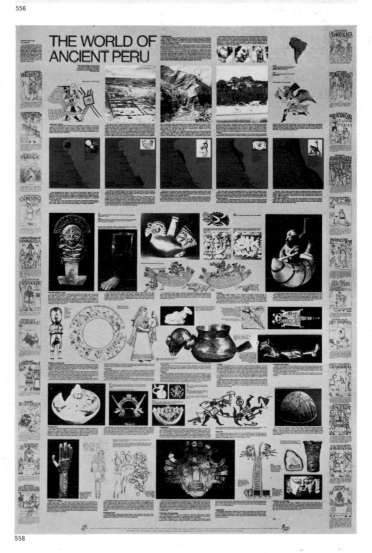

558

559

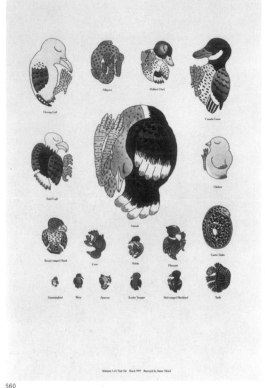

560

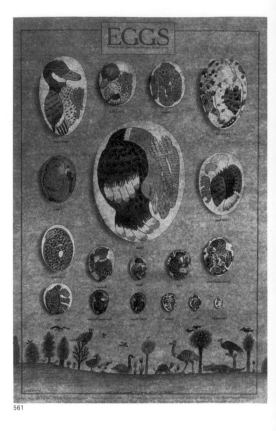

561

559–561 Recto and verso of an educational poster. When this poster is held up, the birds on the verso are visible in their corresponding eggs (Fig. 561). In full colour. (USA)
562 Full-colour poster for children. (USA)
563 Poster to promote specialized education. Referred to here are studies in horticulture. The text mentions the various possibilities in this profession. The lettering is white on a black background. Colour photograph. (USA)
564 Poster referring to the interference of man on the Galapagos Islands and the necessity of preserving local species. (USA)

559–561 Vorder- und Rückseite eines Lehrplakates. Die Vögel auf der Rückseite werden beim Hochheben des Plakates in den zugehörigen Eiern sichtbar (Abb. 561). In Farbe. (USA)
562 «Stiefel.» Mehrfarbiges Plakat für Kinder. (USA)
563 Zur Förderung der Fachausbildung veröffentlichtes Plakat. Hier geht es um das landwirtschaftliche Studiengebiet Hortikultur. Der Text erwähnt die verschiedenen Berufsmöglichkeiten. Weisse Schrift auf schwarzem Grund, Farbaufnahme. (USA)
564 Die Erhaltung der vom Aussterben bedrohten Leguane der Galapagos-Inseln ist das Thema des Plakates. (USA)

559–561 Recto et verso d'une affiche éducative. En mettant l'affiche contre la lumière, on voit les oiseaux dans leurs œufs respectifs (fig. 561). En polychromie. (USA)
562 «Bottes.» Affiche polychrome pour enfants. (USA)
563 Affiche pour la promotion de la formation spéciale. Le texte mentionne les diverses possibilités dans le domaine de l'agriculture, particulièrement l'horticulture. Typographie blanche sur fond noir, photo en couleurs. (USA)
564 Appel lancé en faveur de la protection des iguanes des îles Galapagos qui sont en voie de disparition. (USA)

ARTIST / KÜNSTLER / ARTISTE:

559–562 Simms Taback
563 Doug Barber
564 Agusta Agustsson

DESIGNER / GESTALTER:

559–562 Carol Carson
563 Claude Skelton
564 Agusta Agustsson

ART DIRECTOR:

559–562 Carol Carson
563 Bernice Thieblot
564 Robert P. Moore

AGENCY / AGENTUR / AGENCE:

559–562 Scholastic Magazines
563 North Charles St. Design Organization
564 The Graphic Workshop

Educative Posters
Erzieherische Plakate
Affiches éducatives

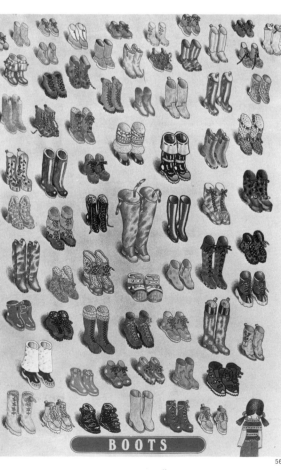

562

563

178

IN 1835, WHEN CHARLES DARWIN LANDED IN THE GALÁPAGOS, HE HAD DIFFICULTY FINDING A PLACE TO PITCH HIS TENT BECAUSE OF THE NUMBER OF IGUANAS. TODAY, AS A RESULT OF MAN'S INTERFERENCE WITH THE ECOLOGY OF THE ISLANDS, THIS SPECIES OF IGUANA IS NOW CLOSE TO EXTINCTION.

BARRINGTON LAND IGUANA

564

565

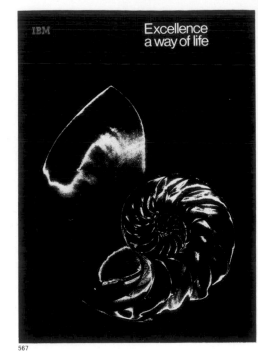

566

567

ARTIST / KÜNSTLER / ARTISTE:

565 Alain Le Quernec
567 Jim Faye/Roger Ewy
568, 569 Jim Faye
570 Carl Futura
571 Alfred Zemlok
572 Terje Roalkvam
573 Tanya Stringham
574 André François
575 John J. Sorbie

DESIGNER / GESTALTER / MAQUETTISTE:

565 Alain Le Quernec
566 Michael Baviera/Ruedi Bauer
567, 569 Tom Bluhm
568 John F. Anderson
570 Stan Jones
572 Terje Roalkvam
573 Carole Wade
575 John J. Sorbie

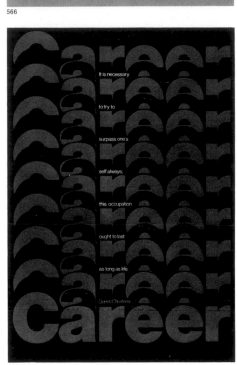

568

569

570

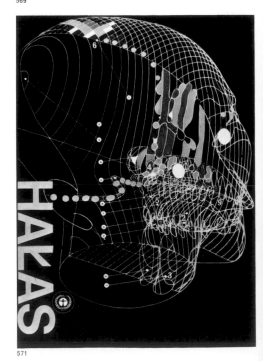

571

NEI TIL OLJEBORING I NORD!

572

Mind your own business.
Find out how: Retailing Orientation Seminar
Thursday, January 25, 10 to 11 a.m., 172 JKB

Whether you're planning to be an executive for a large retail corporation or to manage your own store, you'll be more successful with retail management training. To learn more about this exciting and rewarding specialty, attend the Retailing Orientation Seminar.

Skaggs Institute of Retail Management
School of Management
280 JKB

573

CAN WE WAIT?

For Information Contact Air Quality Program —
Larimer County Health Department
Telephone 221-2100 X500

575

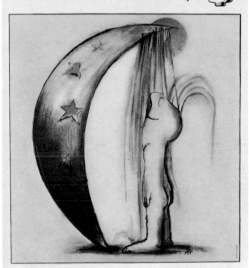

FAITES LE PLEIN D'EAU CHAUDE, LA NUIT, AU TARIF "HEURES CREUSES"
chauffe-eau électrique

574

ART DIRECTOR / DIRECTEUR ARTISTIQUE:

565 Alain Le Quernec
566 Michael Baviera
567 Tom Bluhm
568, 569 John F. Anderson
570 Stan Jones
572 Terje Roalkvam
573 Carole Wade
574 Gilles Dulis
575 John J. Sorbie

AGENCY / AGENTUR / AGENCE-STUDIO:

565 Kan Ar Mor
566 M & M Baviera
567–569 IBM
570 Doyle Dane Bernbach
573 Graphic Communications
574 Bazaine Publicité
575 CSU Art Dept.

Educative Posters
Erzieherische Plakate
Affiches éducatives

565 "We are not condemned to nuclear energy!" Poster from an information campaign. Black on green. (FRA)
566 Poster for internal opinion research at an IBM factory. Black and white on a green surface. (SWI)
567–569 Three posters from an IBM series urging people never to stop learning. In full colour. (USA)
570 Poster as an appeal for energy saving by a gas company, here suggesting shorter showers. (USA)
571 Poster on the subject of reducing noise. (POL)
572 "No searching for oil in the North" (of Norway). (NOR)
573 A well-known expression serves to advertise a training course for businessmen. Full-colour poster. (USA)
574 Appeal to save energy by using power at night. Blue and yellow illustration with some violet. (FRA)
575 Black-and-white poster dealing with the consequences if air pollution continues at its present rate. (USA)

565 «Wir sind nicht zur Kernkraft verdammt!» Plakat aus einer Informationskampagne. Schwarz auf Grün. (FRA)
566 Plakat für eine betriebsinterne Meinungsumfrage der IBM. Schwarz und Weiss auf grünem Grund. (SWI)
567–569 Drei Plakate aus einer Serie von IBM, mit denen zum ständigen Lernen aufgefordert wird. In Farbe. (USA)
570 Aufruf einer Gasgesellschaft zum Energiesparen. «Sing kürzere Lieder.» (USA)
571 Plakat zum Thema Lärmbekämpfung. (POL)
572 «Keine Ölsuche im Norden» (Norwegens). (NOR)
573 Plakat für ein Einzelhandels-Seminar. «Kümmern sie sich um ihre eigenen Dinge.» Mehrfarbiges Plakat. (USA)
574 Aufruf zum Energiesparen durch Ausnutzung des Nachtstroms. Illustration blau und gelb mit wenig Violett. (FRA)
575 «Können wir warten?» Thema dieses Schwarzweiss-Plakates ist die Luftverschmutzung. (USA)

565 Affiche figurant dans une campagne d'information contre les centrales nucléaires. Noir sur fond vert. (FRA)
566 Affiche annonçant une enquête d'opinion lancée dans les établissements de l'IBM. Noir et blanc sur fond vert. (SWI)
567–569 D'une série d'affiches par laquelle IBM fait appel aux employés de se perfectionner sans cesse. En couleurs. (USA)
570 «Ne chantez que des petites chansons.» Appel d'une usine à gaz d'économiser l'énergie. (USA)
571 Affiche contre la pollution sonore. (POL)
572 «Non au forage pétrolier dans le Nord» (de la Norvège). (NOR)
573 «Ne vous mêlez pas aux affaires d'autrui.» Affiche annonçant un cours sur le commerce de détail. En couleurs. (USA)
574 Cette affiche fait appel aux usagers de chauffe-eau électriques de faire le plein la nuit au tarif réduit. (FRA)
575 «Pouvons-nous attendre encore?» Affiche au sujet de la pollution de l'air. (USA)

576

577

ARTIST / KÜNSTLER / ARTISTE:

576, 577 Pete Steiner
578 Kaj Kujasalo
579 Graphicteam
580 Jacques Saxod
582 Vojtech Jiricka
583 Hans Arnold/Bo Kagerud

DESIGNER / GESTALTER / MAQUETTISTE:

576, 577 James L. Selak
578 Kaj Kujasalo
579 Graphicteam
580 Roland Graz
581 Peter Binkert
582 Vojtech Jiricka
583 Hans Arnold

ART DIRECTOR / DIRECTEUR ARTISTIQUE:

576, 577 James L. Selak
578 Kaj Kujasalo
579 Graphicteam
581 Peter Binkert
583 Daniel Burkhalter

AGENCY / AGENTUR / AGENCE-STUDIO:

576, 577 Xerox Corp.
578 Epidem
579 Graphicteam
581 Atelier Binkert
583 Anderson & Lembke

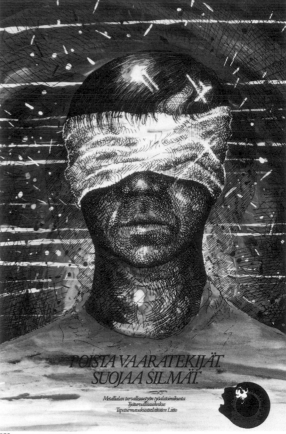

578

581

576, 577 Black-and-white poster for Xerox Corporation pointing out the frequency of accidents caused by alcohol. (USA)
578 This poster deals with the prevention of eye injuries in the metal industry. The background is in the colours of a fire. (FIN)
579 Accident prevention. Full-colour poster for the *Degussa* company. (GER)
580 "No batteries or thermometers in the waste . . . use the special depots in the town or take them to your dealer." Black-and-white poster with green and white lettering. (SWI)
581 "Fire is expensive." Poster for Zurich's fire prevention week. (SWI)
582 The subject of this poster is safety at work. Grey with red, lettering in black. (CSR)
583 "Danger: hydrogen sulphide." The poster indicates the appearance of this gas, symptoms of poisoning and protective measures. (SWE)

Accident Prevention
Unfallverhütung
Prévention d'accidents

Achtung! Sie haben keine Knautschzone.

Degussa

579

PLUS DE PILES
ET THERMOMETRES AUX ORDURES...
...UTILISEZ LES RECIPIENTS
SPECIAUX PLACES EN VILLE
ET CHEZ VOS FOURNISSEURS

580

2 vrtáci = úraz

582

VARNING FÖR SVAVELVÄTE!

583

584

585

588

■ On the occasion of the 30th anniversary of the UN's Universal Declaration of Human Rights, a world-wide exhibition of posters was shown in 1978, some of which are displayed on this double spread as examples of the work exhibited. The original text of the Declaration served as a basis for the artists, whereas quotes were used to underline the points put across. All posters in black and white, and the quotations in red. The subjects dealt with are: equality before the law (Fig. 584); the family (Fig. 585); the right of ownership (Fig. 586); the right to work (Fig. 587); freedom of expression (Fig. 588); education (Fig. 589) and slavery (Fig. 590).

■ Aus Anlass der vor 30 Jahren erfolgten Deklaration der Menschenrechte durch die UNO fand 1978 eine weltweite Ausstellung von Plakaten statt, von denen auf dieser Doppelseite einige Beispiele gezeigt werden. Der Originaltext der Deklaration diente den Künstlern als Grundlage, während auf den Plakaten wiederum Zitate zur Unterstreichung der Aussage verwendet wurden. Alle Plakate schwarzweiss, die Zitate rot. Die Themen: Gleichheit vor dem Gesetz (Abb. 584); die Familie (Abb. 585); das Recht auf Besitz (Abb. 586); das Recht auf Arbeit (Abb. 587); Meinungsfreiheit (Abb. 588); Ausbildung (Abb. 589); Sklaverei (Abb. 590).

■ A l'occasion du 30e anniversaire de la Déclaration des Droits de l'Homme par les Nations Unies, l'International Communication Agency a organisé une exposition internationale d'affiches dont nous présentons ici quelques exemples. Le texte de la Déclaration servait de base aux artistes qui, eux, soulignaient leurs messages illustratifs par des citations. Toutes les affiches sont en noir-blanc, les citations en rouge. Les sujets: l'égalité devant la loi (fig. 584); la famille (fig. 585); le droit à la propriété (fig. 586); le droit au travail (fig. 587); la liberté d'opinion (fig. 588); la formation professionnelle (fig. 589); l'esclavage (fig. 590).

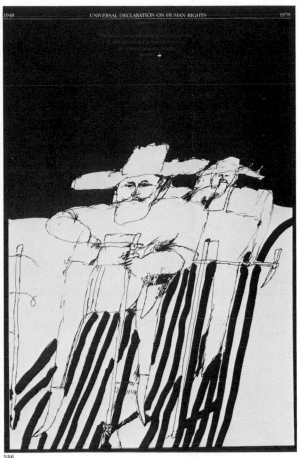

586

587

589

590

ARTIST / KÜNSTLER / ARTISTE:

584 Alan E. Cober
585 Susan Foster
586 Salvador Bru
587, 590 Michael David Brown
588 Geoffrey Moss
589 Tom Teague

DESIGNER / GESTALTER / MAQUETTISTE:

584–590 Ethel Kessler Freid

ART DIRECTOR / DIRECTEUR ARTISTIQUE:

584–590 Ethel Kessler Freid

AGENCY / AGENTUR / AGENCE-STUDIO:

584–590 US International Communication
           Agency

4

Consumer Posters

Dekorative Plakate

Affiches décoratives

591

592

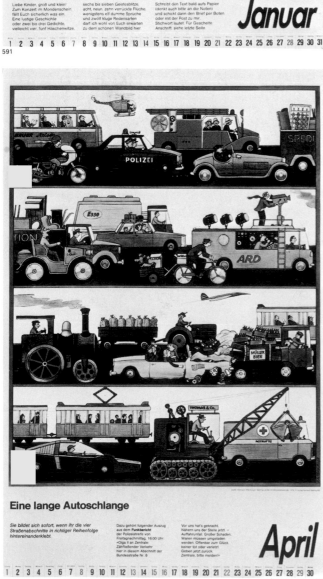

593

ARTIST / KÜNSTLER / ARTISTE:

591 Waltraut & Friedel Schmidt
592 Manfred Bofinger
593 Hermann Altenburger
594 Anne Wilsdorf
595 Tomi Ungerer
596 Etienne Delessert

DESIGNER / GESTALTER / MAQUETTISTE:

594, 595 Kurt Jenny

ART DIRECTOR / DIRECTEUR ARTISTIQUE:

591, 593 Curt Pries
594, 595 Daniel Keel
596 Claude Graber

PUBLISHER / VERLEGER / EDITEUR:

591, 593 Stalling Verlag GmbH
592 Staatlicher Kunsthandel der DDR
594, 595 Diogenes Verlag AG
596 Papierfabrik Balsthal

591, 593 From a children's poster calendar. The moonlight concert in Fig. 591 is supposed to encourage verses, and the cars in Fig. 593 can be stuck together. (GER)
592 Full-colour poster for children issued by the East German state art association. (GDR)
594, 595 Children's posters by the *Diogenes* publishers for the books *Die Riesin* ("The Giantess") and *Kein Kuss für Mutter* ("No Kiss for Mother"). Full-colour (Fig. 594) and black and white (Fig. 595). (SWI)
596 Poster in bright colours on *Telatex*, a nonwoven fabric. (SWI)

591, 593 Aus einem Kinderposter-Kalender. Das Mondscheinkonzert in Abb. 591 soll zum Dichten anregen, die Autoschlange in Abb. 593 lässt sich aneinanderkleben. (GER)
592 Farbiges Plakat für Kinder, vom Staatlichen Kunsthandel der DDR. (GDR)
594, 595 Kinderplakate des *Diogenes Verlags* aus den Büchern *Die Riesin* und *Kein Kuss für Mutter*. Abb. 594 mehrfarbig, Abb. 595 schwarzweiss. (SWI)
596 Plakat in leuchtenden Farben, auf *Telatex*, einem Material mit Textilcharakter. (SWI)

591, 593 Exemples d'un calendrier-affiche pour enfants. Le concert au clair de lune (fig. 591) devrait animer à faire des vers; fig. 593: fil de voitures à composer. (GER)
592 Affiche polychrome pour enfants, publiée par un organisme public de la RDA. (GDR)
594, 595 Affiches pour enfants des *Editions Diogenes* avec des illustrations tirées de deux livres d'enfant. Fig. 594 en polychromie, fig. 595 en noir-blanc. (SWI)
596 Affiche en couleurs vives imprimée sur *Telatex*, un nouveau tissu. (SWI)

Ein Diogenes Kinder Plakat von Anne Wilsdorf aus »Die Riesin«

594

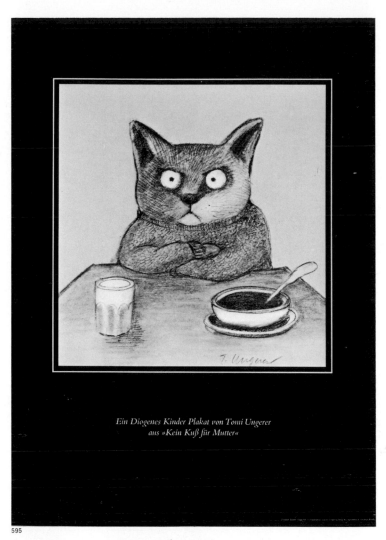

Ein Diogenes Kinder Plakat von Tomi Ungerer
aus »Kein Kuß für Mutter«

595

596

597

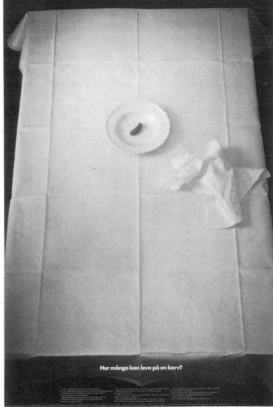

598

ARTIST / KÜNSTLER / ARTISTE:

597 Jan Fridlund
598 François Gillet
599, 602, 603 Jan Bengtsson
600 Heinz von Sterneck
601 Bertil Strandell
604 Waldemar Swierzy

DESIGNER / GESTALTER / MAQUETTISTE:

597–603 Lars Hall

ART DIRECTOR / DIRECTEUR ARTISTIQUE:

597–603 Lars Hall

AGENCY / AGENTUR / AGENCE-STUDIO:

597–603 Hall & Cederquist AB
604 KAW

PUBLISHER / VERLEGER / EDITEUR:

597, 599–602 Upside AB
598, 603 Hedman Repro AB
604 Tonpress

600

601

597–603 From a series of posters by Hedmans Repro AG, proving the high quality of their printing on decorative posters with ironic comments on subjects of general interest. Fig. 597 shows the Head of Information at a nuclear power plant declaring that radiation risks are a lot of nonsense; Fig. 598 poses the question of how many feed from a sausage when taking all "authorities" into account; Fig. 599 deals with the so-called clarity of political statements; Fig. 600 points at the increasingly impotent role of the average person, with all its servile implications; Fig. 601: it seems that the real truth is there is no truth at all; Fig. 602 quotes Balzac on the subject of bureaucracy: the power of giants used by pygmies; Fig. 603 shows a poster that cannot be displayed without permission by a special authority. (SWE)
604 Decorative poster portraying the Beatles. Yellow-coloured faces, hair, hats and background in brown and black. (POL)

597–603 Aus einer Serie der Hedmans Repro AG, die ihre Druckqualität auf dekorativen Plakaten mit ironischen Kommentaren zu Themen von allgemeinem Interesse beweisen möchte. Abb. 597 zeigt den Informationschef eines Atomkraftwerkes, der die Gefährlichkeit von Strahlen für Unsinn hält; Abb. 598 fragt, wieviele von einer Wurst leben, mit Anspielung auf den Umfang der behördlichen Kontrollen; Abb. 599 spielt auf die «Klarheit» politischer Aussagen an; Abb. 600 ist eine Äusserung zu der Zuschauerrolle, die der Mensch angenommen hat, Abb. 601: «Die Wahrheit ist, es gibt keine Wahrheit», Abb. 602 zitiert Balzac zum Thema Bürokratie: die Macht der Giganten, von Zwergen ausgeübt; Abb. 603 zeigt ein Plakat, das ohne Beschluss eines entsprechenden Gremiums nicht aufgehängt werden darf. (SWE)
604 Dekoratives Plakat mit den Beatles. Die Gesichter gelblich, Haare, Hüte und Hintergrund braun und schwarz. (POL)

599

602

604

597–603 Afin de mieux documenter la qualité d'impression, la Hedmans Repro SA a publié une série d'affiches décoratives avec des commentaires ironiques sur divers sujets d'intérêt général. Fig. 597: le chef d'information d'une centrale nucléaire démente l'effet périlleux de la radiation; fig. 598: combien de personnes peuvent se nourrir d'une saucisse? – allusion au contrôle administratif devenant toujours plus sévère; fig. 599 se réfère aux déclarations politiques «claires et simples»; fig. 600 fait allusion au rôle de spectateur que l'homme a adopté; fig. 601: «A vrai dire, la vérité n'existe pas»; fig. 602: citation de Balzac au sujet de la bureaucratie: la puissance du géant exercée par des nains; fig. 603: cette affiche n'a pas pu être suspendue sans l'autorisation d'un comité particulier. (SWE)

604 Affiche décorative présentant les Beatles. Visages en tons jaunes, cheveux, chapeaux et fond en brun et noir. (POL)

603

Decorative Posters
Dekorative Plakate
Affiches décoratives

ARTIST / KÜNSTLER / ARTISTE:

605 Carl Larsson
606 Christine Chagnoux
607–609a Akihiro Orikawa
610 Maurice Sendak

DESIGNER / GESTALTER / MAQUETTISTE:

607–609a Masakazu Taki

ART DIRECTOR / DIRECTEUR ARTISTIQUE:

607–609a Yoshifumi Nozaki
610 Daniel Keel

AGENCY / AGENTUR / AGENCE-STUDIO:

607–609a Dentsu Advertising
610 Diogenes Verlag AG

PUBLISHER / VERLEGER / EDITEUR:

605, 606 Verkerke Reprodukties BV
607–609a Daiichi Kangyo Bank
610 Diogenes Verlag AG

605

606

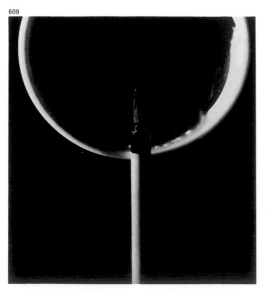

609

608

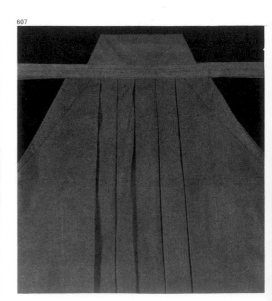

607

610

607a

609a

605 Nostalgic poster in warm colours. (NLD)
606 "The Butterfly Chase" is the title of this poster for children. In full colour. (NLD)
607—609a Details of three posters and complete reproduction of two (Figs. 607a and 609a) from a series. Fig. 607: a red water-colour in a white bowl, Fig. 608: green liquid in a yellow bowl, Fig. 609: red fabric. (JPN)
610 Detail of the illustration by Maurice Sendak for a children's birthday poster by the *Diogenes* publishers. (SWI)

605 Nostalgisches Plakat in warmen Farbtönen. (NLD)
606 «Die Schmetterlingsjagd» ist, der Titel dieses Plakates für Kinder. In Farbe. (NLD)
607—609a Details von drei Plakaten und komplette Wiedergabe von zweien (Abb. 607a und 609a) aus einer Serie. Abb. 607: rote Tusche in weisser Schale, Abb. 608: grüne Flüssigkeit in gelber Schale, Abb. 609: roter Stoff. (JPN)
610 Detail der Illustration von Maurice Sendak für ein Kinderplakat zum Geburtstag, vom *Diogenes Verlag*. (SWI)

605 Affiche nostalgique; chauds coloris. (NLD)
606 «La chasse aux papillons.» Affiche décorative destinée aux enfants. En polychromie. (NLD)
607—609a Détails de trois affiches figurant dans une série et reproductions complètes (figs. 607a et 609a). Fig. 607: encre rouge dans un bol blanc; fig. 608: liquide verte dans un bol jaune; fig. 609: étoffe rouge. (JPN)
610 Détail d'une illustration de Maurice Sendak, utilisée pour une affiche pour enfants, des *Editions Diogenes*. (SWI)

ARTIST / KÜNSTLER / ARTISTE:

611, 612 Klaus Moritz
613 Georges Barbier
614, 615 H. R. Giger
616 Carin Stavrén
617 Elisbeth Zeilon

PUBLISHER / VERLEGER / EDITEUR:

611–615 Verkerke Reprodukties BV
616, 617 Anders Beckmans School

611

612

614

615

613

Ett barn kan tro att en död fågel bara sover.

Rädda Barnen.

616

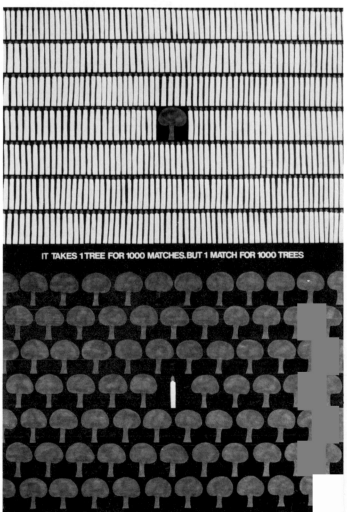

IT TAKES 1 TREE FOR 1000 MATCHES. BUT 1 MATCH FOR 1000 TREES

617

611–613 Three examples from a series of decorative posters, each possessing a nostalgic character. (NLD)
614, 615 Surrealistic posters by H. R. Giger, the Swiss artist. Fig. 614: grey-green, silvery, Fig. 615: brown shades of gold. (NLD)
616, 617 Two examples from an exhibition of students' work of the senior class ''Advertising and Graphic Design'' at the Anders Beckman school in Stockholm. The text to Fig. 616: ''A child would think that a dead bird is only sleeping'', and Fig. 617: ''One needs one tree for a thousand matches, but only one match for a thousand trees''. Both in full colour. (SWE)

611–613 Drei Beispiele aus einer Serie von dekorativen Plakaten mit nostalgischem Charakter. (NLD)
614, 615 Surrealistische Plakate des Schweizer Künstlers H. R. Giger. Abb. 614: graugrün, silbrig, Abb. 615: bräunliche Goldtöne. (NLD)
616, 617 Aus einer Ausstellung von Schülerarbeiten der Abschlussklasse «Werbung und Graphik-Design» der Anders-Beckman-Schule, Stockholm. Der Text zu Abb. 616: «Ein Kind wird von einem toten Vogel glauben, dass er nur schläft», zu Abb. 617: «Man braucht einen Baum für tausend Streichhölzer, aber nur ein Streichholz für tausend Bäume». Beide farbig. (SWE)

611–613 Trois exemples figurant dans une série d'affiches décoratives de charactère nostalgique. (NLD)
614, 615 Affiches surréalistes du peintre suisse H. R. Giger. Fig. 614 en gris-vert et argent, fig. 615 en brun doré. (NLD)
616, 617 Deux exemples d'une exposition présentant les travaux de fin d'études de la classe «publicité et design graphique» de l'école Anders Beckman, Stockholm. Fig. 616: «En voyant un oiseau mort, un enfant croira qu'il dort simplement»; fig. 617: «Un homme a besoin d'un arbre pour mille allumettes, mais d'une seule allumette pour mille arbres». (SWE)

618

619

ARTIST / KÜNSTLER / ARTISTE:

618–620, 623 Jan Balet
621 Niklaus Troxler
622 Ivan Generalic

DESIGNER / GESTALTER / MAQUETTISTE:

618–620, 622, 623 Charles Sahli

ART / DIRECTOR / DIRECTEUR ARTISTIQUE:

618–620, 622, 623 Charles Sahli
621 Niklaus Troxler

AGENCY / AGENTUR / AGENCE-STUDIO:

621 Niklaus Troxler

PUBLISHER / VERLEGER / EDITEUR:

618–620, 622, 623 Galerie Orangerie
621 VWA, Vereinigung der diplomierten
       Werbeleiter

618–620, 623 "December 1977–January 1978", "Homage to the Circus" and "Time Immemorial" are the titles
of works by the artist Jan Balet, which are to be seen on these *Orangerie* posters. A complete poster is shown in
Fig. 619. All three posters are produced in full colour. (GER)
621 Suggestion by *idee* ("idea") magazine to do and observe more beautiful things. In full colour. (SWI)
622 Another *Orangerie* art-poster. Shown here is an example of naïve art. (GER)

618–620, 623 «Dezember 1977–Januar 1978», «Hommage au Cirque» und «Uraltzeit» sind die Titel von
Arbeiten des Künstlers Jan Balet, die auf diesen Plakaten der *Orangerie*, Köln, zu sehen sind. Ein komplettes Plakat
wird in Abb. 619 gezeigt. Alle drei Plakate in Farbe. (GER)
621 Anregung der Zeitschrift *idee*, vermehrt Schönes zu machen und zu beachten. Farbiges Plakat. (SWI)
622 Ein weiteres Künstlerplakat der *Orangerie*. Hier ein Beispiel naiver Kunst. (GER)

618–620, 623 «Décembre 1977–Janvier 1978», «Hommage au Cirque» et «La Naissance du Temps» – ce sont
les titres des peintures de Jan Balet, présentées sur les affiches de la galerie *Orangerie* à Cologne. Une affiche
complète est montrée sous fig. 619. En polychromie. (GER)
621 Le magazine *idee* veut pousser les gens a faire davantage de belles choses. (SWI)
622 Une autre affiche d'art de la galerie *Orangerie*. Ici un exemple d'art naïf. (GER)

620

621

622

623

624

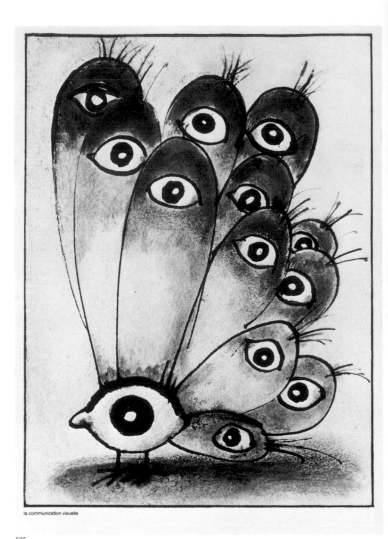

la communication visuelle

625

you are energy...

626

627

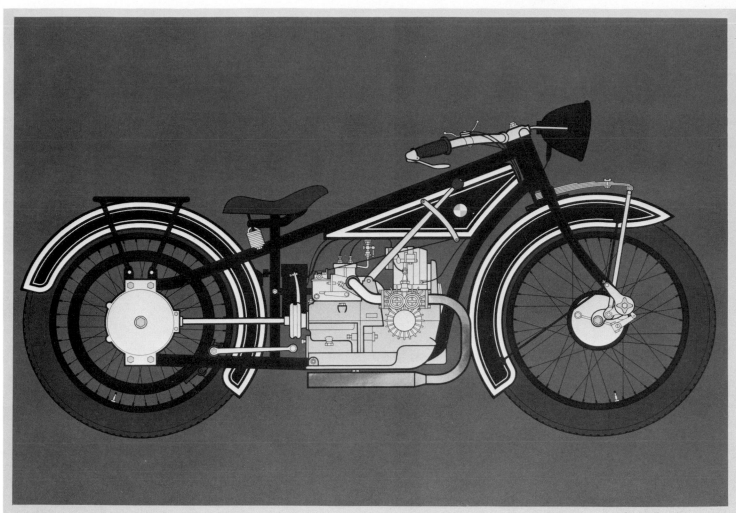

628

ARTIST / KÜNSTLER / ARTISTE:

624 Dietrich Ebert
625 André François
626 T. A. Lewandowski
627 Lanny Sommese
628 Otl Aicher
629 Shuzo Kato

DESIGNER / GESTALTER / MAQUETTISTE:

624 Dietrich Ebert
627 Lanny Sommese
629 Shuzo Kato

ART DIRECTOR / DIRECTEUR ARTISTIQUE:

626 T. A. Lewandowski
627 Lanny Sommese
629 Shuzo Kato

AGENCY / AGENTUR / AGENCE-STUDIO:

627 Lanny Sommese Design
628 Büro Aicher
629 Design Office Kato

PUBLISHER / VERLEGER / EDITEUR:

624 Poterie Française
625 Centre Georges Pompidou
628 BMW, Bayerische Motorenwerke AG

629

624 Poster that can be hung up in the kitchen. Red, brown and white. (GER)
625 ''Visual Communication'' is the title given to this poster. Soft colouring. (FRA)
626 Man as a source of energy. Poster in black and white with a full-colour cable. (FRA)
627 Poster with a poem by Bertolt Brecht (Hitler Choral III). Black on brown-coloured paper with full-colour spots. (USA)
628 Example from a BMW poster series. Here a motorbike constructed in 1923. The text states that BMW still manufactures its motorbikes nowadays according to the same concept. (GER)
629 Poster dedicated to the country-singer John Denver. In full colour. (JPN)

624 Für die Küche bestimmtes Plakat. Braun, weiss und rot. (GER)
625 «Visuelle Kommunikation» ist der Titel dieses Plakates. In zarter Kolorierung. (FRA)
626 «Du bist Energie.» Siebdruck-Plakat in Schwarzweiss mit mehrfarbigem Kabel. (FRA)
627 Plakat mit einem Gedicht von Bertolt Brecht (Hitler Choral III). Schwarz auf bräunlichem Papier mit Farbflecken. (USA)
628 Beispiel aus einer BMW-Plakatserie. Hier ein Motorrad Baujahr 1923. Im Text wird daraufhingewiesen, dass BMW noch heute seine Motorräder nach dieser Konzeption baut. (GER)
629 Dem Country-Sänger John Denver gewidmetes Plakat. Mehrfarbig. (JPN)

624 Affiche décorative pour la cuisine. Brun, blanc et rouge. (GER)
625 «Communication visuelle.» Affiche en tons atténués. (FRA)
626 «C'est toi, l'énergie.» Affiche sérigraphique en noir-blanc, câble en couleurs. (FRA)
627 Affiche présentant un poème de Bertolt Brecht (Hitler Choral III). Noir sur papier jaunâtre avec des taches de peinture. (USA)
628 Exemple figurant dans une série d'affiches décoratives publiée par BMW. On présente ici un moto de l'année 1923. Dans le texte on souligne que les motos BMW sont construits encore aujourd'hui d'après la même conception. (GER)
629 Affiche consacrée au chanteur John Denver. En polychromie. (JPN)

630

631

632

635

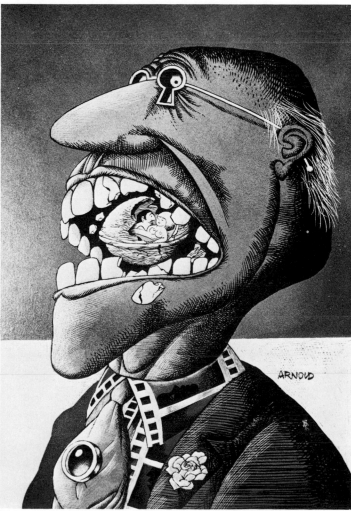

634

ARTIST / KÜNSTLER / ARTISTE.
630—635 Hans Arnold

PUBLISHER / VERLEGER / EDITEUR:
630—635 Vecko-Revyn

630—635 From a series of decorative posters with fantastic subjects. Don Juan in Fig. 630 mostly in blue and red shades; the "Statue of Liberty" in Fig. 631 in a white Ku-Klux-Klan robe in front of the American flag in its actual colours, the rats with white swastikas and white eyes; snake with a brown skin pattern and a green neck in Fig. 632; Fig. 633 with a blue «butterfly» with blue eyes and a red mouth, golden watch with a white clock-face which, like the entrails, is red from below, background in brown shades; the "detective" in Fig. 634 mainly in shades of red and blue; subdued green, yellow and grey colouring with a forceful blue in the diamonds in Fig. 635. (SWE)

630—635 Aus einer Serie von dekorativen Plakaten mit phantastischen Motiven. Don Juan in Abb. 630 vorwiegend in Blau- und Rottönen; die «Freiheitsstatue» in Abb. 631 in weissem Ku-Klux-Klan-Gewand vor der amerikanischen Flagge in Originaltönen, die Ratten mit weissen Hakenkreuzen und weissen Augen; braungemusterte Schlange mit grünem Hals in Abb. 632; Abb. 633 mit blauem «Schmetterling» mit blauen Augen und rotem Mund, goldene Uhr mit weissem Zifferblatt, das von unten, wie auch die Eingeweide, rot ist, und Hintergrund in Brauntönen; der «Detektiv» in Abb. 634 vorwiegend in Rot- und Blautönen; verhaltene Gelb-, Grün- und Graukolorierung mit kräftigem Blau in den Diamanten in Abb. 635. (SWE)

630—635 D'une série d'affiches décoratives avec des motifs fantastiques. Fig. 630: Don Juan en tons bleus et rouges prédominant; fig. 631: «statue de liberté» habillée d'une robe blanche du Ku Klux Klan, drapeau américain en bleu-blanc-rouge, rats avec la svastika blanche et les yeux blancs; fig. 632: serpent brun avec col vert; fig. 633: «papillon» bleu aux yeux bleus, bouche rouge, montre en or avec cadran blanc; intestins rouges, fond en tons bruns; fig. 634: «détective» en tons rouges et bleus prédominant; fig. 635: tons jaunes, verts et gris, facettes des diamants en bleu vif. (SWE)

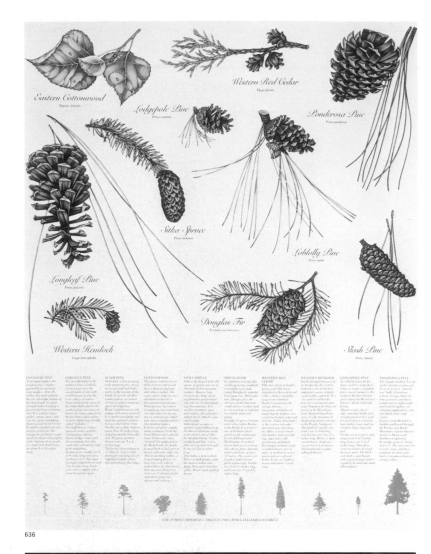

636

637

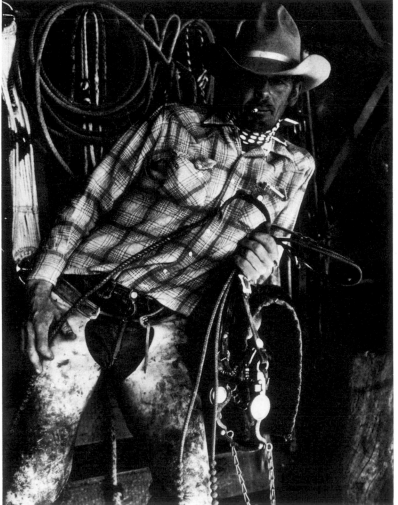

638

639

636 Poster which was used as a decorative supplement to the house magazine *Resource* of the Crown Zellerbach company. The illustrations on this poster are in full colour. (USA)
637 Decorative poster with a space in the middle for messages, which can then be detached. Mainly green with violet. (USA)
638, 639 Small-format posters given away by *Geo* magazine as "rewards" for new subscriptions. Photographs in full colour. (GER)
640 Full-colour poster with a work by Paul Wunderlich displaying his name in large letters. (GER)

PAUL
WUNDERLICH

640

ARTIST / KÜNSTLER / ARTISTE:

636 Dick Drayton
637 Elwyn Mehlman
640 Paul Wunderlich

DESIGNER / GESTALTER / MAQUETTISTE:

636 Nicolas Sidjakov
637 Alex Serniak

ART DIRECTOR / DIRECTEUR ARTISTIQUE:

636 Nicolas Sidjakov
637 Bob Feldgus

AGENCY / AGENTUR / AGENCE-STUDIO:

636 Sidjakov & Berman Associates

PUBLISHER / VERLEGER / EDITEUR:

636 Crown Zellerbach
637 Scholastic Book Services
638, 639 Gruner & Jahr AG & Co
640 Galerie Orangerie

636 Als dekorative Beilage der Firmenzeitschrift *Resource* von Crown Zellerbach verwendetes Plakat. Illustrationen in Farbe. (USA)
637 Dekoratives Plakat mit einer Fläche für Mitteilungen in der Mitte, die sich wieder entfernen lassen. Vorwiegend grün, mit Violett. (USA)
638, 639 Kleinformatige Plakate, die von der Zeitschrift *Geo* als Belohnung für ein Abonnement verschickt wurden. Farbaufnahmen. (GER)
640 Mehrfarbiges Plakat mit einer Arbeit von Paul Wunderlich. (GER)

636 Affiche décorative jointe au journal d'entreprise *Resource*, publié par Crown Zellerbach. Illustrations en couleurs. (USA)
637 Affiche décorative avec un blanc au milieu pour des informations qu'on peut enlever après coup. Prédominance de tons verts avec lilas. (USA)
638, 639 Deux affichettes que le magazine *Geo* envoie à tous ceux qui s'abonnent à ce magazine. Photos couleur. (GER)
640 Affiche polychrome présentant un travail de Paul Wunderlich. (GER)

Paper / Papier: Papierfabrik Biberist – Biber GS SK3, blade coated,
pure white 120 gm² and Biber Offset SK3, pure white, machine-
finished, 140 gm² / Biber GS SK3, hochweiss, satiniert, 120 gm² und
Biber-Offset SK3, hochweiss, maschinenglatt, 140 gm²

Printed by / gedruckt von: Karl Schwegler AG, Zürich

Cover / Einband: Buchbinderei Schumacher AG, Bern / Schmitten
Glossy lamination / Glanzfoliierung: Durolit AG, Pfäffikon SZ